Writing British Columbia History, 1784-1958

Writing British Columbia History, 1784-1958

Chad Reimer

UBCPress · Vancouver · Toronto

© UBC Press 2009

All rights reserved. No part of this publication may be reproduced,
stored in a retrieval system, or transmitted, in any form or by any means,
without prior written permission of the publisher, or, in Canada, in the case of
photocopying or other reprographic copying, a licence from Access Copyright
(Canadian Copyright Licensing Agency), www.accesscopyright.ca.

20 19 18 17 16 15 14 13 12 11 10 09   5 4 3 2 1

Printed in Canada on FSC-certified ancient-forest-free paper
(100% post-consumer recycled) that is processed chlorine- and acid-free.

LIBRARY AND ARCHIVES CANADA CATALOGUING IN PUBLICATION

Reimer, Chad
Writing British Columbia history, 1784-1958 / Chad Reimer.

Includes bibliographical references and index.
ISBN 978-0-7748-1644-1 (bound);
ISBN 978-0-7748-1645-8 (pbk.); ISBN 978-0-7748-1646-5 (e-book)

1. British Columbia – Historiography. 2. British Columbia – History.   I. Title.

FC3809.R445 2009   971.1'0072   C2009-904085-9

Canadä

UBC Press gratefully acknowledges the financial support
for our publishing program of the Government of Canada
through the Book Publishing Industry Development Program (BPIDP),
and of the Canada Council for the Arts, and the British Columbia Arts Council.

This book has been published with the help of a grant from the
Canadian Federation for the Humanities and Social Sciences, through the
Aid to Scholarly Publications Programme, using funds provided by
the Social Sciences and Humanities Research Council of Canada.

Printed and bound in Canada by Friesens
Set in Pitu and Minion by Artegraphica Design Co. Ltd.
Text design: Irma Rodriguez
Copy editor: Joanne Richardson
Proofreader: Jenna Newman

UBC Press
The University of British Columbia
2029 West Mall
Vancouver, BC v6t 1z2
www.ubcpress.ca

To Evan and Jesse

Contents

Acknowledgments

Funding for this research was provided by the Social Sciences and Humanities Research Council of Canada, the Fulbright Foundation, and the BC Heritage Trust Willard Ireland Scholarship.

Portions of Chapter 1 were published in *On Brotherly Terms: Canadian-American Relations West of the Rockies*, ed. Ken Coates and John Findlay. A different version of Chapter 2 was published in the *Pacific Northwest Quarterly*.

This book reflects a life-long fascination with things historical. Along the way, I have incurred many debts of gratitude. Broadly, the public education systems of Manitoba, British Columbia, and Ontario made it possible for me to chase my dream. In an age that too often misunderstands and undervalues the efficacy of learning, it is important to remember the democratic and humanizing impact of high-quality, universally accessible education. More specifically, I wish to thank Jean Wilson, Jean Barman, Marlene Shore, Susan Warwick, Ramsay Cook, George Brandak, and John Findlay.

But most of all, I want to thank my two sons, Evan and Jesse: their light led me out of the darkness.

Writing British Columbia History, 1784-1958

Introduction

> It is an empty land. A European can find nothing to satisfy the
> hunger of the heart. He requires haunted woods, and the friendly
> presence of ghosts ... the decaying stuff of past seasons and
> generations.
>
> — RUPERT BROOKE, 1913

Visiting Canada's westernmost province in 1913, English poet Rupert Brooke encountered a land crowded with sublime mountains, glacial lakes, and dense forests. Yet, amid this natural abundance, Brooke felt an emptiness: the absence of the ghosts of history.[1] Of course, like his compatriots, Brooke was blind to the history of the peoples who had occupied the region for millennia and who had created a land more truly spiritualized than any European newcomer could fathom. To the Englishman, humanity had yet to write its story upon the landscape of British Columbia. And, indeed, just over a century earlier, the area now encompassing British Columbia was unknown to the European world, an empty space on its maps filled in with imaginary seas and passages. But, as with other colonies, the new non-Native society forming on the western coast of North America needed a history to define its own identity and to legitimate its recent dispossession of its Native inhabitants. This book examines the efforts of historians to provide British Columbia with such a history, from the first writings on the region in the late eighteenth century through to British Columbia's centennial in 1958. Most directly, it sets out to answer the question: How and why does a society so new go about writing its history?

It was this question that drew me to the work of British Columbia's historians and suggested to me that the topic was worth doing. As one born and raised in the Canadian west, whose early academic studies focused upon European history, it was a question that gradually yet forcefully pushed its way forward. Indeed, over the years, a distinct feeling of historical inferiority in relation to the Old World was balanced by a sense that the burden of history was heavier there than in my New World home. Europeans, such as Brooke, who travelled through North America remarked upon its lack of history. By contrast, North Americans travelling through Europe felt that they were literally walking through history, the very streets and buildings being physical remnants of a long-recorded past. Brooke himself imagined as much: "So ... a Canadian would feel our woods and fields heavy with the past and the invisible, and suffer claustrophobia in an English countryside beneath the dreadful pressure of immortals."[2] And all the while, Canada's far west province stood out as one of the newest portions of the New World, one of the last sections of the continent to be encountered and brought within the realm of European history. Thus, British Columbia presents a fertile subject through which to study how a society goes about writing its history for we are so very close to the time when it had no written history at all.

British Columbia also represents a particularly clear example for historians of the promise and problems thrown up by new societies – or, more specifically, what Alfred Crosby has labelled "neo-Europes."[3] Physically removed from the confines of the Old World and settling upon the relative tabula rasa of a new land, such societies were presented with the opportunity to invent and define new cultural forms and rules. Like the characters and settings of Vancouver Island novelist Jack Hodgins, individuals could be resurrected with new names and identities or work towards "the invention of the world" around them.[4] At the same time, the lack of a well-established social order and accepted reference points made it difficult either to construct a stable society or to justify the particular form that society took. There existed the twin dangers of a lack of identity and the emergence of traits deemed undesirable by those who hoped to lead and shape the young society. Thus, historians of a new, immigrant society such as British Columbia had to show that it was fundamentally like the Old World from which it sprang, possessing the necessary social and political institutions and the constituent elements of a legitimate history. They also had to establish some distinguishing aspect or element that made it different, thereby taking advantage of the promise it offered.

British Columbia's strikingly peculiar historical situation further rendered it a most difficult historical subject and set it apart from its fellow neo-European societies in North America. The continent's Northwest Coast was only recently brought into the European scheme of things. This delayed "discovery," as Europeans viewed it, was followed by a relatively late incorporation into the modern industrialized nation-state. Throughout, accelerated development and abrupt contacts with the European world have characterized the historical development of British Columbia. As Cole Harris notes, modern and premodern worlds have met with stark abruptness here. "Time seems telescoped in British Columbia," Harris writes, "and the long story of emerging modernity, extending back through European millennia, is compressed into 100 years or so."[5] The challenge posed to its historians, then, has been the very thinness and sporadic nature of European presence and imprint upon the region; the novelty of the area made it difficult to establish a respectable historical lineage. Moreover, this novelty has been perennially renewed throughout British Columbia's history, right up to the present age. Successive waves of immigration have left its population in constant flux as different elements are added to its fluid social mix.

Meanwhile, British Columbia's overwhelming topography and landscape presented the prospect of a very unmodern dominance of geography over history, of nature over humanity. British Columbians' encounter with nature has proven to be a dominant theme in writing on the province. But the society the former struggled to create was predicated on the modern European notion of progress – of humanity's increasing control over the world around it. To legitimate this society, to place it within the realm of modern civilization, writers had to show human agency taming geography, exploiting it, using it. In short, history had to triumph over geography.

Also facing BC historians was the more immediate challenge posed by the profound and rapid changes that, while sweeping across all North America, were telescoped into a few decades in British Columbia. Through the late nineteenth and twentieth centuries, social relations and the economy were remade by the troika of industrial capitalism, urbanization, and immigration. The rise of Darwinian science and a spirit of scepticism unsettled the premises that had held together the mid-Victorian intellectual world. Certainly, there was a strong faith that this era of progress would bring unprecedented benefits, both moral and material. Yet many were unnerved as change rather than continuity now seemed to lie at the root of their world. The popularity of history through the late Victorian era and into this century was a nostalgic reaction against such rapid change, a yearning for seemingly simpler times, when values were clearer and social order more assured.

This book's central argument is that the writing of history was an essential tool in the construction of a neo-European society – and, more particularly, an Anglo- or British-derived society – on the Northwest Coast of North America. It thus examines the role played by historical literature and the historian within society as well as the impact of social context on shaping the history that is written. As with their counterparts elsewhere, BC historians were conscious of the social role played by written history. For them, the latter was one of the necessary elements of any new society. The writing of history, then, has stood as a fundamentally meaning-giving activity: it is one of the most prevalent and powerful ways in which individuals and societies define their place and identity in the world. Indeed, rather than passively reflecting a ready-made history, historians actively shape the narratives they write in order to meet social and personal goals. As one historiographer has noted: "Critics adhering to diverse ideological persuasions have suggested that societies in fact reconstruct their pasts rather than faithfully record them, and that they do so with the needs of contemporary culture clearly in mind – manipulating the past in order to mold the present."[6] Historians, then, bring their own abilities, motivations, and intellectual filters to the task of writing history. By studying these, and their interplay with the material handed down from the past, we can see why and how history was written.

More globally, historical writing worked to incorporate the Northwest Coast within Western European (more broadly) and British (more specifically) civilization. No doubt, this task was a tall one for, as Australian historian Paul Carter asks, "who are more liable to charges of unlawful usurpation and constitutional illegitimacy than the founders of colonies?"[7] Paradoxically, such new societies responded to this challenge by adopting a strategy of "indigenization," whereby they claimed that they belonged in their newly colonized land and that that land belonged to them.[8] The writing of historical narratives was an indispensable tool in this strategy for written history was seen as a fundamental component of civilization – that which distinguished European newcomers from non-civilized Native peoples. Historians worked to justify the dispossession of the region's Native inhabitants by describing the latter as savages – part animal, part child – and perhaps more significantly, as people without history. Native peoples literally disappeared, and the newcomers moved in to claim the now vacated land as their own.

Not only did history "become complicitous in imperial expansion," but it was actively wielded to bring about this colonization.[9] Since the publication of Edward Said's groundbreaking *Orientalism*, a growing body of scholars has revealed how diverse disciplines, or ways of knowing, have contributed to and benefited from the emergence of European empires. Building new disciplines upon the Enlightenment premise that knowledge meant power, the modern European colonial project set out to gain knowledge about far-flung lands in order to manipulate both them and their people for European advantage. Such "technologies of power" ranged from military hardware and strategy to political institutions to cultural forms such as literature and history.[10] For, as Said writes in his more recent *Culture and Imperialism*: "The main battle in imperialism is over land, of course; but when it came to who owned the land, who had the right to settle and work on it, who kept it going, who won it back, and who now plans its future – these issues were reflected, contested, and even for a time decided in narrative."[11] From the time of the Northwest Coast's first encounter with Enlightenment Europe late in the eighteenth century, through the two centuries that followed, the production of historical knowledge about what would become British Columbia would contribute to the unfolding of the European imperial project there.

While British Columbia's historical literature was political in this global sense, it also engaged the more immediate political issues of its day. The province's historical writers were relatively privileged members of the Anglo immigrant society, which was working to construct and assert its hegemony over the province. To this latter end, these writers helped define and enunciate a broader immigrant-settler ideology – one that was as profound in the breadth and depth of its claims as it was in its succinctness. First, it defined residents and immigrants of British descent as "settlers"; they, with their British-derived institutions and culture, were there to stay in ways that the province's other two major groups (Natives and Asians) were not. Second, it asserted that British Columbia properly and legitimately belonged to this Anglo settler society for reasons legal, political, historical, economic, and cultural – in effect, for all reasons. Thus, the region's Native peoples could be made virtual outsiders in their own homeland. Seen as a dying people (due, in large part, to their precipitous depopulation in the decades after the arrival of Europeans), they were denied the vote, banned from preempting and settling Crown land, and pressed to give up ever more of their sparse reserve lands on the grounds that they were not properly exploiting them. Meanwhile, Asian residents and immigrants were defined as aliens and sojourners, their presence a distasteful but, in the end, fleeting reality. Like Natives, Asians were denied the vote and the right to settle on Crown land; unlike Natives, who had no other home to go to, Asians were largely excluded and sometimes even ousted. Exclusion laws, head taxes, physical evacuation: the province agitated for these at different times in its campaign for a "white man's country." On each of these issues, British Columbia's historians gave voice to the arguments of their own dominant society, providing historical narratives in support of them.

Over the course of nearly two centuries, historical writers wrestled with the challenge of constructing a past for the problematic new society that British Columbia represented. The results of their efforts can be divided into three broad genres – promotional history, pioneer history, and professional history – each of which loosely characterizes successive phases. The first genre, promotional history, sought to write the region into history itself for it was through this literature that the Northwest Coast became known to the European world. Possessing little or no first-hand knowledge of the region, these writers were more concerned with the future than the past, with promoting the region as a promising field for settlement, economic opportunities, and imperial expansion. Chapter 1 examines this literature.

Chapters 2 and 3 explore the second genre, pioneer history, which emerged from the more settled and industrialized British Columbia of late

Victorian and Edwardian eras. Pioneer history extolled the efforts of newly arrived Europeans, depicting them as the people responsible for building the province's foundations. This literature also marked the heyday of British imperialist and racialist thinking as writers worked to shape their narratives according to the trinity of civilization, empire, and race. While the community of amateur historians of this time adopted a celebratory view of British Columbia's past, and echoed contemporary prejudices, it did produce one scholar who stood out. Chapter 4 takes up the historical work of Judge Frederic Howay, who was able to free himself from the intellectual constraints of his fellow amateur writers and leave behind a significant body of research. His work provided the example and basis for a more critical, scholarly history of the province.

Finally, the opening of a provincial university made possible the emergence of the third genre, professional history, which is examined in Chapters 5 and 6. Graduates of standardized academic programs, and employed full-time as university professors, these professional historians brought the standards, themes, and conceptual frameworks of their discipline to the writing of provincial history. All too often, those frameworks did not fit the realities of British Columbia's past, and scholars like Walter Sage struggled to construct a satisfactory historical narrative of his adopted home. But the University of British Columbia did produce a first generation of locally trained historians who could draw upon personal experience in their study of the province's past. W. Kaye Lamb and Margaret Ormsby were the most notable members of this generation.

This book ends in 1958, which, at first blush, might seem curious. After all, the following decades produced an explosion of literature on the province as historians took up the same conceptual tools and interpretations that were revolutionizing historical writing in the Western world. Historians now examined how the forces of class, ethnicity, and gender shaped particular aspects of the province's history. More recently, a fresh perspective has been added: drawing on the burgeoning field of postcolonial studies, historians have conceptualized BC history as part of the centuries-long global spread of European colonialism. This book is intended to be a contribution to, rather than a survey of, this growing body of literature. By delimiting its subject, it can focus on the role played by historical writers in the process of colonization. It can also shed light on the process by which individual historians struggled to construct meaning out of the messy reality of the past. And, as has already been suggested, British Columbia's past was particularly messy – or, rather, it proved to be a particularly challenging subject for historians. For this reason, it presents us with a particularly enlightening case study of how historical knowledge is produced. Finally, the writings of British Columbia's historians during this time provide a rich and readily accessible source through which we can study the intellectual and cultural development of the province as it struggled to define its own identity.

1

The Earliest Pages of History

For those in search of a starting point for BC history, the first European explorations have proven to be stubbornly unsatisfactory. Juan Perez espied but never touched land in his 1774 cruise northward, while Captain James Cook's survey of the Northwest Coast four years later was a brief, perfunctory interlude in his third global voyage. Yet these events have long borne the weight of a founding myth. The province's historical writers have routinely presented the activities of European explorers as the "earliest pages" of British Columbia's history.[1] Even decades after these early explorations, the region could be seen only "as through a glass darkly": just as mists and fog shrouded the coast and mountains for much of the year, so the "mists of time" obscured North America's Northwest Coast from the European gaze.[2]

But the inconvenient truth is that the region had been occupied for some twelve thousand years before Europeans stumbled upon it. While lacking written languages and, thus, historical literature, these societies developed complex methods of recording and recounting the area's past. As we shall see, the largely oral histories of British Columbia's First Nations would be ignored by the historical writers studied here. Nevertheless, the former histories would survive and finally break through into the mainstream discussion of British Columbia's past. This happened first in the work of academic historians, who, in the last decades of the twentieth century, incorporated the methods of modern anthropology into their own "ethnohistories."[3]

Even more recently, a tectonic shift occurred in the legal world when the Gitksan Wet'suwet'en nation of central British Columbia pressed a land claim suit against the provincial government. To prove that they represented an organized society that had occupied and used a specific-ally delineated territory since "time immemorial," Gitksan elders em-ployed the methods of historical recording that were indigenous to them – the songs and oral accounts that narrated individual and collective lineages, along with specific and general events in their people's past. The 1991 decision by BC chief justice Allan McEachern represented the apex of the centuries-long position of British Columbia's immigrant society: in the absence of written verification, oral evidence was not a legitimate legal or historical source; moreover, any rights the Gitksan might have possessed were extinguished well before British Columbia became a province.[4] An appeal court chipped away at parts of McEachern's deci-sion;[5] however, the Supreme Court of Canada went further in 1997, sum-marily overturning it. The Supreme Court ruled that Gitksan rights to their traditional land had not been extinguished and that McEachern had erred in dismissing the oral evidence that could corroborate these rights. In an astonishing passage, the Court wrote: "Had the oral histories been correctly assessed, the conclusions on these issues of fact might have been very different."[6]

For us, the full significance of this ruling lay in the fact that it rejected some of the basic premises of the European historical tradition that had arrived in the region with the coming of James Cook – premises upon which the region's historical literature would be based for over two centur-ies. Beginning in the sixteenth century, when Europeans first encountered the western hemisphere, through the eighteenth-century Enlightenment and into much of the twentieth century, Native peoples of the Americas were seen as people without history. This profound and pervasive belief was itself based on two underlying premises. First, Native peoples lacked a history because they produced no written "historical" records as their societies were without written languages. Beginning in Renaissance Europe, but crystallizing as a dominant idea during the Enlightenment, the pos-session of "alphabetical writing" was seen as an essential component of both civilization and history. As Renaissance historian Walter Mignolo writes, the European conviction that their societies were superior to those of other continents emerged from their belief "that people without writing were people without history and that people without history were inferior human beings."[7]

Second, a "developmental myth" took hold in European thought, profoundly influencing intellectual currents then and in the following centuries.[8] In this model, societies developed through various natural stages: from primitive hunter-gatherer to agriculturalist to commercial (and, eventually, industrial) capitalist. Europe had led the way in this evolution, and it was seen as the universal epitome of a high civilization. The Native peoples of the Americas, including those in British Columbia, were placed at the primitive stage. They were seen as bystanders rather than as active participants in the march of civilization; their most useful role was to act as a foil for civilization's protagonists. The result, ethnohistorian Bruce Trigger writes, was that "native people were treated as part of a vanishing past ... seen as more akin to the forests in which they lived and the animals they hunted than as competitors for control of North America."[9]

The oral narratives and historical traditions of British Columbia's first inhabitants, then, had no influence upon the area's earliest historical writers because the latter did not consider them, or the people who produced them, to be historical. From the European perspective, the late eighteenth-century explorations brought the region into history by pulling it out of the realm of imagination and placing it onto the maps of Europe. Prior to the 1770s, the Northwest Coast had been an empty space on these maps, providing ample room for the imagination. Mythical Northwest Passages and other fanciful cartography, along with fictional creations such as Jonathan Swift's Brobdingnag, all found their home on these distant shores.[10] Unfortunately, Spain refused to publish the accounts of early explorers such as Perez for fear that the information might bring other nations into a region over which they held a tenuous claim. British authorities were less secretive: the records of Cook's third voyage, published between 1781 and 1784, provided European readers with the first dependable information on the Northwest Coast. These journals consisted primarily of the record of the expedition's activities, along with the captain's impressions of the Native inhabitants of these new regions. The official publication also provided a historical introduction to the voyages in order to underline the significance of the discoveries made.[11] Accounts subsequent to Cook's presented historical information as well, scant as it was, and in the following decades some attempts were made to tie together the various explorations of the northern Pacific into something resembling a chronological survey.[12]

The journals of other visitors, including maritime fur traders and Royal Navy officers such as George Vancouver, left a more poignant historiographical legacy: the image of the Northwest Coast as an empty, or rather emptied, land. Repeatedly, these writers described a land haunted by the dead, littered with decaying villages and lonesome grave markers. These writers often differed over the purported cause of this depopulation (war, famine, disease), but the overriding image was of a "Country nearly deserted," as Vancouver's journals stated.[13] We now know that the region surveyed by Vancouver lagged behind only the Incan and Aztec civilizations in terms of complexity and population density prior to the arrival of Europeans. Like the latter two, Northwest Coast First Nations were "virgin" populations lacking immunities to Old World diseases; the results were death rates that could reach 95 percent in the decades after coming into direct or indirect contact with their pathogen-riddled European visitors.[14] Unlike the Spanish experience with the Incan and Aztec cultures, though, the first Europeans to arrive on the Northwest Coast did not encounter Native societies at their peak but, rather, populations that had already been decimated by disease. The image of the region's Natives as a dying race, and of the land as empty, was firmly entrenched from the start.

One remarkable fact about the exploration accounts is just how recently they were written as Europe encountered the region at a singularly late date. While the earliest literature on the eastern coast of North America emerged from a Renaissance Europe still shaking off the shackles of the Middle Ages, the continent's western coast first came into contact with a worldview that had been fundamentally altered by the eighteenth-century Enlightenment. Renaissance humanists had begun freeing history from its medieval subordination to theology, but they could not liberate human reason from its subordination to the passions. A truly progressive history, a hallmark of the modern mind, was still hard to achieve. The ensuing Enlightenment effected a revolution in history by more fully secularizing it, looking for human and profane causes rather than divine. Enlightenment history was founded upon a fundamental belief in civilization's progress: history was to be the tale of the progressive triumph of reason over unreason, of civilization over barbarism. This paradoxically future-oriented history saw the past as a realm of superstition and vice that must be overcome, the present as dominated by the conflict of reason and unreason, and the future as the time when humanity would reach its true potential. Humanity's past and future, its history, could be known and controlled; as such, history emerged as one of the Enlightenment's "sciences of man," through which humanity reached out to control itself and the environment around it, ordering that environment and infusing it with human intent and meaning. In the words of Peter Gay, this confidence in humanity's power represented a "recovery of nerve," which was responsible for establishing the fundamental premises of the modern age, most notably the belief in humanity's progressive control over nature and its own destiny.[15]

While Europe's late eighteenth-century explorers shared the fundamental premises of this intellectual heritage, their focus was not primarily on the Northwest Coast's past. Their intent and legacy was cartographical rather than historical, and their journals were more annals than histories. Through this literature, North America's far northwest was plotted onto space, fragments of it named and claimed; but the region had yet to be plotted in time. Indeed, as Paul Carter notes in his study of contemporaneous developments in Australia, what the Northwest Coast explorations created was not so much history as the initial paths along which subsequent history would tread.[16]

Europeans did follow these word tracks into the area. James Cook's journal, posthumously published in 1784, noted in passing that the otter skins acquired on the Northwest Coast fetched high prices in the Chinese market. Cook's remark immediately sparked a flourishing maritime fur trade, involving several nations. The trade came to a sudden end in the 1820s, with the virtual extinction of the sea otter. By this time, land-based fur companies had moved west of the Rocky Mountains, with the British Hudson's Bay Company (HBC) soon dominating trade north of the Columbia River.

Which nation could claim sovereignty over the Oregon Country, as it was then called, was still contested. In 1818, Britain and the United States agreed to leave the region open to joint use and occupation. The issue became ever more heated through the 1830s and 1840s, as American settlers streamed into Oregon and the United States embarked on the most aggressive expansionist movement in its history.[17] In 1844, James Polk was elected US president on a platform that called for American annexation of the entire Oregon Country; Britain saw its imperial interests threatened, and war seemed imminent. Fortunately, cooler heads prevailed and the

1846 Oregon Treaty delineated the present boundary, running along the 49th parallel west of the Rocky Mountains and jutting south around Vancouver Island.[18]

The Oregon dispute is of interest here because citizens of each country, often with their government's assistance, took up pens to assert their nation's right to the Northwest Coast. And a question of history was at the heart of the ensuing debate: which power could claim priority of exploration and occupation and, thus (based on European-derived international law), sovereignty? In answering this question, American and British writers provided the first historical surveys of the Oregon Country, constructing competing chronologies in support of contrasting claims.

American writers made the first and most substantial contribution to this literature. On the orders of the US secretary of state, Robert Greenhow (a translator and librarian at the State Department) drafted a historical brief in support of his government's claims. The subsequent report was then published in 1840 by the US Senate under the title *Memoir, Historical and Political, on the Northwest Coast of North America*. Four years later, with James Polk recently elected as president on a platform calling for the annexation of the entire region up to 54'40", Greenhow released an expanded version of his earlier history entitled *The History of Oregon, California, and the Other Territories on the North-West Coast of North America*.[19] Together, these two works presented the first continuous narrative histories of the Northwest Coast. While the later *History* was more scholarly and decidedly less polemical, both books were firmly based upon primary material (most notably exploration accounts and government records) and reprinted crucial documents in appendices.

The historical narratives that emerged constructed the story of the Oregon Country as an American drama. Even though the United States had come into existence only in the 1770s, Greenhow argued that its historical lineage in the region dated back two centuries because Spain had ceded all of its historical claims to the Americans in the 1819 Treaty of Florida. The more recent presence of American explorers, fur traders, and settlers represented a continued US presence; these and earlier Spanish activities were given prominence in Greenhow's works, while British actions were noted but downplayed.

Greenhow's arguments in support of the US claim to Oregon were echoed in other American works of the time. Three authors – Oregon settlers Thomas Farnham and George. Wilkes, and twenty-six-year-old evangelist Ephraim Tucker – penned books that were largely derivative of Greenhow's work, at points simply paraphrasing his writing and research.[20] The books were decidedly polemical and partisan, and they failed to meet the standards of scholarship seen in Greenhow's *Memoir* and *History*. Nevertheless, the works of this trio echoed the central themes first presented by Greenhow, thereby establishing the beginnings of an American historiography on the Oregon Country.

Most centrally, Britain was depicted as an arrogant, grasping, monarchical power bent on thwarting the just claims of the American people. Of course, this image dated back to the American Revolution; a nagging Anglophobia persisted into the nineteenth century and was stoked to fever pitch by the Oregon dispute.[21] Wilkes spotted Britain's "calculating monarchists" working to impose their "tyranny" on Oregon.[22] Farnham wrote of the "insolent selfishness of Great Britain, her [sic] grasping injustice, her destitution of political honesty," while Tucker darkly warned of English plans to incite Native peoples to attack the United States' western frontier.[23] Likewise, the Hudson's Bay Company was demonized as an agent of Britain's imperial designs. It, too, was an autocratic power, inimical to the settlement of a "free population" in Oregon; neither it nor its government had any rightful claim to Oregon – tellingly, they were dismissed as "foreign."[24] Thus, compromise with Britain was rejected and the annexation of the entire Oregon Country demanded for, as Tucker cried, "Oregon is ours."[25]

The immediate goal of the American writers in the Oregon dispute was to debunk any claim that Britain possessed historical rights to the region; yet even more profound was the dismissal of Oregon's Native peoples. Greenhow had initially questioned whether the history of Oregon could be written since it was "almost entirely in a state of nature," occupied only by "savages incapable of civilization."[26] On the rare occasion that Natives appeared in *Memoir* or *History*, they did not take human form; rather, they posed as darkly mysterious threats, treacherous and violent, willing to rob and murder visiting Americans.[27] Other American historians also alternated between the dismissal and vilification of Oregon's Native peoples. Voicing the theme of the vanishing Indian, a motif that would only become more pervasive as the nineteenth century went on, Wilkes argued that Natives were "rapidly passing away before ... [a] superior race."[28] Meanwhile,

Tucker suggested the danger of the British inciting an Indian uprising on the western boundaries of the United States, a time-worn spectre that depicted Native peoples as easily manipulated pawns, incapable of acting on their own.[29] Natives had no rightful place in this American history of Oregon; they could be pushed aside in the face of American settlers, commerce, and political institutions.

Yet other Americans hoped for a different destiny. Albert Gallatin and William Sturgis had been involved previously with the Oregon Country, the former as an American diplomat at various international conferences, the latter as a naval captain who had visited the region at the beginning of the nineteenth century. Both sought compromise on the issue, eschewing war and arguing that the United States and Britain were "kindred nations" whose people together would settle the Northwest Coast. Their preference was a unified Oregon, perhaps even independent of Britain and the United States; failing that, they sought a peaceful division of the territory.[30] Sturgis pursued his critique even further; he rejected the effectively universal presumption that the region's Native peoples had no claim to land over which they had "actual, undisturbed, undisputed possession ... from a period to which the history of this continent does not reach." He also accused his "covetous" compatriots of neglecting and mistreating Oregon's Natives, prophesying a judgment day "when equal justice will be meted out to Christian destroyer and his heathen victim – and that will be a woeful day for the white man."[31]

Sturgis's was a voice crying in the wilderness. It was Greenhow's narratives, supplemented by Farnham, Tucker, and Wilkes, that formed the basis for an American history of Oregon. The State Department official's works also affected the response from British writers, who recognized the need to counter his solid research and forceful claims. The British government's historical case was laid out in a pair of anonymously written pamphlets, which provided contrasting timelines of the two nations' activities in the region.[32] The government also supported more substantial works by barrister Thomas Falconer and Oxford professor Travers Twiss.[33] Independently, clergyman and King's College lecturer Charles Nicolay, and HBC employee John Dunn, entered the fray with their own historical narratives.[34]

These writers set out to refute the American histories of Oregon – which Falconer dismissed as "very ridiculous trash" – and to construct a British counter-narrative in their place.[35] The British historians rejected the crucial claim that the United States had inherited two centuries' worth of Spanish rights to the region; rather, they argued that, "if Spain had any rights, Great Britain had [already] acquired them," either through international treaties such as the 1794 Nootka Convention or by priority of exploration and occupation.[36] Spanish activities thus receded into the background or were ignored altogether, while subsequent American efforts were derided as "trivial."[37] Instead, in the British narrative, Francis Drake was the first to discover North America's Northwest Coast in 1579; and, two centuries later, James Cook and George Vancouver inaugurated the region's first "continuous occupation," which was carried on by British fur-trading companies.[38]

British writers also sought to counter their American counterparts' demonization of the HBC for they knew that the Company represented their only effective presence in the Oregon Country. Not surprisingly, Dunn proffered the most fulsome praise of his former employer: "[The HBC was] the greatest commercial association that ever appeared in England, next to the East India Company," acting as a determined agent of the British Empire and civilization.[39]

And yet, even in the first British writings on the Northwest Coast, the Company's shortcomings as a founding figure were recognized. Anglican missionary Charles Nicolay acknowledged that the HBC pursued its own economic self-interest as much as, if not more than, the cause of Empire. Echoing some of the American literature on Oregon, Nicolay acknowledged that the Company had used alcohol as a trading item, with devastating effects for Natives, and, more recently, had been at best half-hearted in its efforts at bringing Christian civilization to them.[40] Certainly, the argument that the HBC had saved the region for Britain (and thus Canada) would persist as a central theme in BC historiography; but a nagging ambivalence towards the Company as a less-than-satisfactory founding agent would also persist.

Most of the British writers in the Oregon dispute, though, argued that the HBC had been uniquely benevolent in its treatment of Native peoples and had "point[ed] out to the benighted savage the means of improvement, comfort and happiness."[41] They drew a stark contrast between this treatment and the virtual "war of extermination" undertaken by American agents; Nicolay, for one, concluded that Britain had a moral responsibility to hold on to Oregon to save the region's Native peoples from such a fate.[42]

The greater attention paid to Natives, along with a less harsh portrayal of them, differentiated the British writers from the more mean-spirited American writers. In the British histories, Natives did not assume the role of violent and treacherous threat but, rather, appeared as a population of wards destined to be led by either HBC officials or Christian missionaries. Indeed, Oregon's First Nations provided the means by which British writers could discredit the United States and justify their nation's hold on the region. In this, British historians of Oregon anticipated the myth of "benevolent conquest," which would become a fundamental tenet of BC and Canadian historical writing.[43] As Bruce Trigger notes, British writers on North America and their Canadian heirs "relished comparing the brutal treatment of native people by the Americans with the 'generous' treatment they received from Euro-Canadians" – an interpretation requiring "great self-deception, or hypocrisy" in the face of British and Canadian government policy, the goal of which was the eradication of Native identity and culture.[44]

Paradoxically, British writers in the 1840s could make room for Native peoples because they were more willing than were their American counterparts to see Oregon within a colonial framework. They believed that Britain could exert a firm yet benevolent hand over the region's less civilized peoples because, unlike the United States, their nation possessed centuries of experience in colonizing new lands. Indeed, since its Empire spanned the globe, Britain viewed the entire world through an imperial filter. Accordingly, British writers presented typically colonial arguments for the acquisition of Oregon: it would open up new opportunities for British emigrants, while solving the problem of the home country's surplus population; it would provide new markets and avenues for commerce; it would further Britain's strategic military interests; and it would result in the "spread of our free institutions, equal laws and holy religion."[45]

Meanwhile, American writers on Oregon did not view their own people as colonizers. As Frederick Merk notes, at the heart of the American national ideology was the view of the United States as an anti-colonial power.[46] It had thrown off its own colonial master and, through the Monroe Doctrine, asserted the right to stop European powers from recolonizing the western hemisphere. Even the expansionist creed expressed in the 1840s phrase "Manifest Destiny" was not imperialistic at its ideological core; rather, it was premised upon the notion of consensual, contract government. Americans moving westward would set up their own governments and, in due course, apply to join a federated United States. Native peoples could not be incorporated into this vision because they were "unenlightened" peoples who were incapable of self-government.[47] They thus had to give way to the American settlers then moving into the region, who would seal Oregon's fate as part of the United States. This was not a matter of colonization but of the inexorable march of history.

It had taken an international crisis, with two powerful nations drawn dangerously close to war, to produce the first properly historical literature on the Northwest Coast. Not surprisingly, given the overheated atmosphere, this literature proffered divergent historical narratives for the Oregon Country, introducing themes subsequent historians north and south of the border would inherit. Meanwhile, in the immediate aftermath of the 1846 Oregon Treaty, the British government recognized that it had to strengthen its tenuous hold north of the new boundary if it were to maintain an outlet on the east Pacific. In 1849, it created Vancouver Island as its first colony in western North America.

The fact that the HBC was granted effective power over the new colony meant that, once again, controversy was the source of literature on the region. In the two years preceding Vancouver Island's creation, James Edward Fitzgerald launched a concerted campaign against the plan to grant the island to the Company. An emigration agent and English member of Parliament interested in colonial reform, Fitzgerald felt the new colony was too important to be entrusted to the policies of the fur trade monopoly. The criticisms made by this future prime minister of New Zealand were echoed in the British House of Commons in an 1848 speech by Lord Monteagle.[48] British policy continued unchanged, and efforts got under way to promote settlement on Vancouver Island under the HBC's auspices. But the issue of the HBC's anomalous position in the colony persisted, and this time the Company's critics were more successful. In 1857, after hearings and debate, a House of Commons select committee concluded that the Company's connection with Vancouver Island should be terminated and that the colony should be extended to encompass the mainland west of the Rocky Mountains.[49]

The controversies sparked by the HBC's privileged position on the Northwest Coast were significant for two reasons. First, the debates left a negative image among the British public, who now saw the region as an inhospitable, "howling wilderness," an image that later promotional literature had to confront.[50] Second, the Company's critics raised doubts about whether it was acting as an agent of imperial power and even suggested that it might be a hindrance to the British Empire's interests. The HBC's shortcomings were thereby kept in full view, adding to the Company's reputation as a flawed founding figure of a British Northwest Coast.

Yet, well into the 1840s, the HBC was effectively the sole source of first-hand information on the region.[51] This changed in the following decade; in the aftermath of the Oregon Treaty, a British-American surveying team was sent to mark out the 49th parallel on the ground. Meanwhile, British naval captain George Richards was given the task of accurately surveying the coast north of the border. With naval officers, hydrographers, botanists, and astronomers in tow, these surveying teams were a melding of scientific and imperial motives. Their systematic survey work produced an accurate, first-hand picture of the Northwest Coast above the new international boundary. This, in turn, provided colonial officials with a better idea of the new realm over which Britain was to exercise its sovereignty and power.

Indeed, in mid-nineteenth century Britain and British North America alike, the acquisition of scientific and geographic knowledge became ever more intimately linked to the acquisition of new colonial and national possessions.[52] The clearest embodiment of this scientific imperialism was the Royal Geographical Society (RGS) of London. Through the 1850s, the RGS actively promoted a transcontinental railroad line that would unite all of British North America; it also sponsored the Palliser Expedition, which spent three years surveying the Prairies and Rocky Mountains. Along with Palliser's extensive findings, the reports of Captain Richards, Lieutenant Richard Mayne, Judge Matthew Begbie, and other British officers and colonial officials were read and discussed at the RGS. The RGS also heard from Charles Nicolay and Thomas Falconer, who had contributed historical texts to the Oregon boundary dispute.[53] Taken as a whole, these reports were optimistic about Britain's far west possessions. However, this positive picture did not go unqualified: the long shadow of the HBC dampened the enthusiasm of some towards the region. Captain W.C. Grant arrived in 1849 as Vancouver Island's first independent settler, but he soon returned to England after his settlement efforts failed. Speaking before the RGS in 1857 and 1861, Grant was critical of the Island's prospects and harshly attacked the position and policies of the HBC.[54] Once again, the issue was raised whether the Company hindered or helped British imperial interests.

The RGS's activities had increased British knowledge of and interest in the far distant colonies of Vancouver Island and British Columbia; the discovery of gold in the Fraser River further heightened that interest. It also caught the attention of William Carew Hazlitt, a twenty-four-year-old British War Office clerk who would later become a highly respected historian. In 1858, the year of the Fraser River gold rush, Hazlitt published *British Columbia and Vancouver Island: A Historical Sketch of the British Settlements in the North-West Coast of America.* It is an obvious but significant point that this was the first text to use the term "British Columbia," for the colony had been created and named only weeks before. British Columbia was now a defined, concrete subject, its existence no longer contested. Hazlitt and subsequent authors could now focus on providing a historical lineage for it and on promoting its development. Working from previous histories (most notably those of Greenhow and Nicolay), RGS papers, government documents, and newspaper reports, Hazlitt constructed a scholarly British narrative for this new entity. As with previous English writers, he stressed the priority of British exploration and occupation, from Drake through Cook to Alexander Mackenzie; and, like some of the earlier writers, he displayed a distinct ambivalence towards the HBC. Hazlitt also provided an extended ethnological description of British Columbia's Native peoples, arguing that they were not doomed to extinction: rather, they could adapt if properly converted to the verities of Christian civilization. Of course, the book's overriding goal was to attract British emigrants to the region, and it informed prospective settlers of the various transportation routes to this "New Eldorado." Because of their resources, climate, and agricultural potential, Hazlitt concluded, British Columbia and Vancouver Island could become a "Britain on the Northern Pacific."[55] In this, the text was more concerned with the future than with the past, conscious as it was of the relatively light imprint of Europeans upon the region. The colonies' true history had yet to arrive.

Hazlitt's *British Columbia and Vancouver Island* was part imperial history, part promotional literature. Meanwhile, the events that had helped inspire it (the Fraser River and subsequent Cariboo gold rushes) also produced a spate of practical handbooks, all advertising the promise of gold-related wealth to be found in British Columbia. Some of these were prefaced with brief historical sections; all were primarily concerned with giving practical information on how to get to British Columbia's goldfields and how to go about mining gold once there. While some handbooks adopted a typically Victorian equation between material and moral progress, depicting the "thirst for Gold" as a force bringing British civilization to this wilderness, others expressed doubts about the kind of population attracted by such a materialistic motive. A Chinook-language dictionary was often appended to these works or published separately. The popularity of these dictionaries represented a pragmatic, if implicit, recognition of the fact that Native peoples vastly outnumbered British Columbia's non-Native population at the time.[56] Thus, these works eschewed the often dogmatic and stereotypical treatment afforded Native peoples in other early writings on British Columbia. That being said, the primary purpose of the handbook literature was to aid those who wished to exploit the region's natural resources or take up settlement there; that is, they set out to incite and assist events that would lead to the dispossession of the region's original inhabitants.[57]

A second form of promotional literature, the directory, emerged in the 1860s as the population of British Columbia and Vancouver Island rose with the Fraser and Cariboo gold rushes. Unlike previous writings on the colonies published in distant imperial centres, much of this genre was produced by Northwest Coast merchant interests. San Francisco publishers had a strong, early presence, demonstrating the extensive economic ties between the city and Britain's Pacific colonies. But with the growth of Victoria through the 1870s, the new provincial capital produced its own series of directories. The main purpose of the directory genre was to advertise the commercial possibilities of the area, providing readers with lists of citizens' addresses and vocations as well as information on various local businesses. They were "handbooks of merchant capital," practical guides for the profit-oriented, which saw little need to delve deeply into the scarce history the region had so far acquired.[58] This no-nonsense approach was taken by others as well. For instance, colonial surveyor-general and engineer J. Despard Pemberton published the *Facts and Figures Relating to Vancouver Island and British Columbia* in 1860. Pemberton argued that previous books on the region had not been useful because they spent too much time discussing the colonies' early history, an error the engineer did not repeat.[59]

Meanwhile, the colonial governments of British Columbia and Vancouver Island contributed to promoting the colonies, determined as they were to attract permanent, preferably British, settlers to replace the shifting and largely American population of gold seekers. The colonies' promotional efforts of the early 1860s also sought to repair the negative portrayal of the region that had emerged in previous decades. Accordingly, officials organized a coordinated exhibit shown at the London International Exhibition in 1862. In echoes of William Hazlitt's earlier history, the display and accompanying *Catalogue* extolled the "industrial resources" of Vancouver Island and British Columbia, stressing the region's England-like climate and agricultural potential.[60]

The two colonies also held separate prize-essay contests, with £50 rewarded to the author who best "set forth in the clearest and most comprehensive manner the capabilities, resources and advantages of Vancouver's Island [and British Columbia] as a colony for settlement."[61] The winning essayists, a Royal Navy doctor and an Anglican clergyman, admitted that Europeans had only briefly and lightly occupied the region. To both, hope lay in the future: rich with resources and capabilities, the two colonies promised to become outposts of Empire and Christian civilization as well as commercial centres on the Northwest Coast. In these government-sponsored works, the imperial motif was more prominent than the capitalistic. Meanwhile, history was harnessed to promotional purposes; it provided a brief, obligatory introduction to define the colonies in time, just as descriptions of political and geographic boundaries defined them in space. With the subject thus firmly in grasp, the author and reader could then look forward to a promising future.

The gold rush did not produce a lasting, systematic body of literature on the region, although it did place distinctly materialistic and fickle forces at the centre of British Columbia's early historiography. Promotional efforts and renewed interest in the region were linked as much to imperial and scientific motives as they were to the discovery of precious metals. A more significant literary legacy emerged from the naval officers, missionaries, and settlers who came to the area in the late 1850s and 1860s as part of the new British presence there. Though still sojourners, these men gained extensive personal knowledge of the Northwest Coast and from that experience produced systematic accounts of the region in properly Victorian tomes.

The first of these, Richard Mayne's *Four Years in British Columbia and Vancouver Island* and Alexander Rattray's *Vancouver Island and British Columbia*, were published by London houses in 1862.[62] Mayne served under Captain George Richards, completing survey work that arose out of the Oregon boundary settlement. Several of his reports had been read at RGS meetings, and he was one of three commanders to accompany the 1862 exhibit to London. Meanwhile, Rattray worked as a naval surgeon stationed in Esquimalt during the 1859 San Juan Island dispute, when the shooting of a pig sparked a crisis between Britain and the United States over ownership of these Georgia Strait islands.

The accounts of these two Royal Navy officers, while dependable and relatively moderate, were written from a decidedly imperial perspective, with a maritime orientation and an underlying anti-Americanism. Both also spent little time dwelling on the past, though enough to establish the plot of British exploration and sovereignty of the Pacific colonies. Rattray was clearest in his imperial vision of British Columbia's and Vancouver Island's future as a united colony, the physician in him arguing that the region was ideally suited as a health sanatorium for the Royal Navy.[63] He was equally optimistic about the colonies' economic prospects and suitability as destinations for British emigrants. While Rattray largely ignored the United States, Mayne expressed strong anti-American opinions. The latter's attitudes no doubt were coloured by the San Juan dispute then raging; to this were added an aristocratic disdain for democratic institutions and a suspicion of that portion of the American population that had been attracted by gold fever. As with other British writers, past and future, Mayne drew a stark contrast between an anarchic, violent American far west and the peaceful, orderly colonies north of the border.[64]

Others were less sanguine about the prospects of Britain's Pacific colonies. Duncan MacDonald was a civil and agricultural engineer who visited British Columbia and Vancouver Island from 1858 to 1862, working there with the Government Survey Staff and the Royal Engineers. Like W.C. Grant before him, MacDonald's plans to settle in the colonies came to naught, and he left the region bitterly prejudiced against its prospects. Upon returning to London, he published the 524-page *British Columbia and Vancouver's Island* and delivered lectures discouraging prospective emigration. In these, MacDonald was unremittingly negative about the climate and prospects of the region, labelling it an "inhospitable wilderness" and dismissing it as "England's Siberia."[65] He also depicted the colonies' officials as an "irresponsible autocracy" whose land policy was a disaster, and he took issue with the emerging view of the colonies as a peaceful realm in contrast to the violent American west.[66] Possessing better qualifications than others in the field, MacDonald might have produced a scientific assessment of the region's agricultural and settlement prospects; instead, his *British Columbia and Vancouver Island* presented a disjointed, unsystematic analysis, stronger on unqualified opinions than on reasoned arguments.

A more even-handed and dependable account of Britain's new Pacific colonies was presented in 1865, with the publication of Reverend Matthew Macfie's *Vancouver Island and British Columbia*. Macfie served five years ministering in the colonies, and, with the assistance of the two colonial governments, he embarked upon an 1864 speaking tour of Canada, Nova Scotia, New Brunswick, and Britain to promote emigration to the far west. These promotional efforts inspired him to write *Vancouver Island and British Columbia*, perhaps the most useful and balanced of the volumes to emerge during this time. The text was critical of the HBC and colonial governments headed by James Douglas. In the first such survey of the colonies' political development, Macfie introduced the notion of an autocratic "family compact" that existed between the Company and local governments.[67] Despite these criticisms, Macfie argued that the colonies' resources and climate promised a bright future, and he foresaw the completion of a transcontinental railroad. For the reverend, the latter represented the westward-moving tide of empire, race, and Christianity – all intimately linked to capitalism and civilization – which were in the midst of overtaking the region and providing it with its true destiny as the "England of the Pacific."[68] The materialist impulse of gold had played its role in initiating these forces but would be replaced by more solid agricultural and industrial settlement.

The promotional literature that emerged in the decade after the Fraser River gold rush was often overwhelmingly positive in its portrayal of British Columbia and its potential, and its treatment of the region's Native peoples was similarly optimistic. While earlier histories had largely ignored Natives, Hazlitt, Macfie, and Mayne in particular devoted considerable attention to them.[69] Unlike so many others, these British writers did not feel that the Natives were inevitably doomed to extinction; rather, they largely agreed that Native peoples could adapt to British civilization and thus survive, although they asserted that this was possible only if Natives converted to Christianity and European ways.[70] They also argued that the Northwest Coast's First Nations were not a violent threat and that most of the violence that had occurred was due to European, and most specifically American, provocation.[71] Here, of course, they resurrected the by now routine contrast between the purported US policy of virtual extermination of Native peoples and Britain's policy of benevolent conquest. Duncan MacDonald provided a dissenting view. In keeping with his efforts to discourage emigration from Britain to the region, he portrayed the Natives as a "murderous" and "bloodthirsty" threat.[72] Overall, though, in their desire to jump-start a flow of British immigrants that had yet to materialize, British writers during this time sought to portray British Columbia as an inviting field for settlement and missionary activities. It was in their interest to downplay any suggestion that the region's original inhabitants might have been hostile to such efforts.

Taken as a whole, those who produced the earliest writings on British Columbia were promoters of Empire and civilization. As Brook Taylor notes in his study of early historical writing in eastern Canada, writers of the promotional genre sought to order and civilize what so recently had been wilderness. With such a short tale of civilization's unfolding, the focus tended to be upon the future rather than the past. Indeed, a prehistoric past of wild nature and savage Natives only served to highlight the inroads civilization had already made, and it pointed to the promise of future development.[73] Over the course of the nineteenth century, writers on British Columbia gained more personal knowledge of the Northwest Coast; yet they remained sojourners rather than permanent settlers and viewed the region from the outside through global filters. Moreover, unlike Taylor's promoter-historians in eastern Canada, these writers' personal fortunes were not linked directly to the success of the colonies. Aside from the gold rush and directory literature, the English man-of-letters or Royal Navy officer who took to writing the more substantial work of this period had only a temporary and imperial interest in the region, further frustrating attempts to establish a continuous literary tradition.

From the start the writing of BC history proved to be a problematic task and British Columbia itself a difficult historical subject. The European writers who first turned their attention to the region were acutely aware that there was very little history upon which to build a founding myth. American writers on Oregon could work from motifs such as the Exodus-like trek of settlers along the Oregon trail, the martyrdom of the Whitman massacre, and notions of nationalist expansion that were an expression of the United States' doctrine of Manifest Destiny. Meanwhile, British writers were frustrated by the fact that their portion of the Northwest Coast had attracted only sporadic interest – and that that interest was marked by controversy and was largely speculative in nature. Even the theme of an expanding British Empire could not be applied without difficulties as the first permanent British presence in the region, the HBC, was not an un-equivocal agent of Empire. The Oregon boundary question, the HBC's peculiar status in the colonies, the gold rush: none of these provided a dependable, unchallenged base upon which to build the history of British Columbia.

2

Pioneers, Railways, and Civilization: The Late Nineteenth Century

In 1871, just thirteen years after the Fraser River gold rush sparked the first significant influx of non-Native people into the region, British Columbia became the westernmost province of a fledgling Canadian nation. The rhetoric of the occasion held out the promise of a glorious and prosperous future in which British Columbia would finally grow out of its early years as, in Adele Perry's apt description, "the awkward and disappointing child of the fur trade and British imperial expansion."[1] Yet British Columbia's new status could not hide some inauspicious facts: Native peoples still outnumbered non-Native peoples three to one; a daunting landscape mocked pretensions that it could be tamed; and the region's sparse non-Native population was separated from the rest of Canada by a sea of mountains and thousands of kilometres of ill-charted territory. In the decade and more after joining with Canada, British Columbians anxiously awaited the building of a transcontinental railway that would make its nominal membership in Confederation a reality. The difficulties experienced by the federal government in launching the railway, and thereby fulfilling the Terms of Union, led the province to reconsider whether it should stay in Canada at all. In this uncertain, even disquieting atmosphere, British Columbians would fail to produce a coherent historical narrative that might have quelled doubts about the province's fate.

Yet, the first full-fledged narrative history of British Columbia emerged out of this period, produced neither in the province itself nor in its national or imperial centres but in San Francisco. This is less surprising than it might first appear as the Californian city was the economic centre of North America's Pacific seaboard; until the completion of the Canadian Pacific Railway (CPR), it dominated British Columbia's commerce and linked the province to the outside world.[2] In 1878, San Francisco publisher-turned-historian Hubert Howe Bancroft visited Victoria to begin research that would culminate, a decade later, in the publication of his 792-page *History of British Columbia*. Part of a thirty-nine-volume history of the Pacific coast from Central America to Alaska, Bancroft's provincial history followed upon a two-volume *History of the Northwest Coast*, released three years previously.[3]

Bancroft was an unlikely candidate to fill the role of British Columbia's inaugural historian. Born in 1832 into a Granville, Ohio, family of Puritan stock, he received a high school education at home, followed by a disappointing year at a local college. He then entered the family book-selling business, which sent him (at the age of twenty) to the gold-enriched market of San Francisco. Within a few years, he established his own business, H.H. Bancroft and Company, which prospered through the Civil War and Reconstruction years. Strategically situated in the economic capital of North America's Pacific coast, the company became the largest bookseller, stationer, and publishing house west of Chicago.[4] As his business grew, Bancroft moved north of the international boundary; as early as 1862, he was supplying stationery and books to Britain's Northwest Coast colonies.[5] Bancroft had also entered the publishing field, producing a mining guide and a series of handbooks on the Pacific seaboard. These volumes made only the briefest reference to Britain's Pacific colonies. Nevertheless, they took their place with other handbooks of merchant capital that were released during this time, aiding those who sought information on British Columbia and those British Columbians who wanted to know about other Pacific states.[6] The most significant aspect of Bancroft's handbooks was the fact that British Columbia was included from the start in his emerging vision of a unified Pacific slope.

Ever restless, Bancroft was determined to go beyond the mere business of books and soon began formulating a grand scheme to write the history of North America's western slope. While collecting material for his handbooks, Bancroft had become convinced that the "old-timers" of the gold rush and Oregon Trail represented a rich source for the historian. He also felt an urgent need to collect the reminiscences of the aging pioneers as, with their deaths, much of the early history of the far west would pass away.[7] Through the 1870s, Bancroft oversaw a massive oral history project to record the testimonies of western pioneers. Meanwhile, he and his assistants travelled to the East Coast, Mexico, and Europe, collecting thousands of volumes that formed the basis of the Bancroft Library. As the size of his collection grew, so his geographic focus expanded: "Gradually and almost imperceptibly had the area of my efforts enlarged. From Oregon it was but a step to British Columbia and Alaska; and as I was obliged for California to go to Mexico and Spain, it finally became settled in my mind to make the western half of North America my field."[8]

To take on this ambitious project, too large for one man, Bancroft established a cooperative "history factory" that employed hundreds of assistants and a dozen co-authors. Organized on "business methods and the division of labour," the factory was an operating model of Adam Smith's pin factory. The various tasks of historical production-research, note taking, writing, and editing were divided up among a pool of employees. Overall editorial control remained in Bancroft's hands, although on some volumes his major assistants performed this function as well.[9] Even in the matter of authorship the history factory functioned as a capitalist enterprise: as employer, Bancroft claimed ownership of not only the means of production but also of the products of his employees' labour. What is notable about the subsequent *Northwest Coast* and *British Columbia* is that Bancroft was far more involved in their production than he was in that of other volumes. One-half of the original draft of *British Columbia* was written by three co-authors. None of the latter was American (William Nemos was Swedish, Alfred Bates English, and Amos Bowman eastern Canadian), no doubt contributing to the volume's even-handedness on controversial issues such as the Oregon boundary dispute. Along with drafting half of *British Columbia*, Bancroft exercised editorial control over the remainder, thereby producing a thematic unity to *British Columbia* that made the volume, in the words of Bancroft's American biographer, "one of the most readable of the thirty-nine."[10]

One reason for his direct involvement in the BC volumes was that Bancroft personally collected much of the primary material for them in a remarkable research trip to Victoria. He and his wife spent most of May 1878 in the province's capital, busily collecting material and interviewing individuals who "had taken an active part in the discovery and occupation of the country."[11] Despite some official reluctance, he secured access to colonial government records and HBC accounts stored at the provincial capital.[12] More important, though, were the papers and correspondence of James Douglas (made available by Douglas's family), Simon Fraser, John Stuart, and other deceased traders.[13] Copies of these documents were transcribed by an assistant and sent back to San Francisco. Bancroft then turned from the records of the dead to the reminiscences of the living. With the aid of his wife, he interviewed a number of HBC traders who had lived through the early history of the province. Roderick Finlayson, A.C. Anderson, John Tod, and others produced memoirs that recounted the role of HBC officers as "pioneers of civilization": men who had overcome a forbidding geography, peacefully and humanely pacified a savage Native population, and thus prepared the way for settlement.[14]

The hagiographical portrait painted by these Company men did not go unchallenged; Bancroft spoke with a number of former employees and frustrated settlers who levelled time-honoured criticism at the HBC. In their eyes, settlement under the HBC had been a failure, brought about by the Company's "obstructive, exclusive policy" and the inherent conflict between its fur trade interests and those of the colony's settlers.[15] Bancroft received material from still other sources; prominent individuals such as G.M. Sproat, P.N. Compton, Amor De Cosmos, and clergymen Edward Cridge and John Good drafted remarkably valuable and original manuscripts.[16]

Bancroft's collection efforts left a profound legacy for the writing of BC history. The Bancroft Library represented the first significant archival collection for provincial history, established a full thirty years before British Columbia founded its own archives. When Provincial Archivist E.O.S. Scholefield and University of British Columbia history professor Walter Sage undertook to build up the province's sparse archival collections in the early twentieth century, they would turn to the Bancroft Library, making frequent requests that it send them copies of material it held. Bancroft's efforts also laid the pragmatic foundation for a pioneer history of British Columbia. In contrast to earlier promotional literature, this history looked not to the future but to a pioneer past. It did so by drawing upon the accounts of the early European occupiers of the region (fur traders, government officials, settlers, and others), accounts that had been acquired from the actors themselves in a grand oral history project.

Of course, the sources available to historians shape the history they write. The former determine both what events can and are written about and the eyes through which these events are witnessed. By placing pioneer sources at the centre of his works, Bancroft ensured that the authors of those sources would emerge as history's main players. Certainly, Bancroft recognized that one could not view documents in a naive or simplistic manner, that the historian had to look at the evidence without bias or prejudice.[17] His own work showed a keenly critical perspective, and his willingness to step back from partisan or ideological positions set him apart from others writing the history of the Northwest Coast.

Bancroft's work thus was closer in its approach and methods to that of the more serious, national historians of the time than it was to that of other so-called amateur historians. A man of books, who gathered a massive personal library and viewed history as his true calling, Bancroft no doubt was well aware of contemporary currents in American historical writing. Over the second half of the nineteenth century, this writing was reshaped by notions of a "scientific history" that privileged a "methodology of the document." The inspiration for this new history was German professor Leopold von Ranke. Aided by the early nineteenth-century Romantic critique of the Enlightenment, Ranke and his disciples moved Western historical writing away from the programmatic, didactic tradition of the latter, which viewed the past as a realm of superstition and vice. History was still seen in a progressive way, as the story of humanity's material and moral progress; but now, there was to be greater appreciation of the past on its own terms. For Ranke, the historian's task was to recreate the past "as it really happened" – or more precisely, as it was experienced by the historical actors themselves. The way to do this was through the primary accounts and documents produced by these actors; the historian's focus thus was to be on individual agents and particular events rather than on a priori theories. Schooled in their own tradition of empiricism, American writers adapted the methodological tools Ranke crafted. Now, the historian could approach his or her subject free of personal bias and unearth the true story of the past, which was embedded in the accounts and documents themselves; taking a narrative form, and the vantage point of the actors themselves, the story essentially told itself.[18]

Bancroft's historical work partook of other, more regionalized trends. As a genre, pioneer history dominated western North American historical writing through the later decades of the nineteenth century.[19] Pioneer history resonated in the region's new societies because it spoke to the anxious search for historical legitimacy. Indeed, when *British Columbia* was republished separately in 1890, more than 230 copies were sold within one year, reflecting a deeply felt need in the young province for a dependable, substantial historical text.[20] Pioneer history also rang true because it employed powerful intellectual currents of the English-speaking Victorian world. Individual character and morality were seen as central; but individuals also stood as representatives of larger forces. In more established societies, historical actors tended to be "Great Men" who displayed virtue in the face of challenges and who embodied the great forces of their time. Pioneer history permitted the fledgling societies of western North America to use these same ingredients. In their struggle to build a life in new lands, pioneers stood as virtuous examples to which a fledgling society could aspire. Moreover, pioneers were the agents by which new lands entered the civilized world as they brought Christianity, commerce, and enlightenment to a previously savage wilderness. Ordinary people pursuing everyday tasks could thus be players in the grand sweep of history for they lived in a privileged time and place: North America's far west had only recently come into the ambit of European civilization, and they were present when that happened.

British Columbia, then, was incorporated into a universal historical narrative that had emerged with a modern Europe. This was the story of civilization's progress, a story with an underlying, inexorable trajectory: starting in ancient Greece, civilization had marched ever westward – into Western Europe, across the Atlantic to the eastern seaboard of America, and then into the wilds of western North America. For Bancroft, the history of the Pacific slope, British Columbia included, represented nothing less than the culmination of this universal history, "the ringing-up of universal intelligence for a final display."[21] The sense of geographic occasion the Pacific coast provided, with its meeting of mountain and ocean, thus was matched by a sense of historical occasion. Civilization could march no further west: the final act of history had begun in this, the last region of the globe to be brought into a Eurocentric world.

Bancroft pushed his vision for North America's west coast one step further; he believed that it was here that one would witness a "worn-out world re-animated."[22] In this vision, Bancroft was profoundly influenced by American intellectual currents. One of the most potent founding myths in the United States was the vision of the nation as a City on the Hill, a new land in which a revitalized society could be built, purified of the ills afflicting a tired and overcivilized Europe. Through the nineteenth century, unease grew that the eastern United States was falling victim to the same problems that had plagued old Europe, and an increasing number of Americans looked to their own western lands thinking that there the hope for a better society could be rekindled.[23] The myth of the western frontier emerged: the frontier was seen as an unbroken line moving westward. Here, heroic individuals brought the light of American civilization into new lands and, by their actions, forged the United States' identity as a free and democratic nation.[24] Subsequent historians of British Columbia would wrestle with the question of whether the frontier thesis applied to the province. As we shall see, Bancroft recognized the differences between the unfolding of the American and British-Canadian frontiers. For him, though, the dynamic underpinning the frontier thesis – the march of civilization over savagery – shaped historical developments both south and north of the border.

Bancroft's views on the craft of historical writing itself were of a piece with his grand world view. He believed the writing of history to be one of the highest endeavours of humankind, an "ennobling" vocation that played an active part in the spread of civilization.[25] As we have seen, "alphabetical writing" was a constitutive element in the modern European definition of civilization because it made possible the recording and drafting of a society's history and, thereby, the plotting of that society's progress.[26] Bancroft shared this definition; he argued that an essential difference between civilization and savagery was that the former preserved its past in written form, while the latter did not.[27] While his work described the actions of pioneer historical actors who brought the region into the realm of a European-based civilization, the texts themselves also civilized the region, inscribing it into the empire of written history.

Bancroft's hemispheric and global perspective was clearly shown in the three texts that covered the region that would become British Columbia. The two-volume *History of the Northwest Coast* examined events from the sixteenth century to 1846, when the Oregon Treaty drew the line dividing American from British possessions in the region. What followed were separate volumes for the different parts of the Northwest Coast. While sharing its earliest history with that of Oregon and Washington, *History of British Columbia* emerged as a distinct entity and volume, describing the period from the 1840s to Confederation and the coming of the CPR.

Bancroft and his co-authors constructed a unified narrative from the mass of primary material collected for *Northwest Coast* and *British Columbia*, largely because of the unifying vision described above.

This unifying theme – the region's move into civilization and into history itself – was most apparent in Bancroft's discussion of the region's Native peoples. For him, the history of British Columbia presented another instance of "the great and universal wiping out of savagism by civilization."[28] Accordingly, the defeat or recession of British Columbia's Natives was seen as inevitable; they were a doomed race, "children" whose best hope was to be treated as wards of the state.[29] Here, then, Bancroft's views did not depart from the conventional evolutionary scheme of his era, which by the late nineteenth century had hardened into a "radical biological determinism" that ranked different so-called "races" from inferior to superior, with the latter inexorably emerging dominant over the former.[30]

And yet, while other writers stopped here, with Native peoples thereby dismissed and not worthy of inclusion in any historical narrative, Native peoples did play a significant part in the *Northwest Coast* and *British Columbia* volumes. Alone among historians until well into the twentieth century, Bancroft suggested that Natives had often contributed to British Columbia's economy.[31] And, echoing William Sturgis before him, he intimated that they could lay claim to the Northwest Coast by "natural right."[32] However, Bancroft was not interested in Native peoples for their own sake; they appeared as passive and dependent, not active and independent, agents in their own destiny. Instead, they – or, more properly, their treatment by non-Natives – provided the means by which the march of civilization could be measured, and criticized, for Bancroft recognized the dark side of the historical forces he elsewhere celebrated. Without benefiting from its virtues, he argued, the region's First Nations had been afflicted by the vices of civilization, such as disease, liquor, and misguided missionary activity. Bancroft further railed against "our hypocritical civilization," which criticized the Natives' savagery while committing acts of greater violence, and which justified its coercive and deceitful possession of the land by "the laws of Christian nations that made might right."[33]

Bancroft was most critical of his own country on this score; he described the treatment of Natives in the American west as an "epoch of aboriginal extermination," which represented "the foulest blot in the annals of the nation."[34] Here, Bancroft was at odds with the main trend of the emerging

American historiography on the region, which, starting with the Oregon boundary dispute literature, tended to depict Native peoples as an obstacle that needed to be pushed aside, or worse. One particularly splenetic historian of Oregon called for the "utter destruction of the Indian race on the American continent."[35] For his part, Bancroft contrasted his compatriots' depredations with the benevolent conquest north of the border. For him, British Columbia was distinct, its history an "anomaly," because of the peaceful working out of the universal process of civilization's victory over savagery.[36] The benevolent yet firm policy of British traders and officials had prevented a repetition of the Indian Wars of the American frontier and had left the legacy of a realm ruled by law and order.[37] Of course, this contrast – American violence versus British benevolence, law, and order – was a theme much beloved by British and Canadian writers on British Columbia. Unlike the latter, though, Bancroft did not attribute this difference to the putative superiority of British (and thereafter Canadian) morals and institutions but, rather, to the more mundane and self-interested motives of material profit.

Bancroft, then, introduced a rarely heard sceptical voice into the writing of BC history, a scepticism that grew, in part, from his seemingly congenital nonconformism. At times, Bancroft flaunted his contrariness: he depicted Utah's Mormons in a favourable light at a time when they were widely vilified; he also harshly criticized John Fremont in an age when the filibuster was extolled as California's founding father. Bancroft even expressed disdain for Oregon's Methodist missionaries, whom others had canonized, arguing that they would end up destroying the Natives they sought to save.[38] In other words, Bancroft rejected major tenets of the American historiography on the Northwest Coast, depicting the emergence of an independent British Columbia in a favourable light and eliciting heated charges from his compatriots that he harboured a pro-British bias.[39]

Bancroft's penchant for sceptical nonconformism also revealed itself in his discussion of the Chinese presence in *British Columbia*. While other writers before and after him reflexively redacted Chinese British Columbians from their works, Bancroft made frequent and detailed reference to the contribution of Chinese miners in the various gold regions of the province; he carefully noted the returns they were making, even how many of them were working particular sites at particular times. Implicitly, the picture that emerged contradicted that of the established view of Chinese as sojourners and European and American immigrants as settlers. While the latter moved from one mining site to another in search of a big strike, and the large majority ended up leaving British Columbia altogether, the former's presence was less fleeting. The Chinese, Bancroft noted, tended to stay for longer periods, working sites more methodically; the result was an ongoing Chinese presence in British Columbia through the decades after the gold fever of the 1850s and 1860s.[40]

Curiously, Bancroft was not as assiduous in his description of the building of the CPR. A vast "army of labourers and mechanics," numbering more than seven thousand, toiled on the project, he wrote. What he neglected to mention was that the vast majority of this army was from China. His only reference to Chinese workers was an anecdote that involved a mere 150 men, engaged in a particularly arduous task; moreover, he listed the wages paid to railroad workers but underscored that these were for "white labour only."[41] In the wake of the CPR, Bancroft made note of a large, vibrant Chinatown in Victoria, once again belying the argument that Chinese British Columbians were mere sojourners in the land.[42]

Bancroft's language in describing Chinese contributions to British Columbia was remarkable in its neutrality – remarkable because, in the two decades after Confederation, anti-Chinese sentiment reached a fever pitch in the province. The provincial legislature passed bill after bill designed to exclude people of Chinese descent from the new society and polity forming there. Through the 1870s, the Chinese were prohibited from voting in provincial and municipal elections; they were also barred both from government employment and from working on contracted-out government projects. The following decade, the province decreed that Chinese could not preempt Crown land; at the same time, it tried to restrict immigration of Chinese into the region and to tax those who had already arrived. The federal government disallowed the latter bills, arguing that they were federal matters. However, in 1885 (after the completion of the CPR meant it no longer needed the thousands of Chinese workers that had entered in the previous years), Ottawa relented and passed the first of several head taxes on Chinese immigrants, while also disenfranchising those who had become residents.[43]

Bancroft made note of these moves in a brief but scholarly passage, providing dense footnotes that quoted the relevant bills and acts. It is hard to tell how sympathetic Bancroft was to these measures since he eschewed the harsh anti-Chinese rhetoric that marred the work of other writers. No doubt, as a Californian, he understood the position in which Anglo British Columbians saw themselves. He concluded that "on the Chinese question, British Columbia was, in relation to the dominion, somewhat as the Pacific United States were to the federal government, little hope being entertained by either that any radical change in the law would be made until the matter came home more closely to the doors of their eastern brethren."[44]

While Chinese immigrants and Native peoples played, at best, secondary roles in Bancroft's historical narrative, the Anglo newcomers in the early history of British Columbia entered the drama as pioneering agents of civilization. Most notable were the shrewd officers of the HBC, who had so impressed Bancroft during his 1878 trip to Victoria. In his writing, he described the Company veterans as courageous pioneers who, though few in number, controlled a vast wilderness region from their "outposts of civilization." For him, their greatest legacy was the peaceful pacification of the Native peoples, through which the way was prepared for further settlement and the next step in civilization's march.[45]

Bancroft's sojourn in Victoria, though, had introduced him to various criticisms directed at the Company. He was also aware of the staunch anti-HBC tenor of historical writing south of the border. Seeking to provide Oregon with a founding myth based upon missionary-settlers and a nationalist Manifest Destiny, the latter depicted the HBC as a despotic monopoly: it promoted the interests of a grasping British monarchy and deployed any tactic (including the incitement of Native peoples to violence) to thwart American settlement, commerce, Protestantism, and democracy.[46] Bancroft's own faith in free market capitalism and Jacksonian democracy only increased his willingness to criticize the HBC. With characteristic rhetorical abandon, he wrote of the "incubi of monarchy and monopoly" north of the border. In the face of frustrated settlers on Vancouver Island, he argued, the Company's officers formed a compact to control the colony's government, resisting efforts at wholesale settlement. For this reason, Company officers were not fully pioneers since they sought to keep British Columbia in a half-state of savagery. The HBC consistently subordinated civilization to commerce, resisting anything that would disrupt the Natives' trapping and trading of furs.[47]

However, Bancroft would not participate in wholesale HBC bashing, dismissing the worst of the charges levelled against it and stressing the generosity and humanity of its officers.[48] At the same time, he presented a shrewd analysis of the Company's policies based upon its material interests. To Bancroft, the Company was guilty of only one thing: pursuing its business interests with a calculating coldness. Its policies of resisting settlement and not disrupting Native culture, even its position vis-à-vis British colonial authorities, were governed by the profit motive. The Company, he wrote, "was by no means a free and full representative of the British nation. They were simply an incorporated association, acting for themselves, solely in their own pecuniary interest, and were as deadly opposed to opposition from people of their own nationality as from those of any other nation."[49] Eschewing the jingoism and moralism of other writing south and north of the border (which swung between demonization and hagiography), Bancroft contributed a materialist, interest-based analysis to the debate swirling around the HBC.

As we have seen, Bancroft believed a fundamental unity underlay the history of North America's Pacific coast. The regions north and south of the 49th parallel were drawn into the same story – the spread of civilization into a previously savage land and the "spoliation of its aboriginal inhabitants."[50] And, in this, American and British newcomers were equal partners, part of the same Anglo-Saxon family – "mother and child" – that was at the vanguard of history. Thus, much to the consternation of his compatriots, Bancroft accepted with equanimity the peaceful division of the region between these two colonizing powers. Bancroft's treatment of the Oregon boundary dispute, the event that created this division, was revealing here. Setting aside national partisanship and making extensive use of the existing literature, Bancroft's discussion of the competing claims suggested that British Columbia's separate existence was well founded upon a continuous British presence in the area.[51] In subsequent decades and volumes, the regions north and south of the new boundary parted ways; Oregon's fate was "Americanization" through rapid settlement, while the removal of the HBC to Vancouver Island marked the beginning of a distinct history in Britain's new Pacific possession.[52] Thus, Bancroft's discussion charted a middle path between writing north and south of the boundary that the Oregon Treaty created, with an abiding resentment among British Columbians matched by calls from some Americans to "re-annex" the province.[53]

In the *Northwest Coast* and *British Columbia* volumes, Bancroft was determined to balance the hemispheric forces that had caused him to include British Columbia in his Pacific slope series, with imperial and national forces that had ensured its independence from the United States. While he characterized the beginnings of representative government in sparsely populated, HBC-dominated Vancouver Island as "farcical," he argued that British political institutions had since taken root in British Columbia and that its people enjoyed the same freedom and security of rights as did Americans to the south. Bancroft went so far as to label Britain's colonies "virtually republics," a description no doubt seen as heresy by his American detractors. Likewise, Bancroft viewed British Columbia's entry into Canada as a positive development: just as the Pacific states filled out a transcontinental American nation, so the far west province completed an even younger Canada.[54] More profoundly, Canada and the United States were family, the "offspring of the mother of nations."[55]

At the time, the evolution of self-government and national status was not the dominating theme as it was among historians in eastern Canada. Rather, Bancroft's discussion of British Columbia's post-Confederation history was dominated by the promise and presence of the recently completed CPR.[56] Bancroft recognized that the CPR linked the province's fate to the British Empire and the Canadian Dominion. Significantly, Bancroft tended to stress the imperial and global aspects of the railroad: first conceived as part of an "All-Red" route linking Britain to the Orient and knitting together its worldwide Empire, it was only more recently taken up by politicians in eastern Canada. The CPR, Bancroft concluded, would ensure British Columbia's fate as an "England on the Pacific," fulfilling the mother nation's dream of a Northwest Passage.[57] Even here, though, Bancroft ascended to a grander perspective. Like the transcontinental railroads traversing the United States, the CPR stood as a monument to nineteenth-century industrial progress, linking the Pacific slope to the westward tide of commerce, humanity, and civilization.

H.H. Bancroft's *History of the Northwest Coast* and *History of British Columbia* were remarkable achievements. Backed by a legion of research assistants and co-authors, and utilizing the resources of western North America's largest publishing house, Bancroft collected and drew upon a mass of primary and secondary material that rivals any historical work up to today. Moreover, working from a clear vision of the main trajectory of the Pacific slope's history, he constructed a coherent narrative to plot out

British Columbia's development. Three decades would pass before another work of equal substance and quality was produced.

The CPR reached Canada's westernmost province a scant two years prior to the publication of Bancroft's *British Columbia*. The newly completed rail line brought with it the first significant wave of non-Native immigrants: half a decade after the CPR's arrival, British Columbia's non-Native population had risen eightfold from its meagre numbers at Confederation, and this number more than doubled in the ensuing ten years. Through the 1890s, an astonishingly small number of non-Native BC residents (fewer than one in five) were born in the province; the overwhelming majority of the rest came from eastern Canada or other parts of the British Empire.[58] Thus, immigrants disembarking at the newly created city of Vancouver stepped into a fluid and still-forming social environment. From miners and tradespeople, to entrepreneurs and professionals who sought to make their fortune or name, the better part of these immigrants were excited by the opportunities provided by what they saw as an untouched frontier. At the same time, there were some who recognized that this population of newcomers possessed no strong attachment to the region and that, if the society they sought were to be built, these people had to gain a sense of themselves as indigenous to this new land. A handful of literary-minded immigrants were convinced that knowledge of the province's history was necessary if its new population were to develop such a sense of belonging and identity, and that such knowledge needed to be locally produced.

This conviction sparked a short burst of historical writing in the early 1890s, producing a trio of provincial histories. John Kerr, Oliver Cogswell, and Alexander Begg had recently arrived in BC from eastern Canada and, drawing upon their backgrounds in journalism, publishing, and teaching, they set out to provide their fellow immigrants with the kind of written histories their home provinces possessed.[59] Echoing his fellow Nova Scotian Joseph Howe, Cogswell argued that knowledge of one's history was the necessary basis for love of one's country. By studying the history of far distant lands while ignoring local history, he concluded, citizens "reside in one country and live in the world of thought in another. Patriotism must flag under such circumstances."[60] The provincial government recognized the need for such locally produced history; it supported the publication of Cogswell's text by purchasing it for use in public schools, while Begg received $1,100 from the legislature for the research, writing, and publication of his *History of British Columbia*.[61] In their search for founding fathers, this trio of writers turned to the pioneer, as Bancroft had done before them. They shared the latter's fear that, in the face of rapid change and massive immigration, there was a danger that the few long-time residents who had participated in and knew the province's early history would be forgotten. Unintentionally echoing Bancroft, Kerr argued for the urgency of saving the memory and records of those who had weathered the "storm and stress of pioneer life and made the new condition of things possible."[62]

British Columbia's first resident historians also wished to correct the embarrassing anomaly of having an American outsider provide the first and only provincial history. They sought to bring historical writing closer to their new home, to take possession of it, for dependence on a foreigner as founding historian implicitly pointed to the fact that they were themselves newcomers to the region. Thus, they were harshly critical of Bancroft; they censured him as strongly anti-British, sharing the "bitterly patriotic, half-educated" hostility towards all British institutions of his fellow Americans.[63] Kerr dismissed Bancroft's work as inaccurate and deceitful, while Begg (who felt free to make extensive use of Bancroft's research to support his own arguments) assailed the American's "pessimistic" view of BC history.[64] Taking a spirited anti-American tack, this trio of historians set out to distinguish British Columbia from its southern neighbour.[65]

What the post-CPR historians sought was a more dependable and unequivocal set of founding myths – in short, a properly British narrative. Focusing almost exclusively on British explorers and fur traders, their narratives suggested that there was no shared history of the Northwest Coast prior to 1846. The HBC played an unambiguous role as imperial agent keeping the region British, and the CPR was described in global and imperial terms. This stress upon imperial over national themes would have an abiding presence in provincial historiography. Even Kerr, who, more than his colleagues, tended to stress the province's ties to Canada, argued that British Columbia had joined Confederation because of its loyalty to Britain, not because of any attachment to a new national vision.[66] Meanwhile, through his history, Begg sought to provide evidence of the "continued loyal feeling" of British Columbians to the British throne.[67] The fact that the latter felt it necessary to give such evidence reflected the anxiety he and others felt over the province's distance from Britain and Canada and its proximity to American influences.

In their desire to distinguish British Columbia from its southern neighbour, the post-CPR historians turned to a well-established motif – ironically, one that Bancroft himself had used: the province was distinct because of the "bloodless" victory of civilization over savagery, perhaps the most "easy and frictionless" pacification in history.[68] This proved to be the only significant role British Columbia's newly resident historians could find for the region's First Nations. Begg explicitly asserted that "little need be said" about the province's Native peoples. The latter were seen as people without history, whose timeless past was recorded in myths, not the written documents needed for legitimate history; subsequently, they played no significant role in British Columbia's development and, just then, were on the edge of extinction.[69]

Not surprisingly, the post-CPR histories were apologias for an Anglo immigrant society that was struggling to establish itself in Canada's far west. These narratives were constructed on the same settler ideology that underpinned British Columbia's official Native policy, stretching back into colonial times: until very recently, British Columbia had been an empty land, improperly used by its first inhabitants; with the arrival of British institutions and bona fide Anglo settlers, any and all claims Natives might have had on the region's land and resources had been extinguished; finally, the Terms of Union under which British Columbia joined Confederation simply continued and guaranteed the province's "liberal" policy.[70] Indeed, through the late nineteenth century, British Columbia's Anglo settler society continually pushed for even more reserve land to be opened up and brazenly resisted federal pressure to reassess or provide redress for reserve land that had already been reduced. In the historical narratives of the late nineteenth century, as in BC public opinion, there was no "Indian problem" to frustrate new settlers eager to make full use of the province's underused land. Begg, Cogswell, and Kerr spoke for their compatriots when they described British Columbia as a largely empty land of untapped resources. So recently a savage wilderness, it had now started along the road to prosperity and only needed more settlers like themselves in order for it to become "a great Maritime province."[71]

Just as this promised future excluded Natives, so it barred the thousands of Chinese residents in British Columbia. Arriving in Canada's far west on the eve of the 1891 census, the post-CPR historians stepped into a novel, and no doubt disquieting, population mix: the province's Chinese population was double that of ten years earlier, at just under nine thousand; one in eleven British Columbians was Chinese, and the province was home to 97 percent of all the Chinese in Canada.[72] These writers responded with a reflexive denial. Their histories made no mention of the mass of Chinese miners whom Bancroft had described as methodically working the various goldfields in the province, nor did they credit the thousands of Chinese whose labour built the railway line that had brought them to their new home. Kerr did mention British Columbia's Chinese population, but only to argue strenuously for their exclusion from the province. Here, he rehearsed arguments made commonplace by the ever-strengthening movement to exclude Chinese from all aspects of BC society: their willingness to toil for less money made them an economic threat; their immorality and crime made them a threat to social order; and their disease made them a health threat.[73] Begg's sole reference to Chinese in British Columbia was a failed effort at eloquence, when he referred to the grand westward movement of European peoples meeting the eastward movement of Asians at the Pacific coast, producing "the paradox of the pioneer confronting the Mongolian [sic]."[74] The paradox here, of course, was that the "pioneer" and "Mongolian" were set apart as mutually exclusive – there could be no "Mongolian pioneers."

The provincial histories written in the early 1890s remained isolated texts, of limited use and quality. They failed to match the standard of research and writing that Bancroft's inaugural work had set. Certainly, British Columbia's first resident historians were hampered by the dearth of historical resources and institutions in the province. Most notable was the lack of a full-fledged archival collection; nothing in the province approached the wealth of published and primary material that the Bancroft Library had amassed. The post-CPR historians were also handicapped by their own reluctance to build upon Bancroft's work. To them, the American historian had not provided the trustworthy British founding myths that they sought. At the same time, their own work did not inspire others to take up pen and paper, and it would be nearly two decades before serious attempts would again be made to write provincial histories.

3

A Greater Britain on the Pacific: History in the Edwardian Age

The three decades after Confederation had brought profound changes to British Columbia. Instead of abating, though, these changes only increased in speed and magnitude in the period between the turn of the century and the First World War as the triad of industrialization, urbanization, and immigration remade the province. The fact that these changes were somewhat delayed meant that their effects were telescoped into a shorter period of time here than in the rest of Canada. Between 1901 and 1911, British Columbia's non-Native population more than doubled to over 370,000; by 1921, it had reached the half-million mark, the better part of this increase squeezed into a few years before the First World War. On the eve of the war, an even smaller percentage of British Columbia's non-Native residents had been born in the province (a mere one in six), and a full six in ten came from outside Canada, mostly from Britain and its Empire.[1] As Robert McDonald writes of the time, the province was "a society in the making rather than a society made."[2] British Columbia's economy kept pace with this dizzying population growth, driven by the capitalist exploitation and export of the region's vast resources. Company towns sprang up in the province's hinterland, and the ports and streets of Vancouver teemed with industrial activity. The province had entered a new age: the days of an individualist and pioneer economy epitomized by fur traders, prospectors, and homesteaders had given way to a newly industrialized economy, with its capitalized corporations and bureaucratic organizations.

These rapid and profound changes created the conditions for a flourishing of local history in the prewar decade. The optimistic days of Edwardian British Columbia, when Premier Richard McBride ruled the province with his "Sunny Ways," instilled in many the conviction that mighty accomplishments had been made and that it was the job of historical writers to describe and praise them. At the same time, there was a strong undercurrent of nostalgia and concern that the perennially new society on Canada's Pacific coast needed to be rooted in the land and that it needed to shape its multifarious elements into an acceptable form. More specifically, there was a growing concern that the lessons and records of the past might be lost in the rush forward. British Columbians looked to history to provide the moral guidance and source of identity required by the fluid, still-forming society on Canada's west coast.

The province's golden age of Edwardian history was further fuelled by currents of thought in the larger English-speaking world. Through the late nineteenth and early twentieth centuries, history enjoyed growing popularity as the "queen of sciences."[3] In the wake of the Darwinian revolution, the period was marked by an evolutionary and progressive understanding of the world. A fundamentally historical mode of thinking set in: things were to be explained as they developed and changed – indeed, progressed – over time. Shifts in the currents of historical writing contributed to its popularity. The Romantic movement and Victorian thought had altered the modern historiographical tradition handed down from the Enlightenment. Influenced by Romanticism, Victorian and Edwardian historians turned to the past with greater sympathy and interest, both as having value in itself for the instructive lessons it proffered and as leading on to greater developments. At the same time, they accepted the Enlightenment's fundamental belief in progress, plotting it as the general rise from savagery to civilization. But now there was less emphasis placed upon an unequivocal and universal human nature and reason; rather, Victorian and Edwardian historiography shifted its immediate gaze away from the universal to the particular, focusing upon individuals, distinct peoples, nations, and imperial powers as the agents and manifestations of larger civilizing forces.[4]

The flowering of BC historical literature during the Edwardian era was made possible by the emergence of a distinct community of historically minded people. The seeds of such a community were sown with the formation of localized organizations such as the Natural History Society (NHS) of Victoria and Vancouver's Art, Historical and Scientific Association (AHSA), which would flourish in the decade prior to the First World War. Upon its creation in 1890, the NHS dedicated itself to increasing knowledge of the province's ethnology, geology, flora, and fauna. In 1901, it expanded its mandate to include "historical research," after pressure from more historically minded members caused it to revise its constitution.[5] But the NHS's contributions to BC history proper were modest; it was most active in supporting the provincial museum's collection efforts, while organizing lectures on topics more traditionally associated with natural history.[6]

Meanwhile, from 1894 on, the AHSA functioned as a centre of Vancouver's intellectual life, meagre as that life was. It operated on the belief that, in the words of one of its founders, it was "absolutely necessary in building up a nation to instill vitality by creating a history of those who have taken a prominent part in its discovery and growth."[7] To that end, from its foundation through the war, the AHSA held a regular series of lectures given by prominent individuals on historical topics. Early on, lecture topics varied widely, from the alphabet and Roman art to William Gladstone and Quebec. Beginning in 1908, though, BC history emerged as the dominant theme, with seminal addresses from provincial archivists R.E. Gosnell, E.O.S. Scholefield, and Judge Frederic Howay.[8] The AHSA's *Historical Papers* published three lectures from 1908. Modest though it was, this single volume represented the first attempt at a provincial historical journal.[9]

The focus on provincial history proved fleeting; after the war, the AHSA turned its attention to the establishment and promotion of the Vancouver Art Gallery.[10] Victoria's Natural History Society was even less committed to historical study. The two organizations made their most significant contribution to the production of provincial history by serving as meeting places for an emerging Edwardian community of historians. Members of the NHS included Gosnell, Scholefield, Alexander Begg, and Father Adrien Morice.[11] Howay served as AHSA president from 1910 through 1915, and his addresses, along with those of Scholefield and Gosnell, regularly appeared in other journals.[12] These same men, though, were frustrated by the absence of "some real historical society." They would have to wait until 1922 for the formation of the British Columbia Historical Association.[13]

In the meantime, the Provincial Archives of British Columbia emerged as the dominant institution for the Edwardian community of historians. While British Columbia lagged far behind the rest of Canada in the formation of a historical society and, more significantly, in the opening of a provincial university, British Columbia followed Ontario as one of the first provinces to create an official archives. As elsewhere, government-sponsored collection of historical material predated the emergence of a stand-alone archival department. In 1893, R.E. Gosnell was appointed the first permanent librarian of the British Columbia Provincial Library. The Library Act he helped draft authorized him to "collect and compile data relating to the history of the Province."[14] Gosnell's subsequent collection efforts represented a good, if haphazard, beginning: printed material included some two thousand pamphlets donated by 1890s historian Alexander Begg, numerous published volumes that formed the basis of the future Northwest History Collection, colonial government documents, and private papers.[15]

Despite his efforts to place archival collection on more solid institutional footing, Gosnell's own position remained dependent on political whim, and he was dismissed and rehired according to changing administrations.[16] Finally, the Provincial Archives was created as an independent body in 1908, with Gosnell at its head. The new archivist's first project was to mount an ambitious centenary commemoration of Simon Fraser's voyage down the Fraser River. Through 1908, an exhibit consisting of some of the most valuable primary material collected by the archives travelled to New Westminster, Vancouver, and Victoria. The exhibit was part of a broader pioneer history that sought to commemorate not just Fraser but also other "Old-Timers" who had built the historical foundations for the province.[17]

In its first year, the Provincial Archives received over $7,000 for the Fraser commemoration and accompanying efforts to collect pioneer reminiscences and material.[18] But, in a feast-or-famine cycle that would repeat itself, no appropriation for the department was made the following year, and Gosnell himself was sacked. The archives gained new life in 1910, when, buoyed by a landslide election victory and the boom years of Edwardian British Columbia, Premier Richard McBride's government appointed E.O.S. Scholefield as archivist and ushered in a half-decade of generous funding. From 1912 through 1916, British Columbia spent more per capita on its archives than any other province.[19] McBride rekindled his own interest in the province's past, personally assisting in the collection and publication of historical material.[20]

With generous funding in hand, Scholefield carried out an aggressive collection campaign. He travelled throughout the province on lengthy research trips and even trekked down the Pacific coast to California. Meanwhile, he solicited material from prominent local historians and surviving pioneers, initiated a copying program of HBC records in London, and entered into an agreement with the Bancroft Library, whereby material collected by H.H. Bancroft was transcribed and sent to Victoria.[21] These efforts added tens of thousands of titles to the government's collection, which historians now could consult in a newly constructed wing of the legislative buildings. Scholefield also made material available to historical researchers through publication of primary material and scholarly works. He used the appropriation set aside for his 1913 report to reprint over one hundred pages of original documents, including material relating to the Nootka Sound crisis and Vancouver Island's colonization.[22] The next year, the Provincial Archives launched its Memoirs series: in ten volumes over the next three decades, the Memoirs reprinted documents ranging from exploration and gold rush eras to colonial government papers.[23] Moreover, exhaustive bibliographies were compiled on various topics, including the extensive "List of Authorities" reprinted in Scholefield's 1914 *British Columbia from the Earliest Times to the Present* volume.[24]

By the time of his death in 1919, Scholefield had largely succeeded in his goal of turning the Provincial Archives into "a scholastic retreat for the student, the scholar and the historian."[25] Showing its international reach, prominent Washington historian T.C. Elliott labelled British Columbia's archives "a Mecca for us all."[26] Certainly, the archives remedied the decades-long anomaly whereby the most valuable repository of historical material on the province was housed 2,500 kilometres to the south, at Berkeley's Bancroft Library. Closer to home, the Provincial Archives proved to be an indispensable factor in the formation of a local historical community in the years prior to the First World War. The most prominent members of this community – archivists Gosnell and Scholefield, Judge Howay, Father Morice – could regularly be found at the archives and made extensive use of its holdings in their writings.[27]

The establishment of the Provincial Archives in 1908, and the robust, generously funded activities of its first decade, made possible both a more scholarly brand of history and, for the first time, a history that was locally produced by long-time residents. The archives' founding also helped spark an explosion of historical literature during this period; at long last, work on British Columbia's past reached a critical mass, initiating a sustained interest that would continue. During the buoyant Edwardian era, historical topics were common fare for local newspapers and periodicals such as the *British Columbia Magazine*.[28] More significantly, a half-dozen substantial books, including a handful of multi-volume sets, were published; most prominent among these were three survey histories of the province released with separate historical and biographical sections or volumes. The first of these was *A History of British Columbia*, its 317-page historical section written by then Provincial Librarian Gosnell.[29] In 1913, Gosnell collaborated with Scholefield on the two-volume *Sixty Years of Progress: A History of British Columbia*.[30] Finally, on the eve of the First World War, *British Columbia, from the Earliest Times to the Present* was released; Scholefield penned the work's first volume, Judge Howay its second.[31]

Each of these texts was initiated and produced by market-oriented publishers who wished to capitalize on the yearning for history in a rapidly growing Canadian west. The genre of subscription-based histories (with substantial biographical sections added, often as separate volumes) proliferated throughout the region during this time, with multi-volume series produced on each of the four western provinces.[32] Subscribers would pay to have themselves included in these biographical volumes, asserting their own importance in the region's still-forming societies. Publishers for these series were sometimes companies that existed for the sole purpose of producing the historical sets.[33] Other sets, such as *British Columbia* (1914), were initiated by American publishing houses like S.J. Clarke of Chicago, which opened a regional office in Vancouver to produce its BC volumes.

While outside interests were responsible for initiating and financing these histories, the former turned to the province's local community of historians to research and write them. What the publishers desired were narratives that would appeal to a paying readership: accessible, entertaining, and boosterish. British Columbia's Edwardian historians, though, had more ambitious goals: they sought to construct a localized version of their province's history with scholarly works that would draw upon the primary documents that so recently had been amassed. The clash between these two underlying motives led to a rocky, often testy relationship between historian and publisher. Scholefield in particular chafed under the constant demands of his publishers, railing against their "fee-for-halo" approach and expressing his "holy horror of these combinations of history and biography."[34] Meanwhile, Gosnell vented his frustration by referring to the *Sixty Years of Progress* set as "that hunk of cow dung."[35]

Such disdain was directed at the hagiographical biography sections of these sets, for which the publishers were responsible. There is no evidence the latter exerted any control over these volumes' historical content, and British Columbia's Edwardian historians took very seriously their own contributions to them. As long-time residents, they were keenly aware that the province had only recently come into the ambit of European history. Scholefield tried to impress upon his political masters the brevity of the province's history and to convince them of the urgency of collecting material from that history.[36] Likewise, Gosnell wrote that British Columbia's history – by which he meant the history of continuous non-Native settlement – had truly begun only with the completion of the CPR in 1885.[37]

The unnerving novelty of British Columbia made the Edwardian historians all the more determined to provide their home with a properly documented narrative, rooting their still-forming society in the region's soil. Their first task, then, was to chart British Columbia's tentative move into the empire of history itself. Not surprisingly, the provincial historians took the conventional position that, prior to the first European explorations in the late eighteenth century, the region lay in the realm of prehistory. But their description of this realm is singularly telling: it was terra incognita, a "no man's land" that lay hidden behind the "veils" and "mists" of ignorance.[38] In their lengthy discussion of British Columbia's early history, these writers reflexively adopted the perspective of the historical actors they describe.[39] This perspective was Eurocentric in the most profound way: all events were viewed through European eyes. If these events occurred outside the latter's vision, they literally were not history. The Northwest Coast thus entered the historical period when it became known to Europeans, and the people who had occupied the region for millennia were dismissed as prehistoric.

Moreover, the provincial historians employed a potent set of dichotomies, which further underpinned their distinction between British Columbia's historical and prehistoric periods. The fundamental trait that distinguished these two periods was the existence of an alphabetical language or, more directly, of a written record of the past. The other oppositions spun off from this: history versus myth, fact versus fiction, knowledge versus ignorance, light versus darkness, clarity versus mist. The Edwardian historians moved back and forth between these various oppositions but always with the former partner in the pairing overcoming the latter. So Scholefield could write that the story of the Northwest Coast "has formed no exception to this apparently universal rule – that the era of historical fact has always been preceded by a mythical age."[40] Lacking a written language, the region's First Nations resided in the darkness of myth and superstition, and would remain so even as Europeans discovered them. Likewise, in the absence of reliable facts, European novelists populated the region with their fictional creations: Jonathan Swift's imaginary land of giants, Brobdingnag, or François Rabelais' picaresque heroes.[41] Also rushing into this vacuum of European ignorance were equally fictional accounts of "apocryphal voyages" by the likes of Juan de Fuca and Bartholomew de Fonte.[42] All such flights of fancy were cleared away only when Europeans gained factual knowledge of the region.

What made possible the move from fiction and myth to fact and history, the Edwardian historians argued, was the presence of written records. The first of these had been provided by European agents in British Columbia's history (explorers, fur traders, pioneer settlers), and the recently founded Provincial Archives had amassed the records and made them available to the historian. Both Scholefield and Gosnell viewed their job as archivists as part and parcel of their role as historians; the former was simply the first step in the process of historical scholarship, while their own writing was the necessary second step, the point of the whole exercise. Scholefield labelled the primary documents he so assiduously acquired "the materials from which history is woven." With these in hand, he gleefully set out to debunk time-worn myths, exclaiming at one point: "Another damned lie nailed! This is good business."[43] As early as 1894, Gosnell defined his role as the province's official record collector as being "in the line of original historical research."[44] Even though he lacked formal training as a historian, Gosnell adopted a relatively sophisticated approach to historical writing and documents, recognizing that the latter gave only a partial window upon the past, one coloured by their author's point of view. A complete historical narrative, he argued, in a phrase redolent of R.G. Collingwood, went beyond the facts and documents to capture "the mental attitude, the mainsprings of thought ... the human element of the time and the action."[45]

For British Columbia's Edwardian historians, written records were not solely responsible for drawing the Northwest Coast out of its veiled, mythical past. Maps, notably those of early explorers, also inscribed the region in the European mind. Maps provided Europe with the first dependable knowledge of the region for, as we have seen, the legacy of exploration accounts themselves was more cartographical than historical. As interpreted by early twentieth-century historians, though, these maps contributed to the arrival of factual history to the region by replacing the fanciful cartography that had preceded them. Scholefield made the most significant contribution on this point. As provincial archivist, he pursued an avid interest in the evolution of early geographic knowledge of the Northwest by amassing a large collection of maps and manuscripts. Drawing upon this collection, Scholefield presented a fascinating survey of the region's historical cartography, which revealed the speculative and piecemeal knowledge possessed by European map-makers from the sixteenth through the eighteenth centuries. One particularly striking map reflected European knowledge of the region as late as 1775: while the rest of the Americas was inscribed in painstaking detail, a massive inland sea – *Mer ou Baye de l'Ouest* – sat where British Columbia should be.

Throughout, Scholefield's cartographical survey linked the emerging shape of the Northwest to the grand effort to discern the "true configuration of the earth."[46] He thus posited an essentially modern theme at the root of the region's history: the probing search for knowledge about the world that had driven Europe's global expansion. Indeed, as historical geographer Cole Harris notes, map-making was one of the "technologies of power" employed by colonizing powers; through it, the Northwest Coast was reconstructed through European categories, thereby enabling the subsequent "creation of formal colonial space."[47]

It was the creation of this formal colonial space – most particularly, the province's incorporation into the British Empire – that was the most explicit theme of the Edwardian historical literature. For these writers, the most important trait of "British" Columbia's identity was its membership in this Empire; from the very start to the present age, the province's history was just one chapter in a larger, imperial story. It was, in Scholefield's words, "the story of the rise of British power on the Northwest Coast of North America."[48] The province's move into history itself was intimately linked to the expansion of the British Empire. The first Europeans on the scene, the Spaniards and Russians, were disqualified as founding agents because they left behind no dependable, accessible written records.[49] Rather, it was the accounts of James Cook and George Vancouver that succeeded in drawing the lines that subsequent history would follow. From this start, as well, the form and trajectory of a British imperial story can be seen. Cook was eulogized and even his death plotted as part of a romantic drama: he was the hero who overcame the obstacles and dangers of charting unknown waters, who sacrificed his life for the greater cause of bringing the Pacific world within Britain's orbit.[50] Meanwhile, Vitus Bering was a tragic figure. Unlike Cook, Bering died in vain, as Russia would eventually surrender its tenuous claims to the Northwest Coast.[51] Finally, Spanish explorers appeared as weak, secretive, and, in the end, comical figures; representatives of a declining power, they chased after mythical rivers and lands on the Northwest Coast, and left behind no trace of their fleeting activities.[52]

Britain did follow up on its early presence as the land-based traders of the HBC took over from British explorers and maritime fur traders. The Edwardian historians' favourable treatment of the Company further illustrated the dominance of the imperial theme in their writing. Here, the HBC acted as an imperial agent that "saved the country for Canada, Great Britain and the Empire."[53] The Company's handful of traders and scattered depots acted as both "outposts of civilization" and "outposts of Empire" in a far distant wilderness.[54] They were responsible for the peaceful subjugation of the region's Native peoples, thereby preparing it for settlement. The HBC also staved off American encroachment and, in its founding of Victoria and reign over Vancouver Island, built the foundations for British institutions, law, and order. Certainly, the Edwardian historians were aware of the criticisms other writers had levelled at the Company. They noted in passing that, in its desire to maintain a fur trade economy, it was not always an aggressive proponent of settlement. They also recognized that the Company's dual role as private monopoly and colonial administrator was anomalous when compared to the development of political institutions in the rest of Canada, and they admitted that it often resisted progress towards representative government.[55] But these writers did not share the ambivalence towards the Company that provincial historians before them had felt. In the former's eyes, the HBC had to act the way it did to bring "order out of [the] chaos" of British Columbia's early history.[56]

The HBC thus emerged as a founding agent of British Columbia. It was an imperfect founding figure, given its autocratic nature and its hard-headed pursuit of private profit, but it played a necessary role: it kept the region within the British Empire and prepared the way for settlement, finally giving way once British Columbia was ready for more mature, British political institutions. The crucial trajectory for the Edwardian historians was British Columbia's evolution from far-distant colony towards the status of a self-governing polity within the British Empire.

It was Gosnell who made the most significant contribution here, providing the first systematic analysis of British Columbia's political development in the pre- and post-Confederation eras. The Ontario-raised Gosnell had been trained in the world of political journalism and had close ties to British Columbia's Conservative Party, serving as secretary to three premiers.[57] Drawing on this first-hand knowledge, as well as the government material to which he had access as provincial librarian and archivist, he presented a journalistic analysis of the province's politics. For colonial times, Gosnell plotted the fate of representative and responsible government, noting that British Columbia's development did not fit the contours of the Reform historiography that dominated eastern Canadian writing. In the former, there was no ongoing struggle between executive and popular branches of government, although faint echoes could be heard in the opposition to the political dominance of the HBC. Also missing was a popular movement of the sort that had agitated for representative government in the Maritimes and Ontario; rather, elective institutions were introduced by colonial British authorities.[58] Gosnell described the evolution of domestic BC politics after Confederation as well. Here he showed an acute insight into that chaotic period of jostling coalitions out of which emerged the rise of party politics, which brought stability and economic prosperity, embodied in the administration of Richard McBride.[59]

What is most notable about the Edwardian historians' discussion of Confederation is the imperial, rather than the national, perspective they adopted. Confederation was an important step, to be sure, but Canada's "greater destiny lies in the sister possessions of an Empire in common."[60] While exhorting British Columbians to cultivate stronger feelings of attachment to their Canadian compatriots, these writers did not call for a new Canadian nationalism; rather, their goal was a British imperial "patriotism," spread throughout the Empire.[61] Likewise, the "supreme achievement" of Confederation – the Canadian Pacific Railway – had indissolubly linked British Columbia to Canada, making possible the transcontinental scope of the new nation.[62] The railway, though, was an imperial project not, as central Canadian writers viewed it, a national one. It was "the initial link in that *mightier* chain to unite the Motherland with Canada, and the Orient and Australia on the all-red line of Empire."[63] This unequivocal privileging of the imperial over the national tie distinguished historical writing in the far west from that in central Canada, where "the National interpretation" of Canadian history came to dominate.[64] Like BC historians, this national historiography emphasized the development of British political institutions; unlike the former, though, the latter's primary focus was on the evolution from colonial status to Canadian nationhood, which represented the story's climax.

Meanwhile, on a personal and professional level, British Columbia's Edwardian historians remained in splendid isolation from their counterparts east of the Rocky Mountains. One reason for this was that the province still lacked its own university, so there was no one with direct links to the emerging guild of academic historians to the east. Instead, British Columbia's amateur historical community had been formed around localized organizations and institutions, notably the Provincial Archives. The involvement of this community in two massive national history projects only served to underscore its isolation. Central Canadian historians initiated the twenty-volume Makers of Canada series (1903-8) and the twenty-three-volume *Canada and Its Provinces* (1914-17) in the hope of incorporating Canada's far-flung regions within a single nation-building narrative.[65] A handful of British Columbians contributed to these series (including Gosnell, Howay, and even Premier McBride), but this participation did not result in any lasting links between them and eastern Canadian historians. Howay would later develop such connections, but he was the exception; Gosnell's experience was more typical. In his usual acerbic style, Gosnell labelled his *Sir James Douglas* the "token" BC volume in the Makers of Canada series. Even though the work was heavily edited by federal government statistician and *Labour Gazette* editor Robert Coats (who subsequently was listed as a co-author), Gosnell and Coats worked wholly independent of each other, never meeting or communicating.[66]

The imperial focus of British Columbia's Edwardian historians reflected and reinforced the broader imperialist sentiment that was so strong in the province through the early decades of the twentieth century.[67] This sentiment was perhaps best expressed by Premier McBride, an ardent and public imperialist who stressed the intensely British nature of the province in his introduction to the BC volumes of *Canada and Its Provinces*. Meanwhile, as a young man, the English-born Scholefield had desperately yearned for a career in one of Britain's far-flung colonies, where he could serve to bring about "one mighty, consolidated, and independent" Empire.[68] Fellow archivist Gosnell devoted much of his career to promoting the vision of greater imperial unity. He helped establish the British Empire League of British Columbia and, in journals and pamphlets, lobbied for a program of "Empire consolidation." Inspired by the model of the Canadian federation, this renewed Empire would be based upon concrete arrangements in defence, trade, and political institutions, and not upon ill-defined sentiment. At the same time, the staunchly Conservative Gosnell categorically rejected any move towards autonomy from England, accusing Liberal leader Wilfrid Laurier of plotting such a break for Canada.[69]

In his imperial view of Canada, Gosnell was part of a wider movement that emerged in late Victorian Canada, which agitated for more formalized ties within a renewed British Empire. This movement had weakened considerably by the Edwardian period, and most of its remaining life bled out on the killing fields of the Somme and Passchendaele. But in British Columbia, the imperialist sentiment remained strong, and it would continue to have a profound impact on the province's historical writing. Gosnell, for one, argued that the war had illustrated the need for *greater*, not less, Imperial unity, thereby setting himself apart from the increasing number of his compatriots who used Canada's achievements in the war as the basis for a nascent English Canadian nationalism.[70]

The abiding potency of the imperial theme in British Columbia's historical writing also affected the role played by the United States in these histories. At first glance, it might seem surprising that the sustained anti-Americanism of earlier provincial histories was largely absent in the Edwardian literature, given the fact that British Columbia had been vulnerable to annexation by the United States for so much of its history. The prewar historians did employ motifs introduced by their predecessors, contrasting both the treatment of Native peoples north and south of the border, and the level of violence in the respective mining frontiers. An orderly and lawful British Columbia was set against the violent anarchy of the American frontier.[71] They also criticized the jingoism that was stirred up in the United States during the various boundary disputes in the region. With the exception of the recent Alaska boundary question, though, the prewar historians concluded that Britain and the United States had come to generally fair compromises.[72] Of course, to say otherwise would suggest that Britain, the bedrock of the province's identity, had failed to protect the interests of its subjects on the distant Northwest Coast, and that British Columbia's love for the motherland was unrequited.

The Edwardian historians no doubt drew confidence in the British fate of the province from contemporary events. The promises of Confederation and the CPR were finally coming to fruition, and British Columbia thrived as it strengthened its ties to the Canadian and British imperial economies. Moreover, the decade prior to the First World War witnessed a massive influx of British immigrants, which reinforced the province's feelings of attachment to Britain and ensured that it would not slip into the hands of the republic to the south. Finally, the relative absence of anti-Americanism in their writing can also be explained by the Edwardian historians' views on race. For them, Britain and the United States shared a kinship as part of the same Anglo-Saxon race; they were mother and child of a common civilization, which was rising to world dominance.[73]

Marching alongside and serving the cause of Empire were the forces of commerce and capitalism. Scholefield and Gosnell wrote that British Columbia was destined to become "an industrial and mercantile Britain" on the Pacific coast.[74] The province's place on the Pacific coast made it a transit point to an Oriental market that had enticed Europeans for centuries, while its location as the terminus of an All-Red transcontinental rail line linked it to markets in eastern Canada and Britain. British Columbia was to become a major centre for global commerce, a modern-day Northwest Passage linking Europe to Asia. Indeed, Scholefield argued that, from its earliest times to the present, much of British Columbia's history had been shaped by "the commercial spirit of the Anglo Saxon race, one of the greatest propelling forces that the world has ever known."[75] Moreover, in its abundance of material resources, British Columbia possessed the same elements for industrialization that had propelled England a century before. Sharing the booster mentality of the time, British Columbia's prewar historians applauded the development of these resources by local entrepreneurs and international capitalism. Gosnell argued that private property was the basis for society, and he rejected class-based critiques of capitalism as "specious."[76] Even while they looked back nostalgically to the bygone pioneer days, these writers maintained a strong faith in "progressive" capitalism and concluded their works by predicting the future greatness of a materially prosperous British Columbia.[77] Running through their work was a familiar booster rationale for BC history: the past was to be studied to demonstrate the great promise that the province held, both materially and as part of the British Empire.

The historical literature of Edwardian British Columbia represented a heyday of imperial sentiment and capitalist faith; it also demonstrated the belief that race was a determining factor in the province's history. The pre-First World War historians implicitly adopted and applied the "race idea" that was so prevalent in their society and in Anglo-American thinking more generally. As Kay Anderson notes in her groundbreaking study of racial discourse in British Columbia, this concept was predicated on a "radical biological determinism" that emerged through the later half of the nineteenth century.[78] In a misapplication of Darwinian thinking, races were equated with species: both were immutably, biologically different. History unfolded as a social struggle for survival, in which the fittest, superior race (Anglo-Saxons) won out over inferior ones (Asian, African, Native American). Accordingly, British Columbia's Edwardian historians wrote freely and interchangeably of the "Aryan," "Anglo-Saxon," and "British" race.[79] As with provincial historians before them, they depicted this race as the vanguard of history and civilization. And, of course, people of British descent were seen as the purest incarnation of the Anglo-Saxon race, their expanding Empire further proof of their superiority. While these writers rather grudgingly accepted Americans as part of this race – as children of a British mother – other European peoples (Spanish, Russian) were dismissed as inferior: listless, waning, and retrograde, they gave way to a more vigorous, progressive British people in claiming the Northwest Coast.[80]

The "race idea" was applied with little imagination to British Columbia's own population in the Edwardian historians' discussion of Asian residents of the province. These writers shared with the majority of British Columbians an atavistic anxiety over this "problem" – one they viewed as unique in Canada. They responded by writing Asians out of BC history, making little mention of Asians in their works.[81] In doing so they had to elide significant events in the region's history: the large number of Asians who helped exploit British Columbia's gold resources in the 1850s and 1860s, and the contribution of thousands of Chinese in the building of the CPR. In the brief consideration given them, Asians were depicted as an immutably different race that could not or would not assimilate into "British" Columbian society. They were alternately depicted as inferior to Anglo-Saxon peoples or as a threat due to their numbers and guile. Whatever the picture, these two races represented what Gosnell labelled inviolable "biological spheres," which could not accommodate each other.[82] Moreover, Asians were viewed as interlopers: while Europeans worked to lay the foundations of British Columbia, Asian immigrants had no intention of remaining in the province and sent their earnings home. In this way, the province's historians could skirt the inconvenient fact that both they and their Asian counterparts were newcomers to the Northwest Coast.

Indeed, the pre-First World War historians regarded their work as part of a broader effort to build what Gosnell called a "white man's country" in British Columbia.[83] The year after the 1907 Vancouver Riot, when an Anglo mob rampaged through Asian sections of the city, Gosnell showed his solidarity with the rioters. Japanese cunning and Chinese willingness to work for degraded wages meant they were threats to "white labour," he wrote; the government and other organizations thus had to take measures to protect the latter, and this included restricting Asian immigration.[84] Arguments such as these helped fuel an increasingly powerful anti-Asian movement in British Columbia through the early decades of the twentieth century. Indeed, anti-Asian sentiment and discourse emerged as a distinguishing and constitutive element of the province's dominant society and politics. The provincial government disenfranchised Japanese residents in 1895, two decades after doing the same to Chinese British Columbians; in 1907, this ban was expanded to include East Indians. In 1903, the federal government raised the head tax on Chinese immigrants to $500, ten times its original amount. Four years later, it bowed to pressure from British

Columbia and signed a "gentleman's agreement" limiting immigration from Japan. At the same time, the province's political parties, labour unions, newspapers, and popular organizations (such as the Asiatic Exclusion League) fought for the restriction or, more commonly, outright exclusion of Asian peoples.[85]

What is notable here is that the writing of history was a crucial tool wielded by British Columbia's dominant society in its construction of social boundaries and in its assertions of who belonged and who did not. The Edwardian historians crafted a historical lineage that defined their society as indigenous to the land over which it exercised control. And, according to the thinking of the time, even the most recent British arrivals could lay claim to this lineage. They belonged, argued the editors of Vancouver's leading newspaper, because "they are our kith and kin ... entertaining for British laws and customs and for the British flag the same respect which we ourselves hold."[86] Meanwhile, Asian peoples did not belong because, no matter how long they had been in the region, they remained, in the words of a BC Supreme Court Justice, "perpetual aliens."[87] This oxymoron is telling for it reveals what Edwardian British Columbians meant when they defined other peoples as alien or foreign and themselves as indigenous. These terms were prescriptive rather than descriptive; they were hegemonic constructs, used to assert one group's hold on social, political, and economic power. In the end, it was not one's place of birth that determined whether one belonged in British Columbia but, rather, one's ethnicity and history.

Not surprisingly, British Columbia's Edwardian historical literature also excluded the region's First Nations from the racially homogenous society it sought to delineate. But Natives could not be dismissed as alien in the same way as Asian peoples had been for they were neither recent arrivals nor sojourners whose homeland lay somewhere across the oceans. Indeed, Natives presented a unique challenge to British Columbia's historians: how could the latter define themselves as indigenous to the region, while legitimating the historical dispossession of the province's indigenous peoples? The intellectual and social circumstances of the time made this task somewhat easier. The rise of scientific racism had led to a hardening of attitudes towards Native peoples through the late Victorian and Edwardian periods.[88] Native peoples also appeared to be vanishing: while at Confederation seven in ten British Columbians were Native, this number dropped to one in twenty by 1911, when the Native population hit its all-time low of 20,174.[89] Finally, Native peoples were segregated from the BC polity by legislation, whether through disenfranchisement or the suppression of cultural practices, and they were physically set apart through separate schools and a miserly reserve system that the provincial government stubbornly refused to change despite federal pressure to do so.

This tug-of-war between Victoria and Ottawa came to a head in the years before the First World War and provided the backdrop for the period's historical writing. Seeking a "final adjustment" of the province's Native land question, in 1912 the BC and Canadian governments established the McKenna-McBride Commission to decide where new reserve land needed to be created and where existing reserve land could be cut back.[90] The commission was arguably the clearest expression of the settler ideology that underpinned government policy and public opinion in British Columbia. According to this ideology, many reserves were not being properly occupied or developed and thus, by law, should revert back to the province, which would then sell the land to non-Native settlers. Not surprisingly, provincial historians of this time echoed these arguments. Writing for an eastern Canadian readership in the wake of the McKenna-McBride Commission, Gosnell categorically rejected the argument that Natives had any existing claim or title to British Columbia's land or resources.[91] As with the histories of the 1890s, so for the Edwardian historians: there was no Indian land problem. British Columbia's historical development had already prepared the land for settlement by European peoples. Natives were not significant players in the province's past; they could be pushed aside and made virtual outsiders in their own land.

The Edwardian historians' first step in the marginalization of the region's First Nations was to dismiss them as people without history. For these writers, a people needed a written record of its past to be considered historical. Certainly, British Columbia's prewar historians recognized the need to begin at the beginning; however, for them, the province's history began with the arrival of European explorers and fur traders. The period before this belonged to the realm of prehistory, and the people who resided there were prehistoric. Thus, historians did not need to concern themselves with the region's first inhabitants as any study of them was the task of ethnologists. Scholefield, for one, successfully resisted suggestions that a chapter on Native peoples open his *British Columbia* (1914) volume. Local amateur ethnologist Charles Hill-Tout did write a chapter on British Columbia's First Nations, but it appeared near the end of the book, as an afterthought to the text's lengthy historical narrative.[92] The result of this acceptance of modern, European-defined history's privileging of written records as constitutive of civilization was that the province's historians viewed the past through European eyes. Natives could be seen only as they appeared in accounts left behind by the European explorers, fur traders, and settlers who had so recently arrived in the region.

The marginalization of Native peoples continued on even after Europeans brought the region from prehistory into history. On the rare occasions when they were included, provincial writers depicted Native peoples as exotic, inferior, and savage. Like children, they were capable of contradictory impulses, from innocence to cruelty and depravity; like children, they were not credited with being fully developed moral creatures. Scholefield summarized these views with concise brutality: Native peoples were "ignorant, superstitious and cunning, yet childlike."[93] In these historical narratives, Natives often played the familiar role of threatening backdrop for the main story of European occupation.[94] The region's Native peoples provided the opposition – savagery – against which civilization was defined and by which its progress was measured. In the end, they, like nature, existed to be subjugated.

The fate of British Columbia's Aboriginal peoples, then, was to give way to the Anglo-Saxon peoples who were just then coming into the region in large numbers. Reflecting the fact that British Columbia's Native population reached its nadir in this period, Edwardian writers viewed them as a waning race, a static culture that had been unable to adapt to the coming of Europeans. This belief prompted Scholefield, in his capacity as provincial archivist, to push for the collection of Native material culture; he feared that American and European ethnologists would loot the province clean in their scramble for native artefacts.[95] Yet, the Edwardian historians pulled back from predicting the final extinction of the province's Natives. Gosnell, for one, argued that, because of the HBC, the natives had survived into the settlement period as a "docile and useful ... people."[96] More presently, he added, the plight of Native peoples was actually improving as they progressed along the path to assimilation.[97]

Such views were inconsistent with the racial determinism that dominated these writers' overall perspective. This inconsistency can be explained by their determination to distinguish British Columbia from the American far west. Making use of a well-established motif, the prewar historians drew a sharp contrast between the purported benevolence and peace of Anglo-Native relations north of the 49th parallel and the violence and cruelty on the American side. Such images of a peacefully pacified Native population were part of the rehabilitation of the HBC's historical reputation. The presence of British colonial and Canadian national power, it was further asserted, had continued this policy of benevolence.[98] This was a rare occasion when British Columbia's historians were in step with their counterparts in the rest of Canada. The theme of benevolent conquest was a core tenet in the nationalist mythology that was gaining strength in Canada, thanks in large part to a maturing national historiography. As Elizabeth Furniss writes, this served to define "the Canadian spirit and ... national identity through the continual assertion of history as a narrative of paternal domination of Aboriginal peoples."[99] The dispossession of Native peoples was, thereby, legitimated; indeed, this dispossession was depicted as in the interests of the Natives themselves.

And yet, even in this heyday of racialist thinking, alternative images were introduced into provincial historical writing. In his *History of the Northern Interior of British Columbia*, first published in 1904, Adrien Morice rejected some of the fundamental premises of Edwardian historiography. Morice was a French-born Oblate missionary, who, from 1885 to 1903, ministered to the Carrier people from his post at Fort St. James. In his writing, he criticized existing histories for their dismissal of Native peoples as of no interest to the historian and for their single-minded reliance on written documents. The oral accounts of Native elders "were reliable as genuine history" when complemented by written sources; and Morice did use both as the documentary basis for his historical narrative.[100] A revealing example of Morice's use of oral evidence is found in his account of the 1829 confrontation between James Douglas and Carrier elder Kwah at Fort St. James. Drawing on Native sources, Morice disputed the accounts of other historians, intimating that their written documents were biased. He thereby rejected the hagiographic portrayal of Douglas, which these accounts presented in their search for founding figures for British Columbia.[101]

Moreover, living and working amid the isolated Carrier tribes, the Oblate missionary rejected prophecies of Native extinction. For him, not only would the Native peoples survive physically but their culture and languages would also endure. And he sought to contribute to this survival by compiling extensive and scholarly syllabaries of Native dialects.[102] Nevertheless, Morice viewed Native peoples through a paternalistic filter. As biographer David Mulhall argues, Morice saw himself as the father-king to a flock of child-like Native people. The Oblate missionary tried to maintain a strong hold over the Carrier by refusing to teach them English, thus ensuring that he was their only link with the outside world. "Only in a colonial situation such as existed on the British Columbian frontier," Mulhall concludes, "could Morice satisfy his need for human relations of inequality and acknowledged subordination – for a paternalism long overthrown in his native France."[103]

While Scholefield would label Morice's work "painstaking" and "valuable," the missionary's innovative approach had no discernible impact on the province's Edwardian historians.[104] Morice's oral history sources and plot lines, both of which demonstrated the active participation of Native peoples in BC history, simply had no place in the narratives the prewar writers had constructed. Instead, the main actors in these narratives were those men who had laid the foundation for British Columbia's existence. Odes to "THE PIONEERS" were liberally strewn throughout the Edwardian literature, part of the larger "idealization of the pioneers" that dominated western North American historical writing in the decades prior to the First World War.[105] In an article written in conjunction with the 1908 Fraser Centennial, Gosnell gave a succinct definition of this group of founding fathers: "Men who blazed the first trails, built the first homes, sailed the first ships, laid the foundation walls of our constitution."[106] Not surprisingly, "Great Men" such as James Cook, George Vancouver, Simon Fraser, and James Douglas figured prominently in the pioneer pantheon. Yet, as did Bancroft, the Edwardian historians recognized that the work of planting a European-spawned civilization involved more mundane efforts. The "pioneer army" of miners and settlers that followed the explorers and fur traders made history without realizing they were doing so, simply through "the prosaic every-day hard work of just making a living and homes in a new country."[107]

These men were making history because they were the agents of larger forces. They were history's vanguard, bringing the Northwest Coast into history and planting the seeds of Empire and civilization. The pioneers represented a historical aristocracy for British Columbia, providing legitimation for the new society that was still forming. They also provided that society with moral instruction. The likes of Cook and Mackenzie were stirring examples of humanity, heroism, and courage in the face of hardship; their lives stood as instructive biographies of the rise from humble beginnings to greatness. They and those who followed bequeathed "to posterity a splendid example of devotion and duty."[108] This example, in turn, would provide British Columbia's still-forming society with social stability. Gosnell was most explicit on this: "hero worship," he argued, provided moral order by constraining and guiding the present generation according to the values handed down by previous generations. Not only was social peace thus attained, but the weight of history saved society from confused thinking and class selfishness, which Gosnell felt were threatening Western civilization in the early part of the twentieth century.[109] The pioneer era represented a golden age of heroic, individual efforts that provided a moral yardstick to a society with very little bottom – a society that was becoming more complex as it entered the age of industrial capitalism. The example of the pioneers would help guide this material growth and assist in the larger goal of building a prosperous, sober British society on the Northwest Coast.

The pioneer history constructed by British Columbia's early twentieth-century historians was built along rigid gender lines. These narratives were dominated by male characters, with women scarcely mentioned. A manly pioneer motif was in full evidence here: the main story was of masculine Anglo pioneers wrestling with untamed nature and Natives, overcoming them and thereby ensuring the victory of Empire and civilization in the region. Outside the mainstream Edwardian historical literature, though, a handful of female writers sought to construct a womanly pioneer history. Nellie de Lugrin's *Pioneer Women of Vancouver Island, 1843-66* was the most substantial work to come out of these efforts. Making use of material from the Provincial Archives, and with archivist John Hosie editing, Lugrin gave prominence to the wives of Vancouver Island's "Great Men," while also noting the efforts of more ordinary women. For Lugrin, British Columbia's pioneer women were engaged in "the great issues of loving and mating, of birth and death, and the struggle for existence under terrible odds."[110] Novelists Agnes Laut and Frances Herring made contributions as well, proffering the common fare of explorers, fur traders, and miners.

But while women were included in these accounts (most often as wives of pioneer men), the main actors were nearly all male. Moreover, the narrative voice was the first-person singular, the verb tense the present, and the authors often drew upon their own experiences in the province. As such, these works were examples of "experiential history," the genre within which most female historical writers worked during this time.[111] Indeed, women were largely excluded from the domain of serious historical writing. Of the three discussed here, only Laut appears to have any ties with British Columbia's mainstream historians, and, significantly, she turned to a Victoria women's organization to publish her work. In the prevailing social climate, women were generally viewed as temperamentally and intellectually unfit for the scientific, objective history to which male historians aspired. More female writers were publishing their work than ever before, but these writers were storytellers, not historians, their style literary and subjective. The handful of female historical writers in early twentieth-century British Columbia remained isolated from the exclusively male, mainstream community of historians, and their work had no discernible impact on the latter.

Another factor contributing to the absence of women in the mainstream Edwardian historical literature was the relative absence of women in the province at large. The 1911 census revealed that for every three women in British Columbia's non-Native population there were seven men. To many British Columbians, this situation represented an "imminent moral peril and imperial disgrace."[112] Frederic Howay, for one, was alarmed by this threat, noting that the province's overwhelmingly male frontier had lacked the virtuous influence of women and that a similar lack of women among Chinese immigrants reinforced their alleged decadence and immorality.[113] Overall, the dearth of female pioneers made the construction of an imperial history problematic. As Adele Perry notes, the presence of white women was supposed to be "evidence of British Columbia's transition from savage to civilized."[114] White women's "special role in the colonial project" was to help save the region for Empire and civilization. Their presence would provide the basis for proper settler families, prevent the miscegenation of British men and Native women, and offset the allegedly decadent influence of thousands of Chinese males.[115] But the realities of British Columbia's history did not live up to the needs of a colonizing historical narrative, and the province's Edwardian historians had to go about constructing their histories without the aid of the very powerful motif of pioneer women as civilizing, imperial agents.

British Columbia's stark gender imbalance was yet another problem confronting the Edwardian historians in their efforts to construct a satisfactory narrative for the province. The singular brevity of the European presence, British Columbia's geographic isolation from Britain and Canada, the fluid nature of a society in the making, and the uncomfortably polyglot composition of its population: all these proved to be troublesome facts. And the anxiety they produced is what made British imperial ties so attractive to those of the province's dominant society. For only the power and grandeur of the greatest Empire in the world could overcome the isolation, novelty, and social fluidity that characterized British Columbia in the years leading up to the First World War.

4

The Domain of History: Judge Frederic Howay

The first two decades of the twentieth century produced an outpouring of historical literature on British Columbia. While the quality of this work was uneven, the Edwardian historians did improve the scholarly standards of provincial historiography – most significantly in their increased use of primary documents, which had become available with the opening of the Provincial Archives. However, these amateur historians largely failed to shed the intellectual blinders bequeathed by the Victorian era, with its grand themes of civilization, empire, and race, or to move beyond the hagiography of pioneer history. One member of British Columbia's Edwardian community of historians, Judge Frederic Howay, proved more successful at this. From his first attempts as a published historian, during the 1908 Simon Fraser Centennial, until his death in 1943, Howay published some three hundred books, articles, addresses, and reviews on the history of the Northwest Coast. Howay's work was both prolific and durable. His early historical narrative, *British Columbia from the Earliest Times to the Present*, replaced H.H. Bancroft's survey as the standard in the field and would remain so for over four decades. And the judge's later work on the maritime fur trade would prove to be the most original and lasting primary research undertaken in the province well into the twentieth century.

Of all provincial historians studied thus far, Frederic Howay possessed the most intimate knowledge of Canada's westernmost province. In the words of W. Kaye Lamb, who as a child lived near the judge's home, Howay "grew up with British Columbia."[1] Born in London, Ontario, the year of Confederation, Howay was three years old when his family was drawn west by the Cariboo goldfields. In 1874, the family relocated to New Westminster, where Howay would reside, with brief interruptions, until his death. From his earliest public school days onward, Howay showed an avid interest in history, an interest fuelled by the stories of pioneer British Columbia with which he grew up. Frederic Howay personally knew many of the region's pioneers, including his father-in-law William Ladner, who had built a supply trail to the Big Bend Mines in the 1860s.[2]

Upon graduation from high school, Howay spent three years teaching in communities outside Vancouver. During this time, he was admitted into McGill University's Associate of Arts Program, hoping to pursue historical studies; however, he was forced to forgo the opportunity, evidently due to lack of money. In 1887, with the assistance of a wealthy uncle, who no doubt thought this a better investment than a liberal arts degree, Howay departed for law school at Dalhousie University. Accompanying the future judge on the newly completed Canadian Pacific Railway was another class of 1890 law student, Richard McBride. Both McBride and Howay returned home upon graduation, the former to provincial politics and the latter to private legal practice in the rising communities in the lower Fraser Valley and in the province's interior. In 1907, Howay secured an appointment from the Liberal federal government as judge of the County Court of New Westminster, where he served until his retirement three decades later. Howay's ascension to the bench was due, in part, to his solid Liberal connections. Liberal politics ran in his family, and his appointment may have been his reward for running against Conservative premier Richard McBride, a personal friend and British Columbia's most formidable political opponent, in the 1907 provincial election.

A year later, Howay's career as a publishing historian was launched when, upon the urging of Premier McBride, he contributed to the centennial commemoration of Simon Fraser's descent of the Fraser River. Howay's interest in Northwest Coast history had never flagged; from the time of his return from Dalhousie, he had been collecting historical material on British Columbia and had established links with the community of historians that was forming in the province.[3] The 1908 Fraser commemoration, initiated and organized by Provincial Archivist R.E. Gosnell, provided Howay with the opportunity to indulge a passion for history he had not been able to pursue in his own formal education and career. Through public ceremonies and published addresses, he depicted Fraser as one of "Britain's heroic explorers, to whom we who reap the benefits of their labors owe honor and love and veneration."[4] Howay also joined

McBride in presiding over a reunion of surviving Royal Engineers, labelling them "builders of the West."[5]

Thus, Howay participated in the celebratory and popularizing pioneer history that characterized the province's Edwardian historical literature. While his own research would soon move towards a more scholarly, specialized standard, he continued to produce works for popular and educational audiences. Howay's commitment to furthering education in British Columbia dated back to 1891, when he began a fifteen-year term as secretary for the New Westminster school board; in 1912, he wrote the BC chapter for the province's official grade school text on Canadian history.[6] Through the 1920s and 1930s, he produced a trio of books that his publisher, Toronto-based Ryerson Press, hoped would be adopted as school readers.[7] These texts were pared down versions of his more serious work: straightforward, accessible surveys of BC history, they also appealed to a wider readership in the province. The tone of these books was celebratory, holding up the likes of James Cook and George Vancouver as "heroes" and "builders."[8]

Howay worked as a popular historian as well, writing pieces for journals such as *The Beaver*, founded and published by the Hudson's Bay Company. Here, the judge stressed the picturesque and dramatic, presenting history through a filter "tinged with the colour of romance."[9] For Howay, popular historians not only had to be accurate in their writing but also accessible and readable. To this end, the historian must bring out the "romance and picturesque of the story," its human element, thereby making the past live again for the reader.[10] Finally, Howay contributed to the popularization of BC history through historical organizations: he was an active member of the Art, Historical and Scientific Association of Vancouver, the first president of the British Columbia Historical Association (BCHA), and the provincial representative of the Historic Sites and Monuments Board of Canada.

Howay's popular and educational efforts emerged from his conviction that the historian had a crucial role to play in society, particularly in a society as young as British Columbia's. He was motivated by the goal of making "history a real influence in the lives of our people."[11] Howay knew from personal experience how novel the province was, and how rapidly it was changing in the early decades of the twentieth century. What most troubled him was the danger that his fellow British Columbians would dismiss the province's history as too brief and inconsequential. Speaking before the BC School Trustees Association in 1915, he noted that "there are some who imagine that the history of our province commences with the gold excitement of 1858."[12] To combat such historical vertigo, Howay set out to show that British Columbia's history stretched back centuries and contained "elements of great and romantic interest."[13] In his inaugural presidential address to the BCHA, Howay employed the same metaphors and images Scholefield had used to plot the region's move from fiction and myth into fact and history. The "mists" and "clouds of doubt and darkness" that shrouded the Northwest Coast from European eyes were lifted with the arrival of explorers and fur traders, whose accounts were literally the "earliest pages" of British Columbia's history.[14] The opening of Howay's *British Columbia: The Making of a Province* echoed these themes: the time before the coming of Europeans was "a twilight period, before the dawn," when the region had yet to enter "the domain of history." Only with the "progress of [European] geographical knowledge" did the Northwest Coast see the light of day.[15]

Howay also shared with his Edwardian counterparts the conviction that history could serve to protect the social and moral order of the day. The "heroes" of history provided the examples of virtue and devotion to duty that were acutely needed by the young and fluid society that was forming in British Columbia. History also provided the province's British-derived institutions with legitimacy by plotting their evolution as positive, necessary, and, thus, natural. That Howay should hold such orthodox views is not surprising for he belonged to the intimate social and political elite then ruling the province. A classmate and friend of future premiers Richard McBride and W.J. Bowser, Howay belonged to a number of the fraternal organizations that knit this social elite closer together. As with McBride and so many others among the elite, Howay was a long-time Freemason; the judge was also a member of Victoria's Pacific Club and the Terminal City Club of Vancouver, two of the most prestigious clubs in the province.[16]

Aside from these social connections, Howay was an active member of the province's ruling elite. As a County Court judge for three decades, he executed the rule of British and Canadian law, thereby upholding the sovereignty of the Crown. In his most prominent case, Howay also proved himself to be a staunch defender of property and capital. In August 1913, riots broke out in the Vancouver Island town of Ladysmith when striking coal miners resisted their employer's use of special constables and strike-breakers. The strike and riots caused considerable property damage, though no serious injuries. To pacify the rioting strikers, the provincial government called in hundreds of militia and ended up charging and trying 166 miners.[17] After the conviction of a third of these, Howay meted out unusually stiff sentences. While pontificating about the need to "temper justice with mercy," he sentenced three men and two boys to two years in the penitentiary, the maximum allowed by law. Howay then sentenced twenty-three others to a year in jail, plus a $100 fine, and another eleven to three months, plus fifty-dollar fines. Subsequently, Howay was called upon to defend the sentences to the federal minister of justice. His original ruling had concluded that the rioters had engaged in planned "terrorism," which he followed up by painting the riots as the result of a violent conspiracy.[18] Howay's judgments were considered harsh even by the standards of the time, and most of them were overturned. Twenty-two of the convicted strikers were pardoned, and none of them served his full term, although one did die in prison, apparently from a lack of proper medical attention.[19]

Howay's historical writing at the time showed a similar faith in the means and ends of capitalist development. His 1914 *British Columbia* lauded the province's capitalist class as builders of the province. It also eulogized Robert Dunsmuir as a "pioneer of pioneers" and defended the often ruthless tactics the coal baron used over the course of building his business empire.[20] This celebratory pioneer history was in evidence elsewhere in the book, for instance in its depiction of the Royal Engineers as "builders" responsible for "laying the foundations" of British Columbia's existence.[21]

Such hagiography, though, was not a dominant theme in *British Columbia*'s 727 pages, which examined the period from the gold rushes to McBride's administration. This text represented a significant transition in Howay's work, away from the limitations of the province's Edwardian literature and towards a more scholarly and critical history. Here, Howay was not satisfied with his contemporaries' reliance on individuals to personify and explain larger historical forces; rather, he sought to get to the deeper, often more prosaic forces and structures at work. Accordingly, an abiding materialism lay at the root of the judge's analysis in *British Columbia*. The first such material force in the text was the discovery and mining of gold. From the formation of British Columbia as a colony to its entry into Confederation, he argued, the most significant events in the development of the province resulted from the various gold rushes that washed across it. In a remarkable passage, suggestive of a nascent staples thesis, he wrote: "The Fraser River excitement of 1858 resulted in the formation of the Colony of British Columbia; the Cariboo excitement of 1860-64 caused the building of its great arterial highway and the accumulation of a large bonded indebtedness; the Big Bend excitement of 1866 left the colony in a bankrupt condition, induced a stronger demand for retrenchment, and so driving the people to seek a road to escape the heavy taxation, led to confederation."[22] Howay also moved towards a more systematic consideration of the mining industry, plotting its evolution from its individualistic stage to more capitalized, mechanized efforts culminating in the "business-like development of interior hydraulic mining."[23] His description of other industries (such as coal mining, salmon canning, and agriculture) charted·a similar evolution as well as revealing a consistent Edwardian faith in the progress of capitalism.[24]

An abiding materialism was also evident in Howay's discussion of British Columbia's political development. From the evolution of British political institutions to the various administrations that dotted the province's electoral landscape, politics in *British Columbia* were not essentially about matters of principle; rather, the judge wrote, "financial considerations are dominating factors in politics."[25] The union of the colonies and Confederation were effected for material reasons: both were seen as solutions to persistent financial difficulties.[26] Howay assiduously charted the fiscal condition of British Columbia from the time of Douglas's governorship to the contemporary government, lamenting the "dark days" of deficits and heralding the "dawn" of budgetary surpluses under Premier McBride.[27]

Moreover, Howay followed Gosnell in noting the irregular nature of British Columbia's political history. The judge earlier argued that "the doctrine of evolution" had no place in the formation of the colony as the rapid influx of people in 1858 meant that the job of establishing government had to be completed rapidly and with unusual abruptness.[28] In the second volume of *British Columbia*, he described the province's "anomalous" political situation: its dual governments ruling a meagre population and the HBC's private and autocratic power.[29] The theme of British North

America's steady evolution towards self-government, which dominated the emerging historical guild of central Canada through the early part of the century, was not prominent in Howay's writings. Instead, more prosaic material matters repeatedly found their way into his narrative.

Not only was there something anomalous about the political development of British Columbia, but in Howay's scheme, for most if its history the province was scarcely a unified entity. The division that split British Columbia in two, and that underlay most of his writing on politics, was that between Vancouver Island and the Mainland. This division, which Howay likened to the European balance of power, animated or coloured all major political issues in the volume, from the time of competing colonies through to the turn of the century. This fissure ran so deep "that the province as a whole had no view." As a New Westminsterite, Howay sided with the Mainland, depicting the "small local interest" of the Island as the culprit, dominating the government and retarding the province's growth and unification.[30] A decade later, Howay himself would become embroiled in the tension between Island and Mainland in a controversy that split the BCHA along old regional lines, sparking his resignation as the association's president.

The fundamental, and for Howay lamentable, Island-Mainland fissure waned only with the influx of new immigrants brought to the province by the economic upturn sparked by the completion of the CPR.[31] The building of the railroad itself, though, was the fuel firing the second most significant conflict dominating British Columbia's political life: the province's wrangling with its new federal masters over the railroad, how quickly it was to be built, and where it was to terminate. While methodically setting out the province's case for "better terms" and describing its hallowed tradition of "fighting Canada," Howay never picked up the provincialist banner, remaining sympathetic towards the position of the federal government.[32] At the same time, he did not portray the CPR as the instrument by which a new national dream had been completed. The final spike represented the fulfilment of another grander dream – the age-old search for a Northwest Passage – thereby linking British Columbia to its exploration and fur trade past. As with the Cariboo Road before it, the railway played its role in "man's triumph over the forces of nature."[33] Interestingly, Howay did not view the CPR through the imperial filter of his Edwardian counterparts – as part of the British Empire's All-Red route spanning the globe. Nor did he see the railway primarily as part of a nation-building project, a theme of eastern Canadian historical writing. Instead, Howay focused on the CPR's effect upon the province itself, seeing it as one of many forces that were increasing its population and mitigating its sectionalism.

Politics alone were a largely divisive and localizing force, somewhat secondary to material and financial issues. For Howay, the existence of British Columbia as a unified entity came not with the political union of its two colonies or with joining Canada, but, rather, some two or three decades after Confederation. First, considerable numbers of new immigrants had settled in the province, lessening the pre-existing sectionalism.[34] Second, Premier McBride's "business-like way" and introduction of political parties had brought sanity to British Columbia's books and stability and unity to its political life. Regional differences could now be brokered within each of the major province-wide political parties, which acted as unifying forces much as did the two major federal parties on the national scene. No longer would the fissure running along the Georgia Strait, or the chaotic mix of personal friendships and animosities, dominate. And, indeed, we can see in the second volume of *British Columbia* that the development of the province had been moving towards this unity: the influx of population that earlier had lessened the Island-versus-Mainland rift resulted, on the eve of McBride's premiership, in a redistribution bill that, for Howay, effectively killed these "insane local jealousies."[35] British Columbia had come into its own under McBride, the province's first "native son" premier.

Another significant theme in *British Columbia* was the series of international boundary disputes through which the borders of the province were defined and British sovereignty recognized. Drawing on his university training in international law, Howay set out the competing claims and historical context of boundary conflicts from the Nootka controversy to the Alaska boundary dispute. Overall, the judge sided with Britain, arguing that the United States claimed more than it was entitled to and that inflammatory American public opinion was the primary cause of this. Britain, on the other hand, was seen to be asserting legitimate principles, such as the freedom of the seas. But, in the end, London's desire to keep peace with the United States and its ignorance of the region meant that British Columbia and Canada's interests were compromised in the final settlements.[36]

The resentment expressed here by Howay emerged from his position as a British Columbian and Canadian (Canada was still a colony of Britain in matters of international affairs), who was determined not to fall under the government of the United States but who recognized that the home country was willing to sacrifice its colonies' interests to protect its own. This precarious position was combined with one that plagued all BC historians as the series of boundary disputes revealed the often tenuous hold that Britain and its successors and, thereby, British Columbia, had over the region.

Finally, almost as an afterthought, Howay addressed issues relating to the social development of the province. Here, the judge adopted a moralizing tone largely absent in the remainder of the volume. Native peoples were largely absent from *British Columbia*, the only extended discussion of them coming in two chapters devoted to missionary activities. Here, the judge presented Protestant and Roman Catholic efforts in an even-handed manner for what they shared was more important than any sectarian differences between them. The missionaries' common task was "to change these savage natures, to end the barbarous and degrading customs, to civilize, and then to Christianize these heathen."[37] Indeed, at this early point in his historical career, Howay took a conventional view of Native peoples; they were secondary to the main story, and, in their infrequent appearances, they assumed the role either of dangerous threat or child-like victim.[38]

As we shall see, Howay's depiction of British Columbia's first inhabitants would change over time, becoming more attentive and sympathetic. Even at this early date, though, there were both similarities and significant differences between Howay's views and those of other Edwardian historians. Howay used the same motifs as the latter in describing the Northwest Coast before the coming of Europeans as a prehistoric land – hidden from Europe by the "mists" and "clouds" of ignorance – and the people living there as without history. Howay went even further, describing British Columbia at this time as "in a state of nature – just as if it had come from the hand of God."[39] Native peoples were depicted as part of this landscape, as wild as the animals that roamed the region's dense forests.

Unlike the Edwardian historians, though, Howay acknowledged that Natives had been the first occupants of the region, and he pushed Schole-field to include a chapter on Native peoples at the beginning of Volume 1 of *British Columbia* because they "were there first."[40] In his later *British Columbia: The Making of a Province*, Native peoples were discussed in the second chapter, before Captain Cook and the maritime fur trade. Yet for Howay, as for his contemporaries, the fact that Natives had lived in the region long before the arrival of Europeans did not give them a claim to the land. However, the time-worn argument that Natives were people without history was just one reason why he believed they were disqualified as heirs to the Northwest Coast. The judge also resorted to more legalistic arguments to legitimate the dispossession of Native peoples by British Columbia's settler society. For Howay, Britain had gained sovereignty over the region (and then bequeathed this sovereignty to British Columbia and Canada) through the "law of nations," which European nations had developed to legitimate their colonial expansion.[41] Howay, who had studied international law at Dalhousie, utilized a central premise of this legal tradition in arguing that the first "civilized nation" that brought about Native acquiescence and then undertook "real possession, occupation, and put them to use [could legally claim] the sovereignty of waste lands."[42]

Of course, for Howay, Britain was the first "civilized nation" to do this on the Northwest Coast. Notably, Native occupation of the region had not bestowed sovereignty upon the first inhabitants because the land still lay in a state of nature: it had not been properly occupied by an organized, settled society and state, and it had not been improved or developed through the use of human labour. This was the primary basis upon which Howay's own settler society exercised sovereignty over British Columbia. As a judge, Howay himself acted as an agent of that sovereignty, so it is not surprising that he did not question the right of Britain to possess the region. Tellingly, Howay participated in the BC government's ongoing efforts to frustrate Native claims for land and redress (just then clearly demonstrated in the province's push for reserve cutbacks through the McKenna-McBride Commission). In 1914, Howay served as a provincial government representative on the royal commission established to assess the value of the land around Victoria that had been taken out of the Songhees Reserve to be used by the Esquimalt and Nanaimo Railway. In questioning witnesses, Howay focused on the narrow question of the land's market value; he refused to permit testimony pertaining to the historical process that had produced the reserve and made no mention of the Songhees people themselves. And, of course, the latter were not asked about the value of this land.[43]

While Howay at least acknowledged the Native presence in BC history and believed Native peoples could assimilate into the dominant, Anglo settler society, his views on Asian British Columbians were more exclusionary. Howay made only passing reference to Chinese miners in his discussion of British Columbia's gold rushes, which he saw as pivotal events in the province's history. Moreover, he completely neglected the contribution of thousands of Chinese workers in building the CPR, another watershed for the province. After a detailed discussion of the railway's construction, he concluded that it represented "man's triumph over the forces of nature" – that is, European man's triumph.[44] Howay was uncharacteristically vitriolic in the few references he did make to the province's Chinese and Japanese residents. He repeatedly noted how other British Columbians "despised" Chinese residents, and he revealed his own feelings by labelling them "little yellow men."[45] He also echoed the arguments being made by his contemporaries in newspapers, unions, and political parties: the Chinese represented a serious economic threat because of their willingness to work for low wages; meanwhile, the Japanese were dangerous because of their adaptive abilities and their "wily" minds. For Howay, the presence of Japanese residents was a distasteful "Imperial burden" that British Columbia had to bear due to Britain's efforts to maintain its alliance with Japan. Lest it antagonize the latter, the Canadian government could not act to wholly exclude Japanese immigrants and had to settle for the 1907 "gentleman's agreement" that restricted such immigration.[46]

Howay's views on Asian British Columbians would grow even harsher with time. In the 1914 *British Columbia*, the judge opposed efforts by "well meaning" bodies to push through exclusionist legislation, viewing the latter as an abuse of the law; instead, he argued, market forces should be left to work to restrict Asian immigration. Presumably, these "market forces" included the tax imposed on every Chinese immigrant, which a decade earlier the federal government had raised from an original $50 to $500.[47]

By the late 1920s, Howay saw the "Oriental problem" in a different light; now he supported legislation and other efforts designed to exclude Asian immigration.[48] No doubt, the judge had been favourably impressed by the effects of the federal government's 1923 Chinese Exclusion Act, which halted all immigration from China. In the years after the Exclusion Act, the Japanese replaced the Chinese as the primary menace in the minds of BC opinion makers. Howay was no exception; he argued that the Japanese had "invaded" almost every aspect of BC life and now posed "a very serious economic threat."[49] The growing hysteria in the province over the presence of over 20,000 Japanese British Columbians would culminate during the Second World War, when, in 1942, the federal government evacuated all Japanese residents from the Pacific coast, moved them to camps in the interior and Alberta, and confiscated their property. There is no record of Howay's reaction to Ottawa's extraordinary moves, but it would have been inconsistent with his overall views if he had opposed it. In the end, Asian peoples were excluded from Howay's vision of BC history and society. His writing was built on the province's prevailing orthodoxy, which defined Asian peoples as sojourners who could not nor would not assimilate. In the push for a white man's province, they were dismissed as perpetual aliens.

Despite these failings, Howay's contribution to the two-volume *British Columbia* represented a major step forward in the writing of provincial history. The Howay-Scholefield collaboration replaced H.H. Bancroft's volumes as, in the words of UBC history professor Walter Sage, "the most complete work in the field."[50] It would continue to be so until the publication of Margaret Ormsby's *British Columbia: A History* in 1958. With its prosaic materialism, concern with conflict and disunity in politics, and closer attention to primary research and knowledge of existing literature, Howay's *British Columbia* helped lay the grounds for a scholarly, modern history of the province. A brief comparison of Howay's volume with Scholefield's shows how the former departed from the conventions of other provincial historians. Scholefield's writing evinced a powerful imperialism and nineteenth-century racism as well as a speculative bent that engaged the grand sweep of global history. For him, the driving force of the region's history was the indomitable "spirit of the Anglo-Saxon race," and its destiny was entrance into the British Empire.[51] Certainly, Howay was still influenced by these themes: the materialist force of gold, he wrote, had "brought a wilderness into civilization ... and established British power firmly upon the Pacific."[52] Such rhetorical flourishes, though, were rare. Howay was more concerned with assiduously separating out fact from fiction in the historical record, of discerning what lay within the realm of history: thus his concerted use of primary documents, to which he applied a decidedly more rigorous and sceptical eye than had Schole-field. And, indeed, Scholefield himself believed Howay's volume was superior to his own.[53]

In the two decades after the 1914 publication of *British Columbia*, Ho-way carried out a massive project that would yield over forty articles relating to the maritime fur trade of the late eighteenth and early nineteenth centuries, producing his most significant work of original research. In research trips that ranged near (the Provincial Archives) and far (Boston, California, even Hawaii), Howay assiduously tracked down scores of first-hand accounts and primary documents related to the maritime fur trade. This work culminated in a series of five addresses presented to the Royal Society of Canada between 1930 and 1934. Entitled "A List of Trading Vessels in the Maritime Fur Trade, 1785-1825," the lectures methodically charted all the vessels known to have visited the Northwest Coast between 1785 and 1825. Howay conceived of the work as "an index or guide" to be used by scholars in the field. Drawing from primary sources previously unavailable, notably the accounts of American traders, which had been less accessible than their British counterparts, the "List" provided both details of the vessels and the principal sources of information pertaining to their voyage.[54] More significantly, Howay was responsible for editing and publishing the bulk of the primary material he had located, making it available to other historians for the first time. Howay was a meticulous and scholarly editor, assessing each document's historical value, interrogating its veracity and contribution to the existing record while also describing its historical background.[55] Here, Howay aspired to nothing less than "factual finality," offering up "everything of value that is still extant."[56]

Aside from this significant documentary legacy, Howay also traced the contours and analyzed the significance of the maritime fur trade. After Captain Cook's accidental discovery of the value of sea otter skins, he argued, the maritime fur trade developed as a series of individual efforts. Competition for skins led to violence with the Natives and eventual exhaustion of the fur supply. In this competition, Howay showed how American traders beat out their British counterparts, establishing a monopoly of the trade out of Boston.[57] This monopoly did not win the region for the United States, though, because the maritime trade was essentially ephemeral, a "looting of the coast" that left no mark of civilization.[58] In subsequent writings, Howay would stick to his conclusions on the maritime trade's negative impact on the Northwest Coast – notably concerning the depletion of the sea otter population and the violence visited upon the region's Native peoples. However, he would change his view that it had left no permanent legacy. In his 1942 presidential address to the Royal Society of Canada, a capstone in his historical career, Howay argued that the trade had significant international ramifications: it drew Russia to North America, bequeathing the "vague Alaska boundary line," which subsequently caused conflict between the United States and Britain; in response to Russian actions, it drew Spain northward, into California, and would be a "strong factor" in the Spanish colonies' successful fight for independence; and, finally, it established crucial precedents in international law, including recognition of freedom of navigation in the Pacific Ocean and the principle that continuous occupation, rather than exploration alone, conferred sovereignty over new lands onto a nation.[59]

Howay's research on the maritime fur trade has stood the test of time. Scholars today still recognize him as the preeminent authority on the maritime fur trade and use his work in their own studies.[60] The judge's abiding reputation as one of British Columbia's most important historical scholars rests, in part, on the documentary legacy he left. It is also based on the fact that his work moved into previously unexamined areas, most particularly the workings and significance of the contact between British Columbia's Native and European peoples. As his research on the maritime fur trade progressed, Howay rethought the dismissive treatment he had afforded Natives in his earlier writings. Increasingly, he became interested in the effects the maritime trade had on British Columbia's First Nations. Here, he took what would become known as the "disaster thesis" – namely, the argument that the trade had "seriously dislocated the finely balanced economic and social fabric of the Indians."[61] This devastation was brought about by the extinction of the sea otter, the high level and incidence of violence surrounding the trade, and the introduction of alcohol by the traders.[62]

While such arguments revealed Howay's increasingly sympathetic view of the Northwest Coast's Native peoples, they nonetheless placed the latter in a passive or reactive stance. Howay argued that even the Chinook dialect (which subsequent research has shown was used as a trading language up and down the Northwest Coast well before the coming of Europeans) and the sails used on the Natives' ocean-going canoes were adopted from the newcomers.[63] In the end, European and American traders controlled the trade and its effects. They were the protagonists in Howay's historical narrative, even if their actions were often more sinister and selfish than heroic.

Despite his adherence to the disaster thesis, Howay's work on the maritime fur trade left him with a greater sympathy and respect for Native peoples and their adaptive abilities. The latter's use of the sail and what he considered their quick acquisition of the Chinook language revealed a "natural ability" to adapt to the challenges presented by Europeans.[64] Howay now recognized that Northwest Coast Natives had possessed their "own standards or morality" prior to contact and that even their pagan religion was not "a wholly debased and vile thing."[65] This language stood in stark contrast to the splenetic tone of his 1914 *British Columbia*, in which he used terms such as "savage ... barbarous ... degrading ... heathen."[66]

Reading the trader journals through a more critical filter, and drawing upon recent studies of often sympathetic local ethnologists such as Adrien Morice and James Teit, as well as the work of Franz Boas, Howay presented a picture sharply at odds with prevailing attitudes. Instead of the hackneyed depiction of Natives as child-like, yet cunning and thievish, he could now be moved to describe them as intelligent, statesmanlike, and "absolutely honest."[67] One factor behind Howay's change of mind was that his ongoing study of the maritime fur trade led him to conclude that the trade's frequent violence was not the result of any putative Native savagery; rather, he argued that "the root cause of these troubles in any time will be found in the conduct of the traders themselves."[68] In the end, Howay could write in 1930 that the province's first inhabitants were "advancing along the path toward civilization," that they would survive and be assimilated into British Columbia's dominant society.[69]

Certainly, both Howay's early and mature views of Native peoples were premised upon a trajectory that plotted the inexorable advance of a European-based civilization over Native societies. And yet Howay did contribute positively to the subsequent interest of historians in the province's First Nations. Adhering to the dictates of chronological narrative, he had argued early on that Natives should be included at the beginning of any provincial history. Later, he was careful to remind readers that, when Europeans first arrived on the Northwest Coast, they had found it inhabited; it was, in short, not a wholly empty land.[70] Such a common-sense observation was singularly remarkable in that it was rarely made by other provincial historians. Moreover, Howay recognized the significant biases and limitations of his own written sources, and he regretted that "we have not the Indians' side" of historical events.[71] This latter view suggested the possibility of viewing Native peoples as active historical agents. Not only would Native sources enable the historian to get a clearer view of events but they would also provide clues as to the motives of their authors.

Thus, Howay helped provide future historians with the means by which they could piece together at least a partial picture of Native participation in the earliest days of contact. The reason he could make this contribution was twofold. First, his own experiences as a life-long British Columbian made him alive to the still large presence of Native peoples in the province. When Howay returned from Dalhousie to take up a legal practice with partner Robie Reid in the early 1890s, Natives constituted more than one-quarter of British Columbia's population. As a lawyer, Howay regularly travelled into the province's rugged interior, where this percentage was even higher. Howay also regularly encountered Native peoples in his capacity as a judge; even if these encounters were not in the most favourable of circumstances, Howay could not simply ignore the Native presence in the province.

Second, Howay's treatment of the historical record was essentially "pluralistic." As Lyle Dick notes in his study of the various historical narratives constructed around the 1816 Seven Oaks conflict,[72] writers with personal, local experience in the region were able to produce accounts that included versions from both sides of the incident: the HBC-sponsored settlers and the North West Company employees. They could do so because they accepted evidence others dismissed (such as oral traditions and even songs) and avoided the kind of overarching teleology that led to the privileging of one side over another. Such a pluralistic approach enabled these amateur, local historians to see all actors as active agents. They thus eschewed the kind of "master narrative" other writers constructed, which focused on an active protagonist, with passive agents acting as foils. Not surprisingly, the result was a more even-handed – and most often more accurate – portrayal of this controversial event.[73]

Along with his personal experience, Howay's education contributed to his pluralistic approach to history. The fact that he lacked formal training as a historian meant that he had not internalized the hierarchy of themes and evidence that marginalized Native peoples in the work of Canada's professional historians; instead, Howay's historical method drew upon his legal training at Dalhousie University. Dalhousie's liberal education and critical methodology provided useful tools for the prospective historian. Its law program was the British Empire's first university-based common law school. Established in 1883 as a departure from the practitioner education then dominant, the program sought to establish law as an academic pursuit, focusing on library research and seminar discussions. The curriculum Howay took included a heavy concentration of constitutional history and law, along with international and maritime law. In these classes, students were encouraged to assume a sceptical attitude towards the authorities they read, criticizing them when they presented erroneous facts or interpretations.[74] Dalhousie's critical, historical approach to law built upon the fundamentally historical basis of British common law – that is, the latter's reading of past judgments within their context and the application of the derived principles to the case at hand. Meanwhile, courtroom practice stressed the need to determine the character and credibility of witnesses through the internal logic of their evidence and their consistency with regard to other testimony. It also sought to weigh the relative weight of all available evidence.[75]

Howay spent over half a century learning and applying this legal tradition. And, indeed, his career as lawyer and judge proved ideally suited for historical work. While in private practice, he travelled to areas of historical interest such as the Cariboo. Later, his life as a County Court judge allowed him to devote considerable time to historical researches. During work on the maritime fur trade, Howay was able to spend a month or two each year researching outside of British Columbia while other judges covered for him. At one point he even turned down a promotion to the Vancouver County Court on the grounds that the new case load would cut into his historical work.[76] Other provincial historians found the legal profession equally congenial to scholarly pursuits: Judge Archer Martin and Howay's former law partner Robie Reid were avid members of British Columbia's Edwardian historical community.

While his legal training profoundly influenced his development as a historian, Howay maintained clear boundaries between his professional career on the bench and his historical avocation. The judge showed little interest in the legal history of the province, perhaps feeling that such a theme was of only parochial interest. Howay's only published work on legal history was a single chapter in Volume 2 of *British Columbia* (1914), which presented a superficial, anecdotal treatment of the subject. More puzzling was the fact that Howay's most significant legal judgments had little history in them: his decisions and arguments in the 1913 Ladysmith Riot and the Songhees Reserve compensation case were singularly lacking in historical context, even though the cases raised important historical issues.

Nevertheless, through his legal training and decades of meticulous historical research and writing, Howay developed a rigorous and sophisticated philosophy of history. In his early published work, Howay shared with Scholefield and other Edwardian historians a relatively straightforward view of the historian's task: it was to separate out fact from fiction, history from myth. As he gained more confidence in his historical skills, Howay adopted a more mature philosophy, one predicated upon the historian's posture towards his documents. Howay came to recognize that, while they were the "tap roots" of historical writing, primary documents permitted the historian to view the past only "as through a glass darkly."[77] Partisan faith, patriotism, self-interest: all clouded the historian's vision. In his search for the objective truth, the historian was to approach his documents with a sceptical eye, free of any biases or "pet theories."[78] Significantly, Howay was committed to the same "objectivist creed" that served as the founding myth of an emerging historical profession in North America. This creed – which can be seen as a direct descendant of Leopold von Ranke's earlier "scientific history" – envisioned the historian as an impartial judge committed to the reality of the past, defined truth as corresponding to that reality, and asserted that the historian was able to gain access to that truth. The historian's work would faithfully and objectively reflect the truth of a past that existed independently of the historian and his documents.[79]

Accepting the core tenet of the professionalization project that was remaking the historical discipline at the time, Howay worked to apply the new standards of scholarship to the writing of BC history. An important instrument in imposing these standards was the book review. From 1910 until his death, Howay contributed scores of reviews to Canada's inaugural national historical journal, the *Review of Historical Publications*, and its successor, the *Canadian Historical Review*. The judge was also a regular reviewer for journals in British Columbia, Washington, and Oregon. Howay lauded books that made original contributions through "thorough investigation of the constantly increasing primary sources."[80] Meanwhile, he censured historians who showed a lack of "perspective, completeness, accuracy, and impartiality."[81] As noted above, Howay applied different standards to works intended for a more general readership, stressing their accessibility and style. Thus, Howay accepted, and contributed to, the separating out of two historical audiences – the popular and the scholarly – through the early decades of the twentieth century.

Not surprisingly, Howay was actively involved in the new organizations that were forging a national community of scholarly historians. He assisted in the birth of the Canadian Historical Association as it evolved out of the Historic Landmarks Association, moving to merge the latter into the former at the CHA's founding meeting in 1922.[82] His involvement in the association culminated in 1931-32, when he served as its president. Presidencies in the Royal Society of Canada (1923 and 1941) and the Champlain Society (1942) marked decades'-long membership in those national organizations. Taken together, these links furthered national recognition of British Columbia as a legitimate field of historical study. Indeed, Howay tirelessly pushed these groups to pay more attention to Canada's far west province.[83]

Closer to home, the judge gave critical assistance to the emergence of history as an academic discipline at the University of British Columbia (UBC). Howay served on the university's Senate from 1915, the year UBC opened, to 1942. He also helped the first professional historian specializing in British Columbia, Walter Sage, get started in the field, and he continued to mentor the young professor for some years.[84] Subsequently, Howay visited Sage's seminar in provincial history and lent assistance to students researching the province's early history, while his books remained required reading at the university for nearly three decades.[85] UBC recognized the judge's contributions by conferring upon him an honorary doctor of laws degree in 1932. Finally, Howay bequeathed his own extensive collection of primary and secondary literature, which was particularly strong in maritime fur trade and exploration journals to the UBC Library. Along with the library of Robie Reid (who served on the UBC Board of Governors for two decades and acted as the university's solicitor), it formed the core holding of the university's Special Collections.[86]

Howay also encouraged the move to a more institutionalized history in the province by supporting the establishment of the *British Columbia Historical Quarterly*, the province's first bona fide scholarly journal of history. Howay himself submitted over a dozen articles to the *British Columbia Historical Quarterly*, starting with the journal's inaugural piece in 1937 and ending with a posthumously published work.[87] Some of these articles reflected the judge's abiding interest in the early maritime trade and exploration of the region as well as the publication of primary documents relating to it.[88] The rest addressed diverse topics that later historians pursued in greater detail: the pioneer history of Vancouver,[89] black immigration to Vancouver Island,[90] and two substantial works on British Columbia's Native peoples.[91] Although many of the pieces were not among Howay's more scholarly efforts, several did show signs of his rigorous use of sources and historical argumentation. Their example, in terms of scholarship and expansion of topics, helped advance the standard for the province's history. As *Quarterly* editor W. Kaye Lamb later recalled, only Sage (with a PhD in history) and Howay wrote with any confidence in those early days of the journal.[92]

Despite his support for such scholarly activities, Howay did not welcome all the changes brought about by the rise of academic history. Through the 1930s, he became increasingly critical of the growing influence wielded by university-based historians over historical societies and journals in Canada and the United States. He charged that the Canadian Historical Association threatened to "degenerate" into a club run by history department heads, noting the "deadening effect" such academics had on historical societies and reviews. For Howay, the amateur historian was the heart and soul of any historical society as well as the most active researcher and publisher. In his words, "the energetic amateur can beat them [academics] every time."[93] The judge's worsening opinion of Walter Sage through this time was due, in part, to his growing frustration with the pretensions of an increasingly professionalized historical guild. Howay no doubt felt that he should not have to play second fiddle to anyone in BC history and certainly not to Sage, whose work he would come to dismiss as "valueless."[94] There was likely a touch of envy and disappointment in Howay's attitude towards Sage; unlike the latter, the judge had not been able to pursue a full-time career as a historian, a vocation he almost certainly saw as his true calling.

In the end, Howay's position within the evolution of BC historical writing and institutions was as an anomalous amateur, who, without formal training as a historian, moved the province's history towards more scholarly standards. As such, Howay's life and work counter the argument, put forward in studies on central and eastern Canadian historians, that an emerging academic community was responsible for the rise of more rigorous standards in historical writing.[95] In British Columbia, it was Howay who played the role of preeminent provincial historian in the first part of the twentieth century. And he could do this because the province's historiographical development departed from that of other provinces. Most particularly, the establishment of historical institutions in British Columbia lagged behind their establishment in other parts of Canada and the United States. As British Columbia lacked a university of its own during its first four decades as a province, the training of British Columbia's elite had to occur elsewhere. A late-starting provincial historical association was plagued by regional jealousies, and a scholarly historical journal did not get off the ground until 1937. In this situation, Howay filled a large gap. When historical organizations or journals required someone to cover British Columbia, they came to Howay as they had no university or well-established historical society readily to hand. Furthermore, the late development of provincial history as a subject at UBC, and the bald fact that Howay was a better historian than was Walter Sage, explains why Howay remained an authority on BC history for journals such as the *Canadian Historical Review* well into the 1930s.

Howay's contribution to the 1942 *British Columbia and the United States* was another sign of the judge's scholarly reputation. The book was part of the Carnegie Foundation's series on Canadian-American relations. Planned and launched in 1934, the project brought together North American academics from various disciplines; by the time of its completion, the series had involved nearly every professional Canadian historian.[96] Howay appears to be the only non-academic historian to contribute to the series;

however, his participation had been deemed "indispensable" by University of Toronto professor Chester Martin, who was general editor for the Canadian volumes.[97] Howay wrote the first seven chapters of *British Columbia and the United States*, covering the period from the maritime fur trade to the Oregon boundary dispute and the Fraser River and Cariboo gold rushes. He also provided the original material for three other chapters, which were then reworked by UBC political economist Henry Angus, who provided a conclusion as well. The remaining five chapters were written by Walter Sage. Reflecting his suspicion of both the increasing power of academic historians and Sage's abilities, Howay resisted suggestions that he and the history professor collaborate on their respective sections, insisting that he maintain control of his own chapters.[98]

The text gave Howay the opportunity to address an issue that perennially confronted provincial historians – namely, the relation of British Columbia to its powerful republican neighbour. Through his meticulous research on the maritime fur trade, Howay was well aware of the early American presence on the Northwest Coast. But *British Columbia and the United States* provided only the briefest survey of the maritime trade. Howay was satisfied to repeat his earlier conclusions that Americans came to dominate the trade but that this trade had been fleeting and largely injurious, both to the sea otter population and to the region's Natives.[99] Meanwhile, Howay gave concerted attention to the decades after the end of the maritime fur trade. In these chapters, he expanded on earlier, passing suggestions that the land trade had left a more permanent legacy, most particularly through the presence of the Hudson's Bay Company. Here, Howay defended the Company against the various criticisms levelled at it by American writers; its employees, along with British colonial officials, had treated American settlers with generosity and as equals under the law. For the judge, it was those settlers and Methodist missionaries who had acted badly, notably in their treatment of Native peoples.[100] Thus, Howay made use of a core motif in BC historical writing: the contrast between a violent American frontier and a peaceful, law-abiding British one. Howay drew further distinctions, comparing the American tradition of self-reliance and individualism with the British penchant for obedience to established authority.[101]

This new-found determination to distinguish the province from its powerful neighbour set *British Columbia and the United States* apart from

Howay's earlier work. The controlling theme here was the region's evolution from a "no man's land" to one defined by respective sovereignties.[102] Of course, the line dividing these sovereignties was drawn by the Oregon Treaty. Howay took a relatively even-handed approach to the dispute; he did rehearse the British argument that Spain had ceded all claims to the region through the Nootka Convention and that, consequently, they had no rights to bequeath to the United States. He also censured "hot-headed Americans" who had inflamed US public opinion with their claim that all of the Oregon country belonged to them.[103] But in the end he concluded that "so far as discovery and settlement up to the 1840s were concerned, the claims of Great Britain and the United States were almost on an equality."[104] Here, Howay's primary concern was not to weigh the competing claims to the region; rather, he set out to describe how the Oregon agreement affected British Columbia, most notably by leaving it in the hands of the British HBC.

Certainly, Howay admitted that, well into the nineteenth century, there existed an "essential unity [in] the history of the Pacific coast."[105] Thanks to his decades-long research in the maritime fur trade, the judge's most extensive, long-standing contacts were with historians from the American Pacific Northwest, and a large part of his work was published in journals there. However, like other provincial historians, Howay was determined to show that British Columbia's often precarious independence from the United States had a solid historical basis. Almost certainly, Howay was not responsible for the cheery continentalism of *British Columbia and the United States*, which appears to have been grafted onto the text by editor Angus. The latter also wrote the text's conclusion, asserting that the relationship between the independent states north and south of the border had matured into an "age of good neighbours."[106] It could not have been an accident that the Carnegie series' American editors gave Angus responsibility for two more recent border disputes – over the San Juan Islands and the Alaskan boundary – the latter of which raised nationalist temperatures north of the border in the face of US president Theodore Roosevelt's walk-softly-carry-a-big-stick diplomacy.

For Howay, it was the toehold of the HBC, followed by the establishment of British Columbia as a colony, that kept a portion of the Pacific coast in British hands. But the British imperialist theme was not a controlling motif either in the judge's portion of *British Columbia and the United*

States or in his writings more generally. Howay also did not adopt the nation-building plot of central Canadian historians, as was noted in discussing his 1914 *British Columbia* volume. In the end, Howay's writings revealed a certain impartiality on matters of political and national partisanship. Just as the Liberal, who faced McBride on an election-time stage, could sing the praises of the Conservative premier, so could the historian give the Spaniard Perez credit for preceding Captain Cook.[107] In an attempt at national impartiality, Howay had asked Washington State historian T.C. Elliott to review his chapters in *British Columbia and the United States* from an American viewpoint to see whether he had been too partial to Britain.[108] Elliott expressed no reservations about Howay's treatment, unlike the Carnegie series' American editors, who fulminated against a litany of Howay's transgressions: his "nationalist tone," his "overdone" defence of the HBC, his "homilies on the virtues of the British and the vices of the Americans," and his "invidious" discussion of the Oregon boundary dispute – a reaction that seems rather thin-skinned.[109]

On balance, Howay's work shows that he was concerned more with writing scholarly history than with engaging in special pleading for empire or nation. Because of this focus, his work helped lay the foundations for a more critical, modern history of the province, moving it away from the celebratory, imperialistic, and amateur tradition of Edwardian writers. Admittedly, Howay failed to establish a compelling, unified historical vision or identity for the province, a task that, over the decades, eluded British Columbian's historians. And his work continued to show the effects of a time when racial prejudice – most notably in the guise of anti-Asian sentiment – was an accepted part of BC society. Nevertheless, Howay provided promising insights that others would take up. Possessing a personal knowledge of British Columbia unrivalled among previous and contemporary provincial historians, he implicitly recognized the brevity of European presence in the region. His work as scholar and public historian responded to the imperative of providing such a new society with a written past, while also underlining the importance of the contact situation.

5

A Professional Past:
The University of British Columbia
and Walter Sage

The late establishment of history as an academic discipline was yet another aspect of British Columbia's historiographical evolution that diverged from the rest of Canada. The University of British Columbia opened its doors in 1915, almost half a century after British Columbia became a province. Manitoba, Saskatchewan, and Alberta all founded universities within years of joining Confederation; further east, universities dated back well into the colonial era. The BC government first tried to set up a provincial university in 1890, submitting a university act for the Legislature's approval. But sectional jealousies between Vancouver and Victoria scuttled the bill, and subsequent governments were loathe to tackle the controversial issue. Finally, buoyed by a booming economy and its rising dominance of British Columbia's political scene, Premier McBride's administration passed the 1908 University Act. Seven years later, classes began at UBC in cramped, temporary quarters, and UBC moved to its permanent Point Grey campus in 1925.[1]

British Columbia had belatedly joined one of the most significant developments in recent intellectual history – namely, the rise of the modern university in North America and Western Europe. Certainly, universities had existed long before the ambitious academics and administrators of the nineteenth and twentieth centuries went to work on the time-honoured institution. However, in the last decades of the nineteenth century and the first decades of the twentieth, the model of the modern university emerged and spread. This model comprised a bureaucratic institution, with departments corresponding to clearly defined disciplines. The proliferation and institutionalization of these specialized disciplines were the hallmark of the modern university. Old subjects such as English and history were reconstructed, while novel disciplines such as anthropology were recognized for the first time. Each of these disciplines created a community of scholars, spanning physical distance, who shared certain basic values and modes of inquiry. A discipline such as history came to be defined by the questions it posed and by the means used to answer those questions, both of which shaped the knowledge that it produced.[2]

The emergence of history as an academic discipline in these modern universities was part of a broader "professionalization project" that was remaking the Western world's middle class.[3] Just as medicine was to be practised only by professionally trained physicians, and law by academically trained lawyers, so the study, writing, and teaching of history was to be taken over by professional historians. Passing through the history departments of the rejuvenated modern university, the professional historian possessed three crucial traits. First was a certificate of merit (increasingly, the PhD), which asserted the historian's qualifications to practise the craft. This certificate or degree was acquired upon graduating from a standardized system of training, which had imparted the tools of the trade and provided mastery of a specialized body of knowledge. With increasing frequency, a thesis was required: based on work in primary documents and making an original contribution to existing scholarship, it represented the rise of the research ideal as a fundamental component of the new discipline. It, and other research undertaken by the professional historian, was also to adhere to an "objectivist creed": freeing their work of the biases and flights of literary fancy that had marred their predecessors' efforts, professional historians could now produce a superior brand of history, one that provided a faithful re-creation of a truthful, objective past.[4]

Second, the professional historian pursued history as a full-time occupation and the main source of his or her income. The expansion and increasing accessibility of universities meant that there were far greater opportunities to pursue history as a career. Professional historians themselves controlled who entered and who was promoted within the guild. And, through peer review, they were also the ones to assess the worth of their colleagues' work. Housed within the university, they now enjoyed a certain (if imperfect) autonomy and adhered to the rules and values of their own discipline.

The history department assembled during UBC's early decades was the product of the professionalization of the discipline. Between 1915 and 1945, five permanent appointments were made to the department, and each of these men possessed at least two university degrees in history. A list of the five, noting their years at UBC, is revealing:

Mack Eastman (1915-25), BA (Toronto), MA (Sorbonne), PhD (Columbia)
Walter Sage (1918-53), BA (Toronto), MA (Oxford), PhD (Toronto)
Frederick Soward (1922-64), BA (Toronto), B.Litt. (Oxford)
D.C. Harvey (1928-31), BA (Dalhousie), MA (Oxford)
Albert Cooke (1929-60), BA (Manitoba), MA (Oxford)

As one can see, undergraduate degrees were completed in Canadian schools, most usually at Toronto, while graduate studies – now a prerequisite for employment as an academic historian – were pursued abroad, with Oxford the destination in all but one case. And, of these five, two possessed the crowning PhD, while all had completed dissertations based upon primary research.

UBC's early history department produced the first professional historian to make the province his field. Walter Sage was a charter member of the national school of history that had been forged in Toronto and Oxford. While there is no evidence that Sage had studied British Columbia during his undergraduate and graduate years, he adopted the province as his field soon after his arrival in Vancouver. Walter Noble Sage was born near London, Ontario, in 1888 into a family of teachers. Sage's father was an Anglican archdeacon who taught apologetics and philosophy at Huron College and the University of Western Ontario, while his uncle and mentor, Harry Gerrans, was a mathematics don at Oxford University.[5] After an unsuccessful attempt to gain admittance to Oxford for undergraduate studies, Sage entered the University of Toronto in 1906. While at Toronto, Sage cast about for some direction to his studies and seriously considered following in his father's footsteps as a clergyman. But it was his interest in history (both ancient and modern) that won out, and, as his studies progressed, he fell under the tutelage of George Wrong, whom Sage would admire all his life and to whom he was related on his mother's side.[6]

The imprint of the University of Toronto on Sage, and UBC's history department, was profound. The history department at Toronto, which Wrong had modelled on Oxford's program, was the foundation stone of a national school of historians – a school that was built in the first two decades of the twentieth century. Virtually all of the young history professors taking up positions in Canada's physically scattered universities during this time had some tie to the University of Toronto. And all of UBC's professors did so, either as graduates (Eastman, Sage, Soward) or as students of Toronto graduates (Harvey, Cooke). Along with personal ties, the members of this school also shared a common approach to Canadian history, focusing on the Whiggian evolution of self-government in Britain's former North American colonies. The establishment of responsible government, Confederation, and the achievement of full national status: these were the themes that dominated, while the regional focus remained on central and eastern Canada, where these institutions first developed.[7]

While the University of Toronto represented the first step for most of the young men who would become Canada's first identifiable generation of national, academic historians, Oxford University represented the second. Starting with Chester Martin in 1904, who was awarded North America's first Rhodes Scholarship, a steady stream of young, middle-class English Canadians made the trek to Oxford. Sage ventured east in 1910, taking up graduate studies in medieval and modern history. Oxford, though, would leave a paradoxical legacy among Sage and his contemporaries. First, of course, it underscored the Britishness of English Canada: Oxford was venerated as the intellectual centre of Britain's far-flung possessions. Sage spoke for many when, at the age of sixteen, he wrote his uncle that "it has always been the height of my ambitions to study at Oxford."[8] Meanwhile, Oxford passed on to this generation of Canadian historians the Whiggian school of history, which then dominated British writing, with its focus upon the progressive evolution of English political institutions and the resulting growth of liberty.[9]

Yet Oxford also sowed the seeds of a budding nationalism among this generation. Most immediately, the Canadian Oxonians shared the experience of being dismissed as mere colonials by an insular English upper class that had dominated the institution for centuries. Victoria-born Henry Angus, who became a close friend of Sage while at Balliol and later joined him at UBC as a political economy professor, recalled that Canadians at Oxford mixed more easily with American students than with their English colleagues as the latter were too "self-satisfied" and felt superior to their colonial brethren.[10] While at Oxford, Angus and Sage expressed their frustrations by co-authoring a four-act comedy entitled "The Homecoming," which lampooned the more-British-than-the-British attitude of one returning Canadian Oxford student while giving sympathetic voice to another's growing nationalism.[11] The Whiggian history imbibed by Canada's aspiring historians also contributed to an emerging nationalist historiography as it gave them the tools with which to plot Canada's rise from colonial status to full nationhood. As with Oxford itself, Britain could be both embraced and pushed away.

While Sage would never completely break his emotional and intellectual ties to Britain, he left Oxford with a more ambivalent Anglophilia. Oxford also armed him with the credentials upon which he could build an academic career, and, upon his return to Canada, he searched the country for open postings.[12] After sessional appointments at Calgary College (1913-15) and Queen's University (1915-18), he obtained a permanent position at UBC in the fall of 1918. During this time, Sage concluded that, with the increasing professionalization of history, a "research degree and preferably a PhD seems necessary for advancement in this country."[13] He registered in the new doctoral program at the University of Toronto in 1917; notably, the thesis he proposed (an examination of central Canadian political parties from 1840 to 1867) closely followed the thematic and regional focus prevailing in national historiography at the time.[14]

After Sage obtained a permanent posting in Vancouver, his vocational aspirations drew him into the field of BC history. On the eve of his departure from Queen's, Sage had been advised by O.D. Skelton to take up BC history since the field "was practically untouched." Soon after arriving in Vancouver, Sage concluded that Skelton had been right: Mack Eastman was not interested in the far west and the only provincial historians to date were, in Sage's words, "enthusiastic amateurs."[15] In British Columbia, then, the young professor had found a field he could make his own, unchallenged by other academics.

In 1921, Sage again registered in the University of Toronto's PhD program, proposing for his dissertation a survey of BC history prior to Confederation. His larger goal at this time was to publish a single-volume history of the province that would replace Scholefield and Howay's *British Columbia* as the standard in the field.[16] In his early research, Sage received invaluable assistance from Howay, who just then was hitting his stride as a historian. No doubt convinced that the young professor could further the cause of BC historical writing and its acceptance by the national community of academic historians, Howay made available his rich collection of material for Sage's use. Meanwhile, the latter sent much of his work for Howay to peruse, receiving candid criticisms and suggestions in return.[17]

Benefiting from such assistance, Sage completed his doctoral dissertation and degree by 1925, joining W.B. Kerr as the first two PhD graduates from Toronto's history program.[18] Five years later, a revised version of Sage's dissertation was published by the University of Toronto Press as *Sir James Douglas and British Columbia*. For Sage and other academic historians, the thesis was the clearest embodiment of the new research ideal to which they aspired. It was to be based on an objective study of primary material and was to make an original contribution to existing knowledge on the subject studied. This certainly was how Sage saw his own dissertation and book; he had energetically gathered primary material from the most important collections for the region – namely, the Provincial Archives, the Bancroft Library, and Frederic Howay's library.

Sir James Douglas presented its protagonist as the "Father of British Columbia," the greatest man in the province's history.[19] For Sage, this accomplishment was due to Douglas's strong personality. Although he was autocratic and largely responsible for the colony's "constitutional backwardness," it was the very strength of Douglas's character that enabled British government, law, and order to be installed upon the Pacific coast. It was Douglas who shepherded the region from its primitive fur trade days to maturity and responsible government.[20] While one of the first books published by the newly founded University of Toronto Press, Sage's *Sir James Douglas* did not represent a significant step forward in the writing of BC history. Its epic-heroic tone, its reliance on one "Great Man" to represent an era, and its focus on the fur trade and colonial periods: these were common fare of the province's amateur historians. The dissertation and book also failed to meet the scholarly standards set down by Judge Howay's work, for example in its reliance upon lengthy quotes from largely undigested primary sources. The failings of Sage's dissertation were noted in his doctoral committee's scathing criticisms of the work as "jejune and amateurish"; tellingly, Sage himself did not keep a copy of the thesis in his otherwise voluminous personal papers.[21] Also telling was the fact that Sage had great difficulty getting the work published, undertaking an active lobbying campaign to do so.[22]

Nevertheless, *Sir James Douglas* did represent the first professional contribution to the regional history of British Columbia, as did other articles on the province Sage added to his publishing record through these years. The publication of the book by the University of Toronto Press, along with the appearance of his work in the *Canadian Historical Review*, helped raise the profile of BC history within national academic circles.[23] A product and member of this historical community, Sage set out to Canadianize the writing of BC history by applying to it the themes and concerns of an emerging national historiography. His early writings on the province were dominated by the political and constitutional focus of the latter and its two main concerns: the rise of representative and responsible government, and the coming of Confederation. Sage's abiding interest in colonial politics, the coming of Confederation and BC's political evolution through the early years of provincial status produced his most lasting contribution to the research and writing of provincial history. Disciplined by the contours of national historiography, he presented a more systematic look at a period that R.E. Gosnell had covered in his reporter-like style. Searching for the roots of democratic government, Sage discerned the faint lines of a Reform historiography: a non-elected power – James Douglas and the Family Company Compact – frustrating the efforts of elected representatives such as Amor De Cosmos and John Robson.[24] Sage also collaborated with George Wrong and Chester Martin on the 1929 text, *The Story of Canada*. Here, Sage was responsible for incorporating British Columbia within the larger national "story."[25]

Despite his best efforts, Sage soon realized that British Columbia's political development did not fit the patterns of Maritime and Ontarian historiography. If Douglas fell short of the role of obstructionist villain in a Reform drama, neither was De Cosmos qualified to carry the mantle of Howe and Baldwin as the romantic protagonist, the "great popular tribune denouncing a tyrannical governor."[26] More broadly, British Columbia itself lacked the political maturity required to sustain the type of struggle for representative institutions that had succeeded in eastern Canada (and, indeed, the initiative for such institutions came from the British colonial office itself).[27] Rather, for Sage, the province's political development had been "anomalous" and "backward": it received responsible government only after joining Confederation, and for the three decades following that, BC politics continued to be out of step with the national scene.[28]

A more directly Canadianizing force in the province's past was the coming of Confederation, for Sage the most significant development in the province's history. And, as with colleagues to the east, his depiction of British Columbia's decision to join with Canada combined the high drama of historical uncertainty – to enable historical actors to achieve greatness – with a reassuring aura of inevitability. Sage argued that British Columbia was faced with three options in the "critical years" preceding Confederation: remaining a British colony, being annexed by the United States, or joining Confederation.[29] Of these, the last was the "only practical solution," and British Columbia opted for Canada even though there were great difficulties to surmount.[30] The greatest of these difficulties, British Columbia's geographic isolation, was overcome by the building of the Canadian Pacific Railway. In Sage's scheme, the CPR took on a more familiar guise as the instrument of a grand, nation-building vision.[31] Thus, the prevailing national historiography had a greater influence on Sage than it had on preceding BC historians, who had tended to place the railway within an imperial and global framework.

Throughout his work, Sage stressed the Canadian connection to an extent previously unseen in provincial historiography. For him, the years following the completion of the CPR had effected the "Canadianization of British Columbia."[32] With the railway's completion and the influx of eastern Canadian immigrants like himself, he argued, British Columbia had become increasingly Canadian in sentiment. And yet Sage also realized that British Columbians remained "Canadians with a difference." An imposing geography isolated the province from Canada for much of its history, postponing its discovery, increasing the influence of the United States, and turning West Coast eyes to the Pacific rather than eastward to the Atlantic. British Columbia's position on the Pacific gave it a sense of occasion for it was here that the Occident and Orient met, and it was here that the westward migration of European peoples confronted its final frontier. Sage remained characteristically vague on precisely what prospects would result from British Columbia's position as "Canada on the Pacific." What he did suggest was the notion, commonplace for the time, that the Pacific was the "ocean of the future"; that is, the Pacific would eclipse the Atlantic not only as the most important route for trade but also as the central arena for great power competition.[33]

For Sage, British Columbia's location facing the Pacific produced another of its unique traits: the only significant Asian population in Canada. The racial fissure underneath the province's history ran not between English and French but between Asian and predominantly British peoples. Thus, while he wrote grandly of the promise that the province's geographical orientation would increase its economic and strategic importance, Sage viewed the presence of Asian peoples in the province as a serious and abiding problem. As with the work of other provincial historians, Asians were largely absent from Sage's writing. On the rare occasion that they were mentioned, it was invariably in the context of the "vexed problem of Asiatic immigration" or of cheap Asian labour competing with "white labour."[34] Thus, not only were Asians viewed as one of British Columbia's "peculiar problems" but the only role they played in Sage's writing was that of immigrants.[35] As in the logic of other provincial writers, so in Sage's: Asians did not belong in BC history. They were sojourners, alien outsiders, anything but residents.

Sage did not explicitly propose any solutions to this problem, but his writing did suggest that, at least prior to the end of the Second World War, he supported the legal ban on further immigration from Asia. Moreover, during the war, Sage privately argued that the solution to the "problem of [Japanese] enemy aliens" was their removal from the coast as soon as possible. Sage expressed these concerns in a February 1942 letter to close friend and colleague Henry Angus. With Japan coming off military successes at Pearl Harbor and Singapore, Sage wrote that "enemy aliens should not merely be left loose in BC."[36] It is not clear whether Sage was calling for the removal of the several hundred Japanese Canadians suspected of actively supporting Japan, which had already begun, or of the more than 20,000 British Columbians of Japanese descent who were subsequently evacuated from the coast. What is clear is the fact that Sage shared the views of the majority of BC residents and historians on the "Asian problem" both before and during the Second World War.

A comparison with Henry Angus provides a striking contrast to Sage's thinking. From at least 1930 onward, Angus launched a concerted, lonely attack on government policies and BC public opinion that discriminated against Asian Canadians. In a series of articles published over two decades, he attacked the two main props of legal racism against Asians: exclusionist immigration policies (most particularly, the 1923 Chinese Exclusion Act) and the disenfranchisement of Asian Canadians.[37] Angus continued his efforts through the Second World War. While serving in the Department of External Affairs, he joined fellow British Columbian Hugh Keenleyside (a graduate of UBC's history department who temporarily returned to teach there) in opposing the evacuation of Japanese Canadians, arguing that there were no grounds to justify such arbitrary actions.[38]

Angus's opposition to anti-Asian racism was predicated on a premise that was even more profoundly at odds with prevailing opinion. For Angus, the question was not how to deal with the "vexed problem of Asiatic immigration," as Sage wrote; rather it was whether the nation would rid itself of the discrimination aimed against "Canadians of Asiatic race."[39] Almost alone among BC opinion makers and writers of the time, Angus viewed Asian British Columbians as part of "us" (as Canadian citizens who could call the province their home) rather than as "them" (alien outsiders who could never belong). Kay Anderson argues that Angus's opposition would prove to be "an important breakthrough" in the dismantling of the anti-Asian consensus in Canada's westernmost province, one that would take place only after the Second World War.[40] And, indeed, acceptance of Angus's arguments required a tectonic shift in British Columbia's cultural development. There is no evidence that Walter Sage was capable of such a profound reversal of thinking. References to the "Asian problem" disappeared from his writing after the war; however, rather than changing positions on the question, Sage simply avoided mention of Asian British Columbians altogether. In the end, Sage's intellectual framework would not permit him to employ the presence of a large Asian population in British Columbia – arguably the trait that most distinguished the province from the rest of Canada – as a component in the unique culture he felt the province was developing.

Sage's fitful search for the defining traits of British Columbia's uniqueness did not lead him to search for an autarkic provincial history; rather, he persisted in his goal of bringing the province into the mainstream of Canadian history. In order to do this, he believed, Canadian historiography itself would have to be rewritten. Moving from an early acceptance of mainstream writing to a critique of it, Sage argued that national historiography was overly focused upon central Canada, neglecting the west and British Columbia. Revealing a budding sense of regional discontent, fuelled by the UBC professor's own physical distance "so far from the centre of things," Sage railed against the "Toronto-centric" point of view that prevailed among his colleagues.[41] He commiserated with University of California historian Herbert Bolton, writing that "we here in BC regard the Toronto view of Canada just as you do the New England tradition in the history of the US."[42] To correct this regional myopia, Sage called for a national history that would examine Canada "from sea to sea"; such a history would recognize the importance of all of Canada's regions, from the Atlantic to British Columbia's Pacific shores.[43]

Sage also faulted Canadian historians for being slow to recognize Canada as a North American nation rather than as a British colony. An "overhang of colonialism" had placed a deadening hand upon the work of Canadian historians. Faced with the absence of a clear break between colonial and national periods, the latter stressed the transfer of British institutions and gradual evolution of self-government during the pre-Confederation era, largely ignoring Canada's development across North America. National historians, he concluded, had looked east towards Europe rather than west towards North America in their search for Canada's history and identity.[44]

To effect this desired change in Canadian historical writing, Sage himself turned southward for inspiration, to the work of western American historians and the abiding influence of Frederick Jackson Turner's frontier thesis. Sage first travelled south in 1925 to address the Pacific Coast Branch of the American Historical Association, which was meeting in Seattle. In the two years following, membership on the Pacific Coast Branch board, a summer of teaching at the University of Washington, and a second summer spent at the University of California brought Sage into close contact with the western American historical community. While in California, he was exposed to the work of Spanish frontier historian Herbert Bolton and his hemispheric perspective.[45] Operating in the best tradition of H.H. Bancroft, Bolton argued that the history of the various nations of Latin America and North America could be examined from a common perspective. This common history was founded upon the expansion of European peoples across the hemisphere – people who tailored their European ideas and resources to fit a new land and who founded new independent nations.[46] Bolton had been a student of Turner and the influence of the latter's frontier thesis could be seen in the shared belief that, free of European ties, the frontier created new peoples and nations in the western hemisphere.

This exposure to western American historians was the most direct inspiration behind Sage's efforts to change the historiography of his own country. In a 1928 address to the Canadian Historical Association, Sage proposed a qualified application of Turner's frontier thesis as a corrective for the failings of national historical writing. Here, Sage argued that the westward surge of European peoples across North America was composed not of two movements but of one: a single, interlacing frontier that ignored political borders. His own province, Sage continued, was a prime example of this. Echoing Turner, Sage noted the succession of frontiers that determined British Columbia's development: a fur trade frontier arriving both from sea and land, the northward movement from California of a mining frontier, and, with the completion of the CPR, the extension westward of a settlement frontier.[47]

Sage's reading of Turner's thesis made two notable points. First, his notion of a single frontier viewed from a hemispheric rather than from a national perspective provided a rebuttal to those Canadian critics who dismissed Turner because of the absence of an unbroken, advancing frontier line north of the international border.[48] Second, the priority given to the notion of westward movement was intended to reorient the focus of national historiography. By examining the frontier, Canadian historians could adopt a westward-looking, North American perspective, thereby turning their eyes from the prevailing eastward focus, which had been produced by an emphasis upon constitutional history. Moreover, British Columbia would assume a more prominent place as historians recognized that westward expansion was an essential component of Canada's development.

If Sage was excited about the regional significance of the frontier, he was less excited about Turner's conclusions concerning its cultural and political effects. Sage acknowledged that the frontier had a discernible and lasting impact upon British Columbia and the west, arguing that it was not yet closed in portions of the latter. There still existed a wilderness to be civilized, providing opportunities that, in turn, kept alive the pioneering spirit. This spirit, or "state of mind," was itself a central part of British Columbia's culture and identity.[49] However, as with preceding provincial historians, Sage was determined to distinguish the western Canadian frontier from its American counterpart. To do so, he employed the same theme of benevolent conquest that had become a constituent element of both provincial and national historical writing. He, too, drew a sharp contrast between the violence of the American West and the reputed law and order of British Columbia's frontier. He also stressed the relatively good treatment of Native peoples in the latter, which had given greater legitimacy to the British institutions imposed in the region.[50]

While British Columbia's First Nations thus played a role, it was a passive and decidedly secondary one, for there was scarce mention of them in Sage's writings. Even *Sir James Douglas*, which discussed a fur trade and colonial era during which Natives were an inescapable presence, said little about them. Sage's view of Native peoples was based, in part, on his own personal experiences. Unlike Frederic Howay and other amateur historians, who had witnessed a pioneer British Columbia in which Natives were a larger presence in the population and economy, Sage would have had little opportunity to come into contact with Native people. Born in southern Ontario, educated there and in England, he settled in post-First World War Vancouver at a time when the province's Native population had reached its lowest point. These years also witnessed a crackdown on remaining Native cultural practices (e.g., a stricter enforcement of the law banning potlatches) and moves to silence Natives who might insist the land question had not been settled (e.g., 1927 legislation that prohibited bands from raising money to press outstanding land claims). Sage's impressions of Vancouver two decades after his arrival are telling: writing in 1937, he described it as a city that had only recently emerged from "primitive times," where Native "squatters" and canoes still dotted the landscape.[51] For Sage, who as a student had strolled under the ersatz Gothic arches of the University of Toronto, and the real thing in Oxford, such scenes were exotic and out of place. Sage viewed Native peoples as remnants of a savage past and – even though they had occupied the area for millennia – as squatters or trespassers, people who did not belong.

Also revealing is the professor's account of the unveiling of a Historic Sites and Monuments Board cairn at Nootka Sound in 1924, the only record we have of a direct meeting between Sage and Native peoples. Sage's private account of the event was more farce than epic: the visitors' boat could not land, the dignitaries' speeches were either overly short or could not be heard, and the after-dinner lecture sparked "quite an incident" when

Judge Howay "went after" the speaker.[52] In his published account, however, Sage reformulated the event as a dramatic re-enactment of James Cook's 1778 arrival in Nootka Sound and the reactions of the Nuu-chah-nulth people to that arrival. In this account, the latter were depicted as exotic and timeless; the Native leaders wore "grotesque" war masks over "flashing eyes" and spoke in "intelligible" words. "It seemed as if the mists of time had rolled away," Sage intoned, "and that we were back again with Captain Cook on the deck of the 'Resolution' looking down at the canoes of the Nootkans which surrounded the ship."[53] In Sage's eyes, the Nuu-chah-nulth were not part of the ongoing historical evolution of British Columbia; rather, they appeared as exotic creatures frozen in time, unchanged in the century and a half since the first appearance of Europeans on the Northwest Coast.

Even though academic history had largely discarded the overt evolutionary racism that had marred earlier historical writing, the methodology and themes of the discipline through most of the twentieth century conspired to further marginalize British Columbia's First Nations. The frontier thesis, which dominated historical writing on the US West and influenced Sage's own work, presumed that North America was an essentially empty land into which European peoples moved rather than a region populated and used by a diversity of Native societies.[54] The active agents of Sage's BC frontier were Anglo explorers, miners, and settlers. The first residents of the region had not properly occupied the land because they had neither domesticated it through permanent settlements nor exploited its resources through agriculture and capitalist production.

Likewise, the dominant themes of Canadian historical writing through most of the twentieth century – the political and constitutional development of the nation, most particularly the coming of self-government and Confederation – left little room for Native peoples for the simple reason that, until 1961, they were excluded from the Canadian polity.[55] Canada's professional historians were concerned primarily with the evolution of a British-derived society and its political institutions. As Adele Perry notes, they effectively neutralized colonialism "by describing it as 'settlement.'"[56] At the same time, Canadian historians depicted this process as natural, inevitable, and desirable; it was part of a developmental model in which the establishment and growth of Anglo immigrant societies was the measure of progress. Most often, this was done implicitly, even subconsciously, so ingrained was the dominant mode of thought. Indeed, Sage and his national counterparts viewed *themselves* as the colonized ones, their focus being on how the colonials of Canada had achieved autonomy within the British Empire. In the founding national myth they constructed, Canada was not, and could not be, a force that colonized other peoples.

Along with a new hierarchy of themes that excluded Native peoples from the main story of Canada's past, the nation's professional historians also imposed more rigid definitions of the legitimate methods and sources to be used in producing scholarly history. Most directly, they placed even more emphasis upon the use of written primary material as the basis for writing history. Indeed, twentieth-century academic history marked the final victory in the centuries-long rise to dominance of alphabetical writing and, with it, "the idea that people without writing were people without history."[57] Lacking such records, British Columbia's Native peoples could not speak or write their way into the province's history. The oft-times more pluralistic approach of amateur historians (such as H.H. Bancroft, Adrien Morice, and Frederic Howay) was largely rejected, their sources dismissed as unreliable, their writing as quaint or antiquarian. The emergence and hardening of disciplinary lines between history and anthropology also played a role here. Built on the fundamental distinction between peoples who produced written accounts of the past and peoples who did not, the two disciplines emerged in almost complete isolation from each other, with distinct methodologies, university departments, and communities of scholars. Academic historians could now plead that, even if they were sympathetic to the plight of Native people, the job of studying the latter was not theirs as they lacked the requisite specialized training; thus, the task was best left to anthropologists.

Sage did stand out, though, as one of the first Canadian historians to wrestle with the question of whether the frontier thesis applied north of the border. But the Canadian historical community, at its annual meeting in 1928, was unmoved by his proposals, and the most immediate reaction was an outright rejection of the frontier thesis's applicability to Canada.[58] Generally, Canadian historians were delicately selective in borrowing from Turner's thesis, wary as they were of its view of the frontier as a force that shaped a distinct American character.[59]

Something else working against the acceptance of Sage's proposals was the fact that national historians were just then turning elsewhere for new conceptual frameworks. The 1930s brought profound changes in Canadian historiography as a number of pioneering historians turned away from the political and constitutional focus of the 1920s to a new focus upon environmental and economic forces. This new focus produced two interpretations that remade the contours of Canadian historical writing: the staples thesis and the related Laurentian thesis. The latter was most clearly and convincingly expressed by Donald Creighton in *The Commercial Empire of the St. Lawrence*, released in 1937.[60] The Laurentian thesis posited that a coherent market economy had been built upon a unified geographic system – the St. Lawrence basin. In search of products for export, this commercial empire had expanded outward along natural trade routes, laying the foundations for both a transcontinental economy and a transcontinental Canadian nation. The Laurentian thesis can be seen as a regionalized application of the staples thesis, the arrival of which in full form was marked by the 1930 publication of Harold Innis's *Fur Trade in Canada*. Briefly, the staples thesis argued that the development of Canada could be explained by studying the exploitation of a series of staple resources, such as fish, fur, timber, and wheat. The exploitation of such resources had set the basis for the economic, social, and political makeup of Canada, from its geographic scope to Confederation to the opening of the West. Moreover, staples production in the hinterland was seen to depend upon markets in metropolitan areas, both within Canada and overseas, and it was the expansion of the metropolis into the hinterland that characterized Canadian history. Canada emerged, Innis concluded, "not in spite of geography but because of it" as east-west trade lines reached all the way to the Pacific.[61]

There has been scant appreciation of the extent to which Canada's westernmost province influenced Innis as he formulated the planks of his staples thesis. Innis visited British Columbia on a number of occasions, and the province's topography strengthened his conviction that environmental factors were central in history. "The whole of BC's problems," he concluded, "might be interpreted as a struggle against mountains, rocks and forests."[62] For Innis, the province's history was shaped by its geography, the emergence of its transportation system, and its reliance on staples such as gold and iron ores.[63] Innis's work on British Columbia revealed a characteristically encyclopedic knowledge of the existing literature of the province. While teaching a 1935 summer session course on economic history at UBC, he read through the entire collection of theses in history and economics housed in the library.[64]

The economic premises of the staples thesis had a particular resonance in the writing of BC history. From the start, provincial historians had recognized the importance of material forces and geography upon the development of Canada's far west. Howay in particular had anticipated Innis, arguing in his 1914 *British Columbia* that the political evolution of the region depended upon mining and finances, and suggesting the importance of a single staple in his work on the maritime and land fur trade. Through the 1930s, William Carrothers, a UBC political economist, applied the staples thesis to the province's forest and fisheries industries.[65] Carrothers's work resembled that of Innis in its painstaking use of statistics to study the historical exploitation of a single staple. However, Carrothers's studies were less ambitious and more limited in scope than were Innis's; they did not make the larger connections to cultural and political developments that rendered the latter's staples thesis such an original and influential interpretation.

Fellow UBC political economist Henry Angus also made limited efforts to apply the staples thesis to British Columbia. In 1929, Angus called upon his colleagues to apply contemporary advances in the social sciences and economics to their studies of the province's historical development.[66] More than a decade later, his contribution to the multi-authored *British Columbia and the United States* stressed the importance of resource exploitation. The history of relations between Britain, Canada, and the United States on the Northwest Coast, he concluded, "has been concerned with the fortunes of various attempts to exploit the rich natural resources of the region and with the international disputes incidental to those attempts."[67] Yet for Angus, this staple resource exploitation did not determine British Columbia's political fate. Despite common resources and a distinct geographic unity, political forces bisected the region, with the northern half pursuing an independent path first as a British colony, then as a Canadian province. And Angus himself did not produce a systematic study of BC history based upon the insights of the staples thesis; instead, most of Angus's writings focused on topics such as the Asian question in the far west and Canada's relations with the outside world.

Sage himself recognized that the turn to geographic and economic factors as represented in the Laurentian and staples theses held promising insights for BC history. Setting aside an ill-fitting political-constitutional framework, he attempted to make use of these insights in his contribution to *British Columbia and the United States*. Drafted through the 1930s and published in 1942, his chapters on railway building and mining in the Kootenay region described how the "stern facts of geography" had thrown up serious obstacles in the way of railroad building in the province, rendering east-west travel difficult. Meanwhile, the "inexorability of the geographic factor" and emergence of hard rock mining had profoundly affected the development of the Kootenays.[68] Sage noted that the Kootenays were first opened as a hinterland area linked to Spokane, the metropolitan centre of the "American Inland Empire." With the intrusion of railway lines built by Canadian and British capital, the Kootenay metropolis moved north of the border. While implicitly incorporating the metropolitan-hinterland premises of the staples thesis, Sage also suggested that the social development of the Kootenays was shaped by the nature of its staple resource. The Kootenays were, he concluded, "a mining region whose characteristics were determined by the nature of the industry."[69] These characteristics included a largely American complexion to the region's population, an abiding American influence in its local culture, and cordial relations with the United States.

Sage, though, did not welcome the new historiographical currents of the 1930s with unqualified support; most particularly, he was wary of their regional implications. The Laurentian thesis reiterated the prominence and dominance of the central provinces in Canadian history and historiography. Sage shared with W.L. Morton the concern that the Laurentian thesis relegated western Canada to a hinterland position.[70] Moreover, for Sage, the daunting series of mountain ranges that separated British Columbia from the rest of the nation rendered untenable the notion that a basic geographic unity radiated out from central Canada.[71] Speaking before the Canadian Historical Association in 1937, Sage argued that Canada had originated "not in one but in five or six localities." A truly national "sea-to-sea" history, Sage continued, would examine the development of each of these "Five Canadas," revealing how they contributed to the nation's history.[72]

Sage was also concerned about the pitfalls of geographic determinism, which he perceived in the new modes of thought. He had leaned heavily upon André Siegfried's study of Canada in drafting his address on the nation's five regions. And, as Siegfried pointed out, the struggle between geography and history was the main dynamic at play in Canadian history. "Natural" geographic lines running north-south drew the nation towards a North American identity but also threatened to pull Canada into the United States. Meanwhile, "artificial" historical lines mitigated New World influences by linking Canada to its European past, most notably through its political ties to Britain.[73] Sage recognized that this dilemma was particularly acute in British Columbia. "Geographically," he wrote, "there are six or seven British Columbias and the isolation of the province from the rest of Canada is an essential fact."[74] Natural geographic and trade lines ran south to north, not east to west. And yet, while the logic of geography and economics suggested union with the United States, the often "artificial" lines of history had been a counterweight, leading British Columbia into federation with a far distant Canada.[75] The overwhelming presence of an isolating geography in British Columbia caused Sage to warn his Canadian colleagues that social and political forces also must be heeded in examining the development of Canada's five regions. For Sage, factors such as population mix, cultural mores, and political institutions were decisive in the end. Had they not been, British Columbia would have been absorbed by the republic to the south.

In tackling the perennial issue of where British Columbia stood in relation to the United States, Canada, and Britain, Sage stood apart from previous provincial historians. More confident than they that British Columbia had become Canadian, he did not feel as threatened by the southern republic and was decidedly less negative in his attitudes towards it. Sage had been influenced by the work of western US historians; moreover, he personally enjoyed the company of Americans and maintained an oceanfront cottage in Point Roberts, just south of the border.[76] In his work, the United States did not appear as a looming imperial power, waiting to swallow up British Columbia. He thus felt that no purpose was served by dwelling on the boundary disputes of the past. Sage's reading of the Oregon question, made in the aftermath of the Second World War, was that it provided an example of peaceful cooperation and compromise that could be used as a model of cooperative relations between the United States, Canada, and Britain in the postwar era.[77] Indeed, his vision of a peaceful concord among English-speaking peoples was consistent with a larger move in this postwar period towards the notion of a common North Atlantic community united by fundamental beliefs in the face of the Soviet communist threat. Despite a parting of ways during the American Revolution, Sage argued that Canada and the United States shared a common heritage bequeathed by Britain: that is, the political, legal, literary, and cultural contributions that the latter had made to the world.[78]

Certainly, Sage was determined to underline the historical basis for British Columbia's independence from the United States, as his description of the contrasting frontiers revealed. Also responsible for maintaining this independence was the fact that British Columbia and Canada had never severed their links with Britain. "It was the British connection," Sage wrote, "which allowed Canada to develop as a separate political unit and prevented her absorption into the United States of America."[79] But the presence of an imperial Britain was not as strong in his work as it had been in the works of other provincial historians. After his early years of Anglophilia, Sage himself had developed a strong sense of Canada and British Columbia's North American identity. At the same time, he applauded the evolution of the British Empire into a loose, voluntary Commonwealth composed of autonomous nations on equal footing with the mother country.[80]

In the end, Sage did not achieve his ambition of rewriting provincial and national history. He did, though, come to recognize some of the unique obstacles British Columbia threw in the way of the historian, whether that involved its being "too politically immature" or that "in no portion of Canada has it been harder to overcome the hard facts of geography."[81] Moreover, in his efforts to incorporate the province into the national historical narrative, Sage successfully highlighted the fact that the established interpretations were drafted primarily to explain regions other than British Columbia and, in crucial aspects, did not fit the contours of the province's past. Thus, Sage emerged as the first historian to launch a critique of mainstream Canadian writing from the perspective of the nation's far west – an achievement not to be minimized. Nor should his substantial publishing record be dismissed; in his four decades as an academic historian, he published over one hundred books, articles, and reviews of British Columbia's history, leaving threads for succeeding historians to pick up.

While Sage struggled to tailor established historical frameworks to British Columbia, an original historical vision of his own also eluded him. A largely derivative thinker, Sage continued to look to a delocalized academic culture for inspiration. His intellectual universe remained bounded by university walls; when this failed him, he was unable to draw upon a more intimate and personal knowledge of the province (as could Frederic Howay before him and as would Margaret Ormsby after him). Sage failed to write the single-volume history of British Columbia that he had conceived in 1921 and that might have provided such a vision. He did make significant suggestions as to how Canadian history could be rewritten in order to provide greater recognition of British Columbia, but neither he nor his colleagues followed through on these prescriptions. Indeed, he showed a strong and abiding penchant for programmatic and suggestive addresses rather than intensive, analytical research. This is one reason why the painstaking work of the amateur Judge Howay has weathered the years better than have the writings of Professor Sage.

If Sage was frustrated in his ambition to provide British Columbia with a compelling historical vision or fresh historical survey, he did leave a more significant legacy in his roles of teacher and administrator. As professor of history from 1918 to 1953, and as department head from 1931 to 1953, Sage worked to establish BC history as an academic subject and to train a first generation of professional provincial historians. Sage was able to expose students to the currents of North American academic history, while also incorporating his own writings and those of British Columbia's amateur historians.

Sage did not become department head until 1931, and his most significant impact on the teaching of history at UBC would wait until then. In the meantime, the two men who preceded Sage left their own imprints on the department, shaping it along the lines of two distinct historiographical traditions. Mack Eastman, who was head for the department's first decade, had completed graduate work at the Sorbonne and took a PhD at New York's Columbia University. Thus, he was armed with the keenly critical tools and socioeconomic perspective of both French and progressive US historical writing.[82] During Eastman's tenure, Western Europe from medieval to modern times was the focus of the history program, and his own Reformation and Renaissance class was the core course. The overarching theme of these offerings was "a progressive interpretation of the development of Western civilization up to our times."[83]

While Eastman's tenure ended when he accepted a position at the League of Nations' International Labour Office in Geneva, his legacy continued on after his departure. One graduate of the early history program, Sylvia Thrupp, would obtain a doctorate from the University of London and go on to become one of her generation's leading scholars on the social and economic history of medieval Europe.[84] Before finding a permanent appointment at the University of Chicago, Thrupp taught economic and medieval history at UBC from 1935 to 1944. She was also given most of the responsibility for the historiography and methodology course that was at the core of honours and master's programs.[85] In her courses, Thrupp tried to instill in her students the keenly critical edge and socioeconomic approach to which Eastman had been committed. Margaret Ormsby (who arrived as a student a year after Eastman left the department) would later remark upon the lasting reputation UBC's first professor had left behind.[86]

The department changed tack when D.C. Harvey, an Oxford graduate from Nova Scotia, took over as head in 1928.[87] Harvey was determined to bring the department more in line with established programs in the rest of Canada; he oversaw a move away from Eastman's socioeconomic approach towards a more political-constitutional history.[88] He also set out to "strengthen [the] Canadian courses" and shifted the program's focus from Western Europe to Britain.[89] For Harvey, this change was justified because "the British character and institutions was the basis of [Canada's] national life and institutions."[90] This link between Canadian and British history was a hallmark of the national school of history to which Harvey belonged. It also had particular relevance to the young society still forming in British Columbia (as we have seen, both public opinion and the province's historical literature tended to stress the imperial tie above all others). As A.B. McKillop notes, in writing of central and eastern Canada in the previous century, the teaching of British history and literature "provided a frontier society with an instant cultural and intellectual inheritance."[91]

While their focus remained on Western European or British history, respectively, Eastman and Harvey did make room for BC history. From 1920 on, students enrolled in the honours stream were able to pursue BC history through supplementary reading in non-honours courses or as part of their graduating essay.[92] The same held true for graduate students after the department brought in a master's program in 1926. The following year, the first seminar specifically devoted to BC history began. Taught by Sage, it was open to both honours and master's students.[93] While this seminar was replaced in 1929 with one focused more broadly on Canadian history, Sage devoted the second half of the latter to a "minute study" of BC history.[94]

Walter Sage finally took over as department head in 1931, after Harvey left to become Nova Scotia's provincial archivist. Sage did not discard the British Canadian imprint left by Harvey for, as we have seen, his own education and work had been shaped by the same national historiographical currents that had influenced Harvey. But as head until his retirement in 1953, Sage channelled a greater share of the department's resources towards provincial history, thereby building what he called a "school of provincial historians" at UBC.[95] Sage had been given responsibility for the department's early BC offerings; as department head, he built a stronger institutional basis for provincial history. One result was the creation in 1936 of an ambitious survey course in western Canadian history, which, like the earlier seminar in Canadian history, devoted its second half to British Columbia's history, from the exploration era into the twentieth century.[96] As he had done in his own writing, Sage applied the themes of Canadian and western American academic writing in his teaching of provincial history. These included: the evolution of British Columbia's political institutions and its entry into Confederation; the relevance of the staples thesis in industries such as the fur trade, mining, and forestry; the applicability of the frontier thesis; and Sage's own "Five Canadas" concept.

Sage also encouraged his students to undertake research in BC history through the honours and master's programs, which were set up in the years after the First World War. Honours students would meet in seminars or undertake individual directed readings, which would teach them, in Eastman's words, "how to do intensive and accurate work in one or more fields ... [that would] involve a study of Bibliography, Research methods, etc."[97] The master's program involved students more directly and extensively in primary research. While at first, course requirements were relatively informal, the crowning achievement was a "thesis embodying original work."[98] In Sage's eyes, the honours and master's programs were part of his department's effort to build "a research school at the University of

British Columbia."[99] As early as 1921, Sage lobbied to get master's studies in BC history under way.[100] A decade later, he was determined to use his new position as head to steer students into provincial history. He argued that only academically trained historians could make proper use of the primary materials collected by UBC and the Provincial Archives in order to write provincial history.[101]

In 1936, Sage started an MA seminar on British Columbia that he would teach until his retirement in 1953, and which would be required of all master's students whether they majored in the topic or not.[102] The master's seminar was more ambitious in scope than its honours predecessor, although both brought students into direct contact with primary documents. The graduate class was explicitly designed to "train research students in the history of British Columbia." Topically, seminar students were faced with the task of placing British Columbia within its national and continental context (significantly, there was no mention of the imperial or British context). Also, inspired by recent currents in historiography and heeding his own advice, Sage's seminar spent over one-half of its time on the post-Confederation era. The province's political history was discussed, as was its socioeconomic development. Particularly novel topics included the history of settlement, urban development, and cultural history. While it is unclear whether any single class actually completed the survey set out in the seminar outline, the outline did contain possible directions and topics for research.[103]

Meanwhile, as department head, Sage actively guided honours and master's students into BC topics not yet covered by the existing literature.[104] A 1937 memorandum entitled "Studies Completed and Fields Assigned in British Columbia History" reveals that Sage had developed a clear program of action for provincial history. The memorandum lists forty-two undergraduate essays and master's theses either completed or assigned to specific students as of that year. All the topics relate to BC history and range from conventional political and economic studies to the less common examination of social issues such as those surrounding the province's Japanese population.[105] Sage's efforts did yield results: from 1935 to 1945, nineteen MA theses on BC history were completed, with their subjects reflecting those of the graduate seminar. Prior to that, only six had been produced, including Sylvia Thrupp's 1929 work on Cranbrook and Margaret Ormsby's 1931 study of the Okanagan. During this time BC theses had overtaken non-BC theses: from 1935 to 1945, only eight of the latter were produced, while from 1926 to 1934 fourteen were produced.[106] About two dozen more BC-related master's theses would be added in the decades after the Second World War.[107]

The body of theses produced by UBC's history graduates placed the writing of BC history on more solid, scholarly foundations. Much of this work was published in the *British Columbia Historical Quarterly*, the province's first bona fide historical journal. Fifteen graduates contributed twenty-seven articles during the journal's existence (1937-58), while later theses would find their way into *BC Studies* when that quarterly was founded in the early 1970s. Moreover, UBC's honours and master's programs represented a crucial step in the formation of the first generation of professional historians to be trained in the province. Graduates included W. Kaye Lamb and Willard Ireland, who served successive stints at the Provincial Archives and as editors of the *British Columbia Historical Quarterly*. Also, Sylvia Thrupp and Margaret Ormsby returned to teach at UBC after receiving doctorates abroad. And, of course, Ormsby would continue contributing to BC history throughout her academic career. Building upon the contributions and suggestions made by Sage through his provincial history courses, this generation would turn its attention to a more systematic writing of BC history.

6

W. Kaye Lamb, Margaret Ormsby, and a First Generation of BC Historians

The opening of the University of British Columbia in 1915 made possible the formation of a first generation of university students born and educated in the province. Like postsecondary institutions in the rest of Canada, UBC served a local constituency, with all but a tiny fraction of its student body coming from within the province.[1] Emerging from the young university during the interwar years were academic historians who possessed direct and personal knowledge of British Columbia. W. Kaye Lamb and Margaret Ormsby, the two most prominent members of this generation to turn their attention to their home province's history, would prove more successful than their teachers had been at drawing upon influences from outside academia in studying their chosen field. With Lamb, Ormsby, and other graduates of UBC, writing on the province's past once again moved towards more locally produced history, a move that repeated an earlier homeward shift among British Columbia's amateur historians.

As we have seen, UBC's early history program was designed to forge the next generation of academic historians, with the honours and master's programs passing on the tools of the historical trade through advanced study and research. Meanwhile, undergraduate and graduate historical societies further instilled the standards and values of the discipline. Formed in 1919, the undergraduate Historical Society was dedicated to the serious "study and discussion of historical problems." The society consisted of history department faculty and twenty selected students, mostly those in the third and fourth years of the honours program. Monthly meetings of the society consisted of the presentation of student papers on the evening's topic, which ranged from international labour movements to the status of Ireland and India, followed by often animated discussions.[2]

The early dominance of international topics reflected the fact that Mack Eastman and Frederick Soward were the most active faculty in the Historical Society during this time. Upon becoming department head, Walter Sage was able to inject more local content, dedicating the 1931-32 year to papers on BC history. Margaret Ormsby would later recall that the Historical Society, in tandem with the honours program, pulled together a "notable" and "extremely stimulating" group of young historians at UBC.[3] In 1934, the Graduate Historical Society was formed, and it was open to the department's growing number of master's students, along with alumni and former undergraduate Historical Society members. Meeting in a seminar room on campus, the Graduate Historical Society provided a forum for students to present their own primary research, including work on the province's past.[4]

Many alumni of UBC's early history program would go on to prominent careers in academia and government. Hugh Keenleyside and Norman Robertson, both Historical Society members in the early 1920s, ascended to high positions within the Department of External Affairs. Keenleyside, a student of Eastman's who taught history at UBC from 1925 to 1927, returned to the province to serve as chairman of BC Hydro through the 1960s. Another Historical Society alumni and Eastman student, Harry Cassidy, pursued doctoral studies in social policy. He and W. Kaye Lamb saw service as two of the young academics hired to carry out Premier Duff Pattullo's reform agenda before he moved on to Ottawa as part of the "government generation" that remade the federal state.[5] And, more significantly for our purposes, this first generation produced a handful of distinguished academic historians. Renowned medievalist Sylvia Thrupp, Provincial and Dominion Archivist Lamb, and Margaret Ormsby: all were members of the select Historical Society and graduates of the honours and master's programs in history. The latter two would have the most significant impact on the writing of BC history.

William Kaye Lamb was born in New Westminster in 1904 to a Scottish father and Ontarian mother. The young Lamb grew up near the home of Judge Frederic Howay. In subsequent years, he was a regular visitor to the homes of Howay and Robie Reid, making use of their voluminous private libraries and conferring with them on historical matters. Building on his close connection to the province's tradition of amateur history, Lamb turned his attention to acquiring the tools of the professional, academic historian. He enrolled at UBC and soon took a prominent place among the "notable" group of students forming around the history honours program. Graduating in 1927, Lamb taught at the university for one year before a Nicol Scholarship sent him to the Sorbonne for three years of study, where he worked under André Siegfried. Illness interrupted Lamb's stay in Paris and brought him home, where he completed a master's degree at UBC. Doctoral studies under Harold Laski at the London School of Economics followed, and a dissertation on the British Labour Party earned Lamb his PhD in 1933.[6]

Upon his return to British Columbia, Lamb was appointed provincial archivist, the first to possess an advanced university education and training in historical research. In 1940, Lamb moved back across Georgia Strait to become the UBC librarian. Eight years later, he left for Ottawa, where he accepted the position of Dominion archivist and where he worked until his retirement in 1968. Lamb returned to Vancouver yet again, continuing to publish books and articles until his death in 1999. While nationally and internationally Lamb is best known for his role in modernizing the nation's Public Archives through the post-Second World War era, he also made significant contributions to the writing of BC history through his decades-long interest in his home province's past.[7]

As provincial archivist, Lamb undertook a fundamental reorganization of the institution aimed at making it an indispensable research tool for the provincial historian. Lamb's predecessors, John Forsyth and John Hosie, had failed to discipline the rich but ill-organized collection that E.O.S. Scholefield had amassed. Upon stepping into Hosie's shoes, Lamb quickly realized that the archives lacked an accurate record of its own holdings and that, without such a record, serious historians would be greatly hampered in their research efforts.[8] With the goal of building "a complete library" for the Northwest Coast and British Columbia, Lamb catalogued the archives' Northwest Library according to the Dewey decimal system. The manuscript collection was also reclassified and an exhaustive index compiled, and order was brought to the budgeting process and staff organization. Meanwhile, Lamb's own collection efforts did not depart from the pre-Confederation focus of his predecessors, a focus reinforced by his personal interest in the maritime and land fur trades and subsequent colonial era. Notable acquisitions here included the private papers of James

Douglas, John Work, and W.F. Tolmie, along with the journal of Captain Richard Mayne.[9]

As provincial archivist, Lamb automatically assumed day-to-day control over the British Columbia Historical Association. He immediately initiated and oversaw a reorganization that resuscitated the moribund organization, which had been crippled by petty regional jealousies. With the aid of Robie Reid and Judge Howay, Lamb launched the *British Columbia Historical Quarterly* in January 1937, serving as editor for its first decade.[10] Under Lamb, the *British Columbia Historical Quarterly* served as the main public forum for scholarship on the province's past. *Quarterly* authors included Lamb and Sage (each with a PhD), prominent amateur historians such as Howay and Californian Henry Wagner, as well as UBC graduate students.

The *British Columbia Historical Quarterly* was Lamb's creation, and as an active, vigilant editor, he shaped the journal's direction during its most productive years. Lamb later recalled that, of the early contributors to the *British Columbia Historical Quarterly*, only Howay and Walter Sage wrote with confidence, and he spent much time "fixing up" articles prior to publication.[11] Most likely, some *Quarterly* articles that are listed as pieces co-authored by Lamb were originally written by one author and reworked by Lamb to such an extent that he then added his name to them.[12] Thus, in his role of editor, Lamb helped raise the standard of scholarship in provincial history, ensuring that articles appearing in the *Quarterly* adhered to the scholarly criteria that his own academic training had instilled in him. Lamb also used the *Quarterly* to publish primary material he had collected while at the Provincial Archives, thereby making that material more accessible.[13] Tellingly, with Lamb's departure for Ottawa, the journal struggled to meet its quarterly deadlines and finally sputtered to a halt in 1958.

Lamb also produced a lasting legacy for provincial history with the publication of a series of exploration and fur trade journals. In these, Lamb pulled together and meticulously edited the accounts and papers of historical figures such as Daniel Harmon, Simon Fraser, Alexander Mackenzie, and George Vancouver. Admittedly, much of this material had been published previously; however, as Lamb noted, earlier editions were all too often faulty, whether in the creative licence taken by previous editors or in their use of unreliable original manuscripts. Lamb himself set out to present the "authentic text" based upon the complete original manuscript (where possible) made accessible by annotation and detailed indexes.[14]

Finally, Lamb contributed a significant body of his own writing to the province's historiography, taking advantage of his position as provincial archivist to gain access to fresh primary material. He made use of documents from the Hudson's Bay Company Archives (just then opening its doors to researchers) to describe the fur trading company's policies, presence, and activities in the far west both before and after the Oregon Treaty.[15] Meanwhile, new acquisitions by the Provincial Archives (such as the Douglas Papers and material relating to Richard Blanshard's brief, comic-opera governorship) were the basis for work on the fur trade and colonial periods.[16]

Given the concentration of the province's archival collection upon British Columbia's early history, it is not surprising that Lamb's writing remained focused upon the pre-Confederation era. Along with his work on the HBC, he was interested in the peculiar political status of Vancouver Island and British Columbia as colonies. Throughout, Lamb's vision of the province was influenced by its early maritime orientation. His examination of the early lumbering industry from the 1840s to 1860s, the first systematic look at the topic, underscored the fact that Vancouver Island dominated British Columbia's economy, and its political life, through this time. Lamb also noted that this Vancouver Island-based economy was largely export driven and dependent upon overseas markets, while turning his attention to a much neglected aspect of the province's history – namely, the rise of a dominant forestry industry.[17]

Lamb's maritime orientation also extended to the Mainland and, most particularly, to the Port of Vancouver. Harbouring an interest in shipping that dated back to his childhood, Lamb produced a series of articles on the Canadian Pacific Railway's trans-Pacific Empress liners in the half century after their inauguration in 1892.[18] Through these articles, Lamb suggested that British Columbia was unique in the country in the extent to which it looked westward to the Orient rather than eastward to the rest of Canada. Moreover, Lamb here presented the trans-Pacific steamships as a natural extension of the CPR: the two formed a modern day Northwest Passage that earlier provincial historians had seen promised in the completion of the CPR. Years later, Lamb would examine the terrestrial leg of this passage in a book-length study of Canada's first transcontinental railway.[19]

Nor should Lamb's abiding interest in ships and shipping be surprising. As Ormsby would recall, Lamb, Howay, and Reid were men of the sea and coast.[20] Living in port towns (whether Vancouver, New Westminster, or Victoria) these men recognized the pull of the sea upon British Columbia, and their most important work focused upon its early, maritime days. And indeed, the impact of the province's indigenous amateur history tradition – the strength of which lay in its documentary pluralism and its focus upon the uniqueness of British Columbia's early history – was profound. Lamb also followed in the tradition of Gosnell and Scholefield in his belief that the archivist's primary task was to assist the process of historical research and writing, although he was unique in that he was also fully trained as a professional historian. Even as Dominion archivist, Lamb rejected calls for the establishment of independent archival schools, arguing instead that such training should be offered within established history departments. Speaking before the Canadian Historical Association in his 1958 presidential address, Lamb expressed his regret that "the career of an archivist has entailed one sacrifice. I was trained as an historian, but acquiring manuscripts for other people to use is such a time-consuming occupation that I have only an occasional moment to spend on historical research."[21] Given the impressive body of work Lamb left behind, one is left to wonder what he might have produced if he had pursued an academic career – although this work might not have focused on his home province as it was archival work that drew him professionally to BC history.

Like Lamb, Margaret Anchoretta Ormsby was born in British Columbia (at Quesnel in 1909) and was an early graduate of the province's undergraduate and graduate history programs. Her father was an Anglo-Irish immigrant who had brought his family to British Columbia's interior to homestead; her mother was a Presbyterian Scot and school teacher. Soon after Margaret's birth, Ormsby's father moved the family to the north Okanagan, where he worked as a merchant and then fruit farmer, eventually settling in Coldstream on the shore of Kalamalka Lake. Here, in a home environment that encouraged sociability and the life of the mind, Margaret Ormsby spent her final grade school days before leaving for UBC in the autumn of 1926.[22]

As a young undergraduate at UBC, Ormsby found the intellectual stimulation she sought in the tight group of students that formed around the honours history program and the Historical Society. She also found herself in the midst of a raw, new campus: the university had moved to its Point Grey site a year before Ormsby's arrival; only two brick buildings had been erected, while other temporary structures were in various stages of completion. The unfinished grounds had only recently been cleared of their dense forest of trees, and Ormsby's first winter on campus was spent in a "sea of mud."[23] The experience of the young British Columbians attending the provincial university during this time contrasted sharply with those of their teachers. Eastman, Sage, Soward, and others had apprenticed amid the ponderous, Victorian architecture of the University of Toronto and had subsequently passed through the medieval halls of Oxford or the Sorbonne. In contrast to these centres, to which generations had turned in their search for wisdom, the raw frontier scene of Ormsby's UBC possessed an aura of newness, of fresh beginnings on the edge of the continent, ocean and towering mountains within sight.

The sharp juxtaposition of an active intellectual life and untamed wilderness would be at the core of Ormsby's emerging vision of British Columbia. At UBC, Ormsby worked to acquire the skills of academic history. Meanwhile, her own research focused on the Okanagan Valley, and she completed an honours thesis and a master's thesis on the region, both of which contributed to the series of local studies produced by history students during this time.[24] Then department head D.C. Harvey had taken Ormsby under his wing and had encouraged her interest in local history, but the initial inspiration for Ormsby's focus came from her own Okanagan upbringing and the direct influence of amateur Okanagan historian Leonard Norris.[25] The moving force behind the formation of the Okanagan Historical Society (OHS) and the main contributor to the evolution of a distinct Okanagan historiography, Norris opened Ormsby's eyes to the history of the valley. It was Norris who encouraged her to study the Okanagan for her UBC theses, and he provided her with assistance along the way.[26] Ormsby joined the OHS in her undergraduate years, and, in the following decades, she contributed a steady steam of articles on the pioneer history of the Okanagan Valley to the society's *Report*, also serving as editor of the journal for seven years (1935, 1948-53).[27]

Indeed, Ormsby's Okanagan background had a profound and abiding effect on her thinking and work, leaving her with a hinterland perspective. She expressed strong pride in being a "farmer's daughter" from British Columbia's interior. At the end of each academic year, she would flee the confines of Vancouver to find respite in her family's Coldstream house, also spending the last two decades of her life there after her retirement.[28] As UBC colleague John Conway would later reflect, Ormsby's "heart was always in the Okanagan."[29] Intellectually, Ormsby's Okanagan background and links to the valley's historians left her with a hinterland perspective. As she recalled later, she had "always lived on the edge of everything."[30] Ormsby was convinced that the root of British Columbia's distinct identity lay in the hinterland for it was there that the juxtaposition between civilization and wilderness was sharpest.

Ormsby emerged from UBC's master's program in 1931 determined to pursue a career in academic history. Once again encouraged by Harvey, she gained admittance into the doctoral program at Pennsylvania's prestigious women's university, Bryn Mawr. At Bryn Mawr, Ormsby focused on the work of the progressive historians and their analyses of American history as her major field, with secondary fields in European history and economic thought. Even though Bryn Mawr offered no courses in the area, Ormsby turned her attention closer to home with her 1937 dissertation, which was completed after spending 1934-36 as an assistant in UBC's history department. At the suggestion of Walter Sage, Ormsby's thesis examined British Columbia's post-Confederation relations with the Canadian government.[31]

After teaching at a private girls' high school in San Francisco, Ormsby returned east to lecture at McMaster University from 1940 to 1943. Here, and through earlier research at the Dominion Archives in Ottawa, she came into close contact with eastern Canadian historians. Throughout this time, her work took on a strong national orientation. Ormsby's PhD dissertation had been generally sympathetic to the Dominion government in its struggles with British Columbia, portraying the views of provincial politicians as narrow and petty. When part of the thesis appeared in the *Canadian Historical Review*, Ormsby's first scholarly article was even more favourable to the federal government as it examined BC-Dominion relations in the 1870s from the perspective of the federal Liberal Party. This emphasis was due in large part to *Canadian Historical Review* editor Donald Creighton's demands that Ormsby's piece be of "national interest" – that is, that it reflect the prevailing focus on central Canada, which dominated the nation's historical writing.[32] Canada's national historical journal, Creighton sniffed, was interested in "the centre rather than the periphery."[33]

Perhaps because of this very dismissal of regional history as peripheral, Ormsby refused to be "captured" by eastern Canadian historians, and her time at McMaster only reinforced her sense of British Columbia's distinctiveness.[34] Yearning to return home, in 1943 she accepted a temporary appointment as replacement lecturer for Frederick Soward, who had been seconded to the Department of External Affairs in Ottawa for the duration of the war.[35] Three years later, Ormsby became the first woman to be hired on a permanent basis by UBC's history department. She was one of only three such hirings throughout Canada prior to the 1960s (Hilda Neatby and Jean Murray at the University of Saskatchewan were the others).

Ormsby's academic achievements were due, in part, to the relatively strong presence of women at UBC in general and in the history department in particular. When Ormsby arrived at the muddy Point Grey campus, she joined a student body that was 43 percent female, twice the national rate.[36] Moreover, the history program she entered had a gender mix not seen in the university's other departments, which were overwhelmingly dominated either by men (sciences, engineering) or women (home economics, nursing, teaching).[37] Through the 1920s, fourteen of the twenty-eight history honours students were women; these numbers dropped to eighteen of sixty in the 1930s and to twelve of thirty-seven in the 1940s.[38] In the master's program, three of seven theses were completed by women in the 1920s, nine of twenty-eight in the following decade, and three of nine from 1940 to 1945.[39] Eight of these female graduates would go on to complete doctoral studies in history or related fields; all but one of them had to study abroad as the handful of eastern Canadian institutions that offered doctoral degrees were resistant to accepting female students and faculty.[40] The strength of UBC's early female history students was further demonstrated in their success in winning scholarship and prize competitions. In the heyday of the 1920s, eighteen women won such competitions, compared to fifteen men. As with history numbers overall, the following decades saw a decline in female award winners: ten of thirty-two in the 1930s and twelve of thirty-seven in the 1940s.[41]

UBC's student historical societies also welcomed and encouraged women to participate. The undergraduate Historical Society that Ormsby found so stimulating was modelled on the University of Toronto's Historical Club, founded by George Wrong in 1904. One difference, though, was that Toronto's club barred women from membership, a stubbornly retrograde policy that did not change until the 1960s.[42] From its inception on, women represented half of the students chosen for UBC's Historical Society. They actively contributed to the society's meetings and served equally in leadership positions. The experiences of students such as Ormsby, Sylvia Thrupp, Isabel Bescoby, and Helen Boutilier corroborate Lee Stewart's conclusion that "women who chose not to conform to the pressures of 'feminine behaviour' that required underrating their intelligence ... were likely to be found in these clubs."[43]

Yet while it provided a relatively welcoming environment for female students, UBC's history department was no equal-opportunity employer when it came to faculty postings. Upon her return to Vancouver in 1943, Ormsby joined Sylvia Thrupp in the cramped offices of the "Zoo," where female faculty were segregated from their male colleagues to prevent any improprieties.[44] Thrupp's experience showed the limits of the history department's acceptance of female faculty and more closely followed the pattern of fellow female academics. Arguably the most brilliant graduate of the department's honours and master's programs, Thrupp completed a PhD in medieval English history at the University of London before returning to teach at UBC in 1935. For nearly a decade, she toiled as an instructor on a year-to-year basis, receiving half the pay of assistant professors – a rank her male colleagues received either immediately upon appointment (particularly if they possessed a PhD) or within a few years.[45] Through this time, department head Walter Sage was adamant that Thrupp not receive a permanent position. However, responsible for the care of an ailing father, she remained in Vancouver until 1945, when a Guggenheim Fellowship and offer of an assistant professorship took her to the University of Chicago.[46] From here, Thrupp embarked upon a career as one of the preeminent medievalists in North America and Britain.

The loss of Thrupp may have convinced Sage that he needed to be more forthcoming with permanent positions if he was to retain home-grown talent such as Ormsby, whose ongoing appointment came a year after Thrupp's departure. Apparently, it took additional pressure from UBC president Norman Mackenzie to overcome Sage's reluctance to hire Ormsby as the history department's first female faculty – although, in return, Ormsby assumed the decidedly non-professional responsibility of escorting the president to official social functions when the latter's wife could not attend.[47] Indeed, the personal experiences of Ormsby and Thrupp contrasted to the norm established by their male colleagues, most of whom had supportive wives to take care of any familial duties.[48] Ormsby remained single throughout her life, and Thrupp married a fellow academic only after her permanent posting in Chicago. Both women were also responsible for the care of aging parents at crucial points in their careers, a responsibility from which their married male colleagues were generally free.[49]

More broadly, the professionalization project that produced several generations of Canadian historians systematically excluded women. The formative institutions of that generation (the University of Toronto, Oxford University, the Rhodes Scholarship) all either actively discouraged female students or barred them outright. If a woman took an alternate route to obtain training as an academic historian, she was faced with the kind of hiring policies outlined by Toronto's W.P.M. Kennedy in 1925: "Our policy is not (whether rightly or wrongly does not matter) to give higher appointments to women."[50] It was a position that remained unchanged at Toronto for four decades. Meanwhile, the organization that bonded together Canada's professional historians was a virtual men's club. For decades, women were excluded from serving on the executive of the Canadian Historical Association, and the first forty CHA presidents were men. Hilda Neatby broke this monopoly in 1962, with Ormsby following four years later.[51] Finally, the political and constitutional focus of the national school left little room for women. Until the First World War brought suffrage, women were excluded from the Canadian polity, and men continued to dominate the nation's political development in the century that followed.

Ormsby's experience as a pioneering woman in the male domain of Canadian academic history had a significant impact upon her legacy in the writing and study of BC history. In short, it threw up powerful constraints to her devoting herself fully and exclusively to the province's past, lest she be doubly marginalized: first as a woman and second as a parochial historian. Reflecting upon her career, Ormsby admitted that she had feared such marginalization. In this light, her statement that she "always lived on the edge of everything" takes on a multilayered meaning as both geographical (the edge of the continent, the edge of the hinterland) and professional (a woman in a man's profession, a provincial historian in a national historical guild).[52]

Overall, Ormsby was less overtly determined than was Walter Sage to build up the BC history curriculum in the history department. She did not view the establishment and promotion of provincial history as her goal, whether in teaching, supervising of students, or as department head.[53] Ormsby did assume Sage's responsibilities for teaching courses with BC content upon the latter's departure. She carried on with the master's seminar on British Columbia offered every other year, although the course focused as much on research methods as on the content of provincial history.[54] In 1968, she resurrected the western Canada course that had been allowed to lapse with Sage's departure and started a survey course on British Columbia in the early 1970s.[55] However, Ormsby's teaching load ranged far beyond provincial borders and included medieval Europe; American social, economic, and intellectual history, taught in the "progressive tradition"; and post-Confederation Canada, a course she had introduced and that became her own.[56]

Moreover, in her roles as graduate student supervisor and department head, Ormsby did not see herself as a salesperson for provincial history and largely avoided steering students into the field.[57] This reticence is reflected in the declining number of graduate essays and theses on provincial history produced during Ormsby's tenure in comparison to the number produced during D.C. Harvey and Walter Sage's tenure: seventeen such theses and essays were completed in the 1930s, fourteen in the 1940s, and twenty in the 1950s. In the 1960s, this number dropped to eleven.[58] That being said, Ormsby did provide strong support when students decided to pursue BC history: of the sixteen honours essays and twenty master's theses she supervised in her decades at UBC, only two were not on BC topics.[59] And, of course, Ormsby was head when the department finally established a doctoral program in 1964. Ormsby herself oversaw four of the earliest PhD students, three of whom studied aspects of BC history: Jean Friesen (at the time, Jean Usher) on Anglican missionary William Duncan, Patricia Roy on the British Columbia Electric Railway, and Robin Fisher on Native-European relations throughout the nineteenth century. Thus, one of Ormsby's most significant legacies was to contribute to the formation of a core of doctoral students who, in the following decades, would start to bring provincial historiography in line with the monumental changes in historical writing of the 1960s and 1970s.

Ormsby also contributed to the lowering of barriers for female participation both in Canada's historical profession and, more specifically, in the scholarly study of BC history. Looking back on her career in retirement, Ormsby took most pride in the assistance she gave to female students in pursuing their studies and careers.[60] Ormsby served as advisor for the two women who were among the first to pursue doctoral studies in the department. Roy later noted that Ormsby subsequently helped her secure a job at the University of Victoria; and Friesen recalled that, with Ormsby as head and supervisor, and with Margaret Prang and Jean Elder also on faculty, her own work and that of other female graduate students could not be dismissed out of hand.[61] Meanwhile, Prang and Elder credited their colleague for making it easier for them to secure jobs in the department and to lead it, as Prang would do upon Ormsby's retirement in 1974.[62] Patricia Roy, who was a leading force in developing, and who eventually chaired, the University of Victoria's history program, believed that Ormsby succeeded in making "British Columbia history a respectable pursuit."[63] One might add that she helped make academic history a respectable career for women in both the province and the country.

And yet, despite her best efforts, there is strong evidence to suggest that some of Ormsby's colleagues did view her as doubly marginal, an opinion that wreaked havoc on Ormsby's tenure as Canada's first female history department head from 1964 to 1974. During this time, UBC's Department of History quadrupled in size to meet a huge influx of students. The "sleepy" and "parochial" department of the 1950s, dominated by Canadian faculty and with a focus on British and Canadian history, was profoundly altered by a new generation of faculty, many of whom had trained at prestigious American universities in recent historical methods and whose focus was on western European and American history.[64] The latter's aggressive push for changes, most particularly in curriculum and department governance, was seen by Ormsby as a challenge to her own authority, and a virtual civil war raged throughout her tenure. Witnesses to and participants in the rift later recalled that, as is so often the case with academic politics, the conflict often degenerated into petty, personal attacks.[65]

Certainly, issues of principle were at stake, the most important being the insurgents' effort to modernize the department and the history it was teaching. But also at play was the new faculty's opinion of Ormsby herself. They tended to dismiss her scholarly reputation as being too weak to justify her being head. Robin Fisher, who, as a doctoral student, had a ringside seat to the conflict, sympathetically diagnosed his supervisor's difficult position, saying that Ormsby started out with two strikes against her: first, as a Canadian and provincial historian and, second, as a woman.[66] The new generation of faculty in the department saw themselves as heirs to the Enlightenment tradition and its focus on questions of putatively universal interest. Explicitly, the department's earlier focus on Canadian history, and Ormsby's own work on national and provincial history, was seen as parochial and particular. Less explicitly, the same Enlightenment tradition that created the modern discipline of history also prejudiced it against the feminine as a particular instance of the universal masculine. Only with difficulty could historians envisage history, both written and as a discipline, as having a woman's face.

While her fear of being marginalized had limited her efforts to promote the study of BC history as a teacher and administrator, Ormsby devoted all her research and writing efforts to the subject. The volume of her work did not match that of Frederic Howay or Walter Sage; however, Ormsby succeeded, where those two had not, in providing an original, overarching vision of the province's past. Most prominently, her 1958 *British Columbia: A History* proffered a coherent narrative of the province's development. *British Columbia* was produced as part of government-sponsored efforts to celebrate the centennial of British Columbia's founding as a colony. Ormsby was chosen by the BC Centennial Committee to author the book because she appeared best suited to produce a "readable general history" that met the highest scholarly standards by Douglas Day, 19 November 1958. A fluent writer, she had just been promoted to full professor and was hitting her stride as a historian.[67] Apparently, Walter Sage had expected to be selected for the job and was disappointed when he was overlooked, although the recently retired professor's age and health problems were no doubt factors in the committee's decision.[68]

Ormsby began work on *British Columbia* in the summer of 1956. A research team made up of half a dozen UBC students was put at her disposal and the parliamentary dining room set aside for their use.[69] Ormsby and her team gathered a wealth of primary material never before available to provincial historians, including government papers from 1914 to 1943 to which Premier W.A.C. Bennett had authorized access.[70] Relieved of her teaching duties for the 1957-58 academic year, she could focus fully on shaping this material into a continuous narrative. Remarkably, Ormsby met the deadline set by the Centennial Committee, and the 558-page *British Columbia* was released with fanfare during Douglas Day celebrations at Fort Langley. The first scholarly provincial history since the multi-volume work of Scholefield and Howay, Ormsby's *British Columbia* became the standard in the field immediately upon its release, and it would remain so for decades to come.

British Columbia appealed to both academic and general audiences because Ormsby consciously and skilfully employed the conventions of narrative history. She admired the writing style of Donald Creighton and shared his conviction that history was a literary art as well as a scholarly endeavour: the historian had to remain true to the facts but she also had to shape those facts into an intelligible, compelling story.[71] Of course, as recent historians of history have stressed, this was not simply a matter of sifting through the material of the past for the inherent story or meaning buried within; rather, the historian, like the novelist, played an active role in structuring her narrative. And the form of that narrative had a content of its own. Historical narrative imposed a beginning and end upon the flow of history, and its underlying structure asserted that one story was the main one, providing both meaning and a teleology to the past.[72]

Just as important for Ormsby, the conventions of narrative left individual people in history. After the Second World War, in response to the dehumanizing totalitarianism of first fascism and then communism, North American historians tended to adopt a liberal democratic focus on the individual.[73] Also, many of Canada's most prominent historians turned to biographical history as a reaction against the economic and geographic history of the 1930s, which had stressed "the sway of impersonal forces."[74] Ormsby saw her work as contributing to this trend. She further argued that the historian had to eschew the merely abstract and strive for a "humanized history" that would capture a truer sense of the past – a sense of the past as it was experienced by those who lived it.[75]

Ormsby's *British Columbia* was constructed on this philosophy of personalized history. For her, the province's frontier conditions challenged and stretched the faculties of even ordinary people, allowing them to realize a potential rarely achieved by those of like means in the more constrictive societies of urbanized Europe and eastern North America. These conditions also permitted energetic and colourful individuals to emerge as moving forces in British Columbia's development. Arguing that studying such individuals was the best way to capture the "elusive shining quality that was distinctive" in the province, Ormsby constructed a pantheon of political figures (most notably James Douglas, Richard McBride, and Duff Pattullo) who emerged as protagonists in the drama of *British Columbia*.[76] As with Creighton's biographical narratives so with Ormsby's: prominent individuals were depicted as representing larger forces and developments. For instance, Ormsby wrote of "The People's Dick," Premier Richard McBride: "More than anyone else he typified the spirit of the age: the optimism which verged on recklessness. Sensing that British Columbia had some distinctive quality – not quite Canadian, or British, or American, or even a blend of all three – he dreamed of developing its vast natural resources through grandiose schemes which would make it almost an empire in itself."[77]

The optimism of British Columbia's leading men, and its society more generally, was founded upon a bedrock faith in material progress, a faith that had emerged as a virtually unquestioned orthodoxy in the Western world during the Victorian age and that dominated the better part of the following century. Believing that the province represented an almost unlimited field of potential wealth and resources, Ormsby wrote that British Columbia's "energetic men ... [were] impatient to unlock the treasures enfolded in the mountains" and that their policies encouraged the rapid material growth of the province.[78] *British Columbia* itself shared this underlying materialism, firmly placing the text within the tradition of provincial historiography. But while previous historians had largely limited themselves to the fur trade or gold rush eras, Ormsby addressed the advent of an "industrialist-capitalist system."[79] Overall, she applauded the capitalist exploitation of the province's natural resources, believing that an optimistic faith in material development was central to the province's identity. As a hinterlander, she realized that development brought "comfort, leisure, education and civilization" to the isolated communities of the province.[80]

Yet Ormsby also voiced criticisms of the changes wrought by industrial capitalism. She pointed to the growing political power of ascendant capitalist interests and noted that industrialization had created new class tensions between a capitalist elite and a working class made singularly radical by the province's resource-based economy.[81] Ormsby's analysis here

was not Marxist; rather, it was inspired by the progressive American historians whom she had studied at Bryn Mawr and who had an abiding impact
on her teaching and writing. Progressive historians argued that conflict
based on material interests lay at the root of American history and that
the central tension was between "the people" and "the interests."[82] The
ongoing opposition in *British Columbia* between entrenched power and
those challenging it echoes this latter tension, and the formation and actions of the province's competing factions were shown to be based upon
their material interests. For example, the professionals and merchants
agitating for political reform and union with Canada did so not out of
high-minded idealism but because doing so "promised the enlargement
of professional, commercial and political opportunity" for themselves.[83]
Unfortunately, the reliance on prominent political figures meant that much
of *British Columbia* was narrated from their perspective, thereby seriously
constraining the extent to which Ormsby could apply a materialist critique
to British Columbia's history.

Along with class tensions, Ormsby also faulted the province's frenetic
economic development with creating serious environmental problems.
Basing her critique as much on aesthetic grounds as on systematic analysis, Ormsby decried the "despoliation of nature" that had produced
"drowned" valleys, "scarred" mountains, and "polluted" cities, thus destroying the very natural beauty that distinguished the province.[84] Indeed,
Ormsby recognized the contradictory relationship British Columbians
(and western North Americans more generally) had with nature and natural resources – a prescient recognition sharply at odds with prevailing
opinion. Largely "people of plenty," her compatriots nevertheless "found
that they could survive in the remote wilderness and make profit from
their enterprise only by destroying the very source of their support."[85] Here
again, one can see the influence of Ormsby's hinterland perspective as this
paradox was most evident away from British Columbia's major cities, where
raw development met pristine wilderness.

Ormsby also discerned the pragmatic substance underneath the often
partisan surface of the province's politics. Thus, while scholars in subsequent decades have tended to characterize the province's political history
as polarized along class lines, with rigidly ideological political parties
divided into opposing camps, Ormsby argued that British Columbia had
a long, abiding tradition of pragmatic, activist government. From Douglas's

road-building schemes and social reform plans to McBride's efforts at knitting together a web of railways to Pattullo's "Little New Deal," British Columbia's free enterprise political leaders had not been reluctant to wield the powers of the state to encourage and direct the province's economic growth and to undertake social programs.[86] Indeed, Ormsby intimated that British Columbia's "maverick" reputation in the rest of Canada was not deserved because, within the province, most of the people were indifferent to the aptness of party label so long as a government improved the hospital insurance system, bridged rivers and lakes, and flung highways across the mountains (as did the Social Credit government).[87]

The province's geography further undermined partisan differences. "Whatever a man's political philosophy," Ormsby wrote, "the obstinate topography of the province remained an incontrovertible fact."[88] This "obstinate topography" had produced some of the basic tenets of British Columbia's shared political culture, from its estranged posture towards the federal government to the central importance of transportation policy. Growing up in the province's interior, Ormsby recognized that it was the hinterlander who had the most direct interest in policies that linked the isolated pockets of the province. Writing as a resident of one of these isolated valleys, relatively cut off from her winter home in Vancouver, Ormsby recognized that, "in large part, our political history is also the history of transportation in the Province."[89]

Not coincidentally, the prominent protagonists of *British Columbia* shared Ormsby's sensitivity to the challenges and potential of the hinterland. Both McBride and Pattullo had started their careers in the northern hinterland, and both envisioned the development of this "New British Columbia." Pattullo, she wrote, "knew the hinterland intimately, and ... considered that the real British Columbia existed outside Vancouver."[90] The success of McBride and Pattullo, Ormsby suggested, was due in large part to their ability to conjure up the promise of the hinterland.

A focus on individuals and the surface events of politics took up much of *British Columbia*'s narrative. While Ormsby thus worked to present a "humanized history" of the province, she also moulded the deeper structure of that history. *British Columbia* was organized around a series of succeeding oppositions, which were the animating force behind the narrative. Much of the cohesiveness and energy of the book was created by the tension of the fundamental oppositions Ormsby charted in these pages.

The first of these oppositions is the pull between maritime and continental orientations.[91] Europeans had first stumbled upon the Northwest Coast from the sea, and the maritime influence continued in British Columbia's links with Britain and in Victoria's dominance of an ocean-based economy. Continental influences were introduced by the land fur traders and culminated in the coming of the CPR, Confederation, and the rise of Vancouver. Yet, throughout, British Columbia remained a Pacific province. As with preceding provincial historians, Ormsby recognized that the meeting of sea and mountain provided the province with a sense of occasion and location. It remained a place of drama as it was associated with the Northwest Passage, with East meeting West, and with being the final region to be swept up in the westward surge of European civilization.

Another opposition was introduced with the beginnings of a settled society in British Columbia and persisted through the nineteenth century. This opposition pitted a hierarchical, or "closed," model of society, built upon entrenched privilege, against a more "open" model of society, one adhering to liberal notions of meritocracy and democracy. The closed model was represented in the system of hierarchy and privilege put in place by the HBC as British Columbia moved from fur trade era to colonial era. The old traders and new colonial officials formed themselves into a "Family Company Compact," which gave way to a "British faction" as the colonies grew. With their entrenched position being based upon control of land and government offices, both the Compact and the British faction soon found themselves facing opposition. First came the settlers, who fought against the Compact's land monopoly. They formed into a "Canadian faction" composed of eastern Canadian merchants and professional men who were seeking access to political power and commercial opportunity.[92]

In *British Columbia*, the tension between open and closed societies was reinforced by regional oppositions, the most prominent of which is the competition between Island and Mainland. New Westminster, and then Vancouver, had been the foci of British Columbia's Canadian element, while the old Family Company Compact and British faction were centred in Victoria. By the 1860s, Ormsby wrote, "it had become second nature for the colonists of British Columbia to reject whatever the Vancouver Islanders accepted." And these tensions spilled over into the Confederation period.[93] While agreeing with Frederic Howay that this rift was healed only with the ascension of Premier McBride, Ormsby did not share the judge's partiality to the Lower Mainland.[94] For her, the tension between Vancouver and British Columbia's hinterland succeeded the older Island-Mainland opposition. Indeed, Ormsby was at her most trenchant in describing the city's rise to dominance: an "imperious and voracious metropolis" that sought to extend "its economic power until it held most of the province in its fee."[95]

The Vancouver-hinterland opposition also expressed itself as the tension between an industrial and commercial urban centre and its largely agricultural rural counterpart. Until recently, historians have largely ignored the rural and agricultural history of the province. It was Ormsby who provided the rare exception to this; she remained proud of her own background as a "farmer's daughter," and her natural early interest in the history of the Okanagan Valley produced a handful of articles on the province's agricultural development.[96] Not surprisingly, Ormsby was most concerned with the problems and challenges of Okanagan Valley fruit growers such as her father. Some of her articles described these challenges, along with the farmers' efforts to meet them either through marketing boards or an abortive attempt at a provincial United Farmers party. And yet Ormsby did not pursue the province's agricultural history in any systematic way, and a concern for the province's agricultural development was not a prominent theme in *British Columbia*.

While most of *British Columbia* focused on political and economic developments, Ormsby did address some aspects of the province's social history. She placed great emphasis upon the social and cultural bonds that, to her, were essential for the building of orderly communities. An abiding concern throughout *British Columbia* was the shape of "social life" at various times in the province's history: from the lonely if literate life of an HBC post to colonial dances and balls attended by the governor and Royal Navy officers to the city life of Victoria and Vancouver. Status distinctions both reflected and reinforced the factional and class divisions animating Ormsby's narrative. The "rigid class structure" imposed by the HBC meant that employees and officers did not socialize. And the exclusion of Canadians from the subsequent Company and British elite, cemented by marriage and high society functions, reinforced their exclusion from power. At the same time, Ormsby's examination of British Columbia's "social life" was founded upon her conviction that the presence of an accepted code of civility helped hold societies together.[97] For this reason, she tended to focus upon high society and culture. Consequently, she did not take the step towards the more systematic, bottom-up social history that would profoundly alter the direction of historical writing in the following decades.

It was primarily through her focus upon "social life" that women are introduced into Ormsby's narrative. As a female historian working in a vocation dominated by men, it is not surprising that she included women in her vision of provincial history. On several occasions in *British Columbia*, Ormsby shifted the narrator's perspective from its usual concentration upon the men who dominated politics and the economy. Taking up the point of view of women, she suggested what life would have looked like to Amelia Douglas (James's wife), female colonists on Vancouver Island, or the wives of British Columbia's members of Parliament.[98] She also showed a sensitivity to the domestic plight of women such as Amelia Douglas and Susan Allison, women who were socially isolated and burdened with the responsibility of large families.

Operating without the benefit of an established body of feminist scholarship, Ormsby nevertheless forged a nascent feminism from the combined influences of her family background, academic career, and the intellectual premises to which she adhered. Ormsby's parents had actively encouraged her intellectual and academic aspirations. Applying a catholic reading of the British sense of "fair play," they stressed that women should have equal access to an education and a career.[99] Ormsby's description of her father's attitude no doubt reflected her own ideal: "He treated women with respect for their innate ability and with a courtesy that was old-fashioned."[100] Moreover, as we have seen, the UBC history department of Ormsby's undergraduate and master's studies had provided a welcoming and fertile environment for female students, while doctoral studies at Bryn Mawr further encouraged Ormsby's historical ambitions. In her subsequent career, as a history professor, department head, and president of the Canadian Historical Association, Ormsby was in the vanguard of female academics. Having struggled to make a career in history, Ormsby took particular pride in the female students at UBC whom she was able to send on to graduate studies.[101] In the end, the intellectual foundation of her feminism was the belief that the tenets of a humanism rooted in the Enlightenment were truly universal. In other words, women were fully human: they had as much potential as did men to develop as individuals (intellectually, morally, etc.) and, thus, should be given the opportunity to do so.

The premises of Ormsby's feminism, however, limited its scope when it was applied to the study and writing of history. Accepting the notion of a universal humanism, Ormsby was unable to counter the very tradition of Western historiography that had marginalized women. As Joan Scott has noted, Western historical writing presumed a "Universal Man" – specifically, the Western European male – to be the proper agent of history and, thus, the proper subject of historical writing. The experience of women as women was marginalized because it represented "but a particular instance," or exception, to the universal masculine standard.[102] On a professional level, Ormsby can be forgiven if she feared that too strong an advocacy of feminist themes would further marginalize her, for such advocacy would call into question the "universalist ethos of scholarship" upon which the modern historical profession was built.[103]

While opening the door for the participation of women in British Columbia's history, Ormsby also moved towards a cultural pluralism not seen in previous provincial historians. The province itself had moved in the same direction after the Second World War. The six-year struggle against a genocidal Nazi regime helped spark what Kay Anderson labelled a "breakthrough in white attitudes" in British Columbia.[104] Institutionalized racism and exclusionist policies, which had constructed an official homogeneity in the face of British Columbia's polyphyletic reality, were no longer constitutive tenets of society and political culture. Between 1947 and 1949, Chinese, Indian, Japanese, Mennonite, and Native British Columbians were re-enfranchised by the provincial government; federally, the 1923 Chinese Exclusion Act was scrapped (although immigration from China and other parts of Asia was still tightly constricted). Even before the war, Ormsby belonged to a generation of UBC students that had been exposed to the questioning of the era's shibboleths by professors Henry Angus and Frederick Soward, who openly and aggressively criticized the anti-Asian policies of the day.[105] Moreover, the Historical Society broke with convention by admitting at least one Japanese Canadian student into its ranks at a time when British Columbians of Japanese descent were barred both from voting and from entering the professions. The society also regularly addressed topics related to east and south Asia, along with the question of race.[106]

In *British Columbia*, Ormsby was careful to note the heterogeneity of the province's population through its history, from colonial Victoria (with its Chinese, Hawaiians, African American, and English) to the polyglot streets of modern Vancouver.[107] She also applauded the increasing racial tolerance of British Columbia after the Second World War and pointed to the contributions of new, non-British immigrants.[108] In Ormsby's intellectual world, the mix of diverse people injected vitality into societies, creating opportunities for more animated and stimulating exchanges. Ormsby's look at the social development of the province remained limited and episodic, however, and suffered from serious omissions. She did not tackle the issue of race in a systematic way, even though she recognized that British Columbia's rapid transformation had produced "ugly and growing racial tension" through the early decades of this century.[109] Most particularly, she failed to address the extent to which racial prejudice had been a constituent element of the province's emerging identity, remaining studiously neutral when looking at the anti-Asian, exclusionist stance of someone like Richard McBride. Although her intention was to praise the young premier for his more positive attributes, Ormsby was surely correct when she eulogized McBride as the embodiment of the province's spirit during the early twentieth century.[110] For there is no doubt that McBride's vociferous and adamant trumpeting of racially exclusionist policies gave clarion expression to the opinions of the province's dominant population.

Also noteworthy was *British Columbia*'s neglect of the role and presence of Native peoples. In his otherwise laudatory review aired on CBC radio in December 1958, renowned naturalist and author Roderick Haig-Brown stated that *British Columbia* suffered from "one notable omission ... Dr. Ormsby's failure to recognise the Native peoples."[111] Ormsby had given extended and positive portrayals of Okanagan Valley Natives in her honours and master's theses at UBC.[112] But while amateur historian Leonard Norris had opened Ormsby's eyes to the past and presence of Okanagan's First Nations, academic history stressed other priorities – namely, the formation of a literate society based upon European patterns of political, economic, and social activity, spheres from which Natives were largely excluded.[113]

Thus, Native peoples received only passing references in *British Columbia*, and, when they did appear, they most often played the conventional role of threatening backdrop to the adventures and activities of Europeans. Alexander Mackenzie was met by "disdainful, insolent and angry Indians" at the Pacific coast, and the "need for defence against hostile

Indians" helped unify the young communities of Vancouver Island.[114] Largely absent from *British Columbia*, though, was the hackneyed and smug tack of earlier provincial historians, who contrasted the putatively benevolent treatment of Native peoples by British and Canadian authorities with the violence dealt out by their American counterparts. Yet Ormsby was not fully immune to this powerful convention, at one point crediting the HBC with a wise policy of "benevolent paternalism."[115]

At the same time, Ormsby did not add the opposition of civilization versus savagery to the series of tensions upon which *British Columbia* is built. She eschewed the racialist notions of earlier writers and would not strip Native peoples of their humanity. Her early theses had portrayed Okanagan Natives as intelligent and moral, comparable to Europeans. There was an underlying sympathetic note to *British Columbia*'s discussion of the Native wives and Métis children of the fur traders. And Ormsby condemned the reserve policy of the BC government after Confederation as "unenlightened" and a "disgrace."[116] Thus, Ormsby rejected a central tenet of the settler ideology upon which earlier writers had built their histories. If British Columbia's Native land policy was unjust, one might presume that some remedy was needed, that there was indeed an Indian land question. Ormsby did not go this far, but she did add her voice to the increasing number of those who criticized the conditions under which the nation's Natives lived. The neglect of Native peoples in *British Columbia*, then, was due less to personal animus or prejudice and more to the fact that the thematic priorities and narrative structure of the work left them with only small, supporting roles to play.

While *British Columbia* was generally silent on the presence and role of Native peoples in BC history, Ormsby did help plant the seeds for a major shift in provincial historiography with regard to the question. Of the four doctoral dissertations Ormsby supervised in the last five years of her career at UBC, two focused on the province's First Nations. Published in the 1970s, the work of Robin Fisher and Jean Friesen would mark a watershed in BC historical writing. Fisher and Friesen belonged to a new generation of historians who benefited from the rise of social history methods in academic history, the increasing cross-fertilization with disciplines such as anthropology, and the ever-waning influence of racialist ideas in provincial society. This generation would radically rethink the place of previously marginalized groups (Natives, Asians, women) in the province's history.

Ormsby's discussion of selected aspects of British Columbia's social development in *British Columbia*, limited as that discussion is, emerged from her primary focus on the internal dynamics and contours of BC history. Along with this focus, though, Ormsby also addressed the province's relation to the world outside its borders. Her doctoral studies and time spent in central Canada had left a strong national orientation to her early work. In 1948, speaking before the Canadian Historical Association, she argued that British Columbia's "Canadianization" began with the influx of Canadians in the decades following the 1858 Fraser River gold rush, predating the watershed events (i.e., the CPR and Confederation) that Walter Sage and others believed linked the province's fate to Canada. Here, Ormsby also argued that a "Canadian faction" was the force behind the province's political evolution and that a strong pro-Canadian sentiment among British Columbia's population had been responsible for the decision to join Confederation.[117]

However, Ormsby soon abandoned this overtly national orientation. In *British Columbia*, she argued that the province's historical development departed in significant ways from that in the rest of Canada. For instance, the former's political development did not fit the latter's reform historiography of democratic forces struggling heroically against executive privilege. Individual reformers were presented as distinctly less impressive than executive figures: Amor De Cosmos was a "profound egotist" driven by personal ambition, and John Robson was a prejudiced and "irritatingly rigid" man.[118] Governor James Douglas appeared as a far more significant and esteemed figure. In *British Columbia*, Douglas did not play the role of intractable autocrat, although Ormsby admitted he had erred in delaying the introduction of representative government; rather, she spoke only of Douglas's "supposedly autocratic attitude" and stressed his achievements, particularly the planting of British institutions in the Northwest.[119] Moreover, *British Columbia* radically brought forward the date of the province's "Canadianization." While an "abiding sense of community with the rest of the Dominion" had been on the rise, particularly in the wake of the Second World War, Ormsby suggested it was debatable whether British Columbia had yet to be fully integrated into Canada.[120] Speaking again before the CHA (this time in her 1966 presidential address), Ormsby explicitly rejected the argument that a strong pro-Canadian feeling had drawn British Columbia into Confederation and that the CPR had successfully nurtured such a sentiment.[121] Instead, British Columbia's geography and distinct identity had made it a virtual "empire in itself," with closer links to Britain and Asia than the rest of Canada, and it was led by men who viewed themselves as "British Columbian Canadians," even "provincial patriot[s]."[122]

Ormsby, then, did not share Walter Sage's determination to integrate British Columbia into the story of Canada's development. The contrast with another prominent western historian, W.L. Morton, is also telling. Born a half year prior to Ormsby, Morton too was a product of a local provincial university. Both drew upon their personal roots in crafting narrative histories of their home provinces. However, whereas Ormsby's *British Columbia* stressed that province's distinctiveness and splendid isolation, Morton's 1957 *Manitoba: A History* depicted its subject as an extension and "crucible" of the Canadian experience.[123] The agrarian-based society, Ontario political institutions, and French-English cultural lines that formed Manitoba had all been transplanted from the east. "It is perhaps in Manitoba," Morton asserted, "that the Canadian experiment in political bi-nationalism and cultural plurality is at its most intense."[124] Ormsby would not have written those lines about British Columbia, nor could she have, for she recognized that the province departed in fundamental ways from the Canadian pattern Morton saw in Manitoba. Democratic institutions had been handed down from colonial authorities, agriculture was a poor cousin to lumbering and mining, and the presence of large Asian and Native populations, rather than a French-English binationality, was the distinguishing cultural trait.

Moreover, in terms of personal and professional connections, and inclusion in national projects, Ormsby was even more isolated than Sage had been with regard to Canada's clubby historical community. A number of factors contributed to this: geographic isolation, the fact she was a woman, and the dismissal of BC history as unworthy of scholarly study. Once again, Morton's career stood in stark contrast to Ormsby's. A graduate of Oxford, he emerged as one the nation's most prominent historians, producing works on Manitoba and national history and editing the

Canada Centenary Series from its inception in the late 1950s onward.[125] In the latter post, Morton adopted a rigidly "national" perspective, arguing that "the principal leitmotifs [were] French-English duality and integration of the regions in the nation-state."[126] He thus worked to keep the number of regionally focused volumes to a minimum. This meant that British Columbia would not receive its own volume but, instead, be subsumed in E.E. Rich's volume on the HBC's expansion to the Pacific coast. Admitting the awkwardness of this, Morton nevertheless argued that "the separateness of British Columbia was by no means equivalent to that of the Maritimes, or of French Canada ... The remedy [to the awkwardness] cannot be to give a separate volume to British Columbia. It is not worth it in the scale of the Series."[127] Thus, unlike Ormsby, who refused to be "captured" by the central Canadian historical guild, Morton tended to look east rather than west to explain his region's historical development.

Despite her stress upon the province's distinctiveness, though, Ormsby never questioned British Columbia's membership in Canada; nor was she worried that the powerful presence of the United States threatened that membership. While Sage and Frederic Howay had been much less anxious than had earlier provincial historians about the threat of American annexation, the former devoted much more attention than did Ormsby to the impact of the southern republic on British Columbia's development. Ormsby did acknowledge that fear of US expansion affected James Douglas's often unauthorized efforts to protect against American encroachments and that it was also an underlying reason for the British and Canadian push to incorporate the region within Confederation.[128] However, throughout her work, Ormsby showed no real interest in constructing sharp distinctions between British Columbia and the American states to the south. Thus, she departed from a fundamental motif in provincial historiography, which had contrasted the violence of the American frontier (particularly with regard to the treatment of Native peoples) with the law, order, and benevolent policies north of the border.

In the end, Ormsby was more concerned with discerning British Columbia's distinctiveness than she was with relating it to either Canada or the United States. A singular aspect of this difference – one that other provincial historians had consistently noted – was the persistence of strong historical and cultural ties to Britain. Prior to Confederation, she argued,

British Columbia was an "outpost of empire": its existence and development could only be explained within "the setting of empire" rather than within the context of an expanding Canada.[129] Yet Ormsby went further, intimating that, even well into the twentieth century, the British fact remained much stronger in British Columbia than it did elsewhere in Canada. Ormsby saw these ties in the isolated valley communities of the province's hinterland, where a literate, ethnically British population kept in touch with the larger world through their interest in British and imperial affairs.[130] Thus, Ormsby's vision of British Columbia's distinctiveness was never parochial. She looked beyond provincial and national horizons and linked British Columbia to global and universal influences and developments.

And yet Ormsby did not view British Columbians simply as ersatz Britons at the edge of the civilized world; rather, it was the juxtaposition of cosmopolitan people with a raw and open wilderness that created in the province something new. She recognized that, for most of their history, British Columbians had been confronted by the region's daunting geography, "by the stark presence of mountains, the vertical physiography of the continent, and by the rough ocean waters which separated them from 'Home.'"[131] This geography posed serious problems for British Columbia: it isolated the latter's cities and towns from each other, often threatening their very existence, and it worked to limit mental horizons, creating a myopia that literally could not see past the next mountain range.

But, for Ormsby, British Columbia's frontier situation also created the promise of something new and vibrant: "Of all men, the Westerner is the man who knows that he is on the edge of civilization and on the verge of something new."[132] British Columbia's frontier towns, she argued, were unlike others in western North America in their sophistication and in the presence of a relatively well-educated population. Here, where the physical obstacles of geography were more determinative than the social constraints of more established societies, a person could develop her potential to the fullest. Ormsby's stress on the individual was crucial. Adhering to a humanism with roots in the Enlightenment, Ormsby's optimistic individualism was predicated on the fundamentally modern and liberal project of self-development, filtered through a Turner-like view of the frontier as the crucible for a new people. Individualism, optimism, and a certain élan:

these were the adjectives Ormsby used most often in describing the BC spirit. She was confident that British Columbians could reconcile themselves with their sublime geography and forge an ideal society built on "love for the citizens rather than a love of the soil."[133] The province, then, had the potential to be the final fulfilment of modernity's promise. Freed from the shackles of tradition-bound, hierarchical societies, individuals could become fully developed, yet remain anchored in the kind of intimate societies that were required for that development.

Conclusion

When Margaret Ormsby sat down to write *British Columbia: A History*, fewer than two centuries had passed since Europeans made their first fleeting encounters with the Northwest Coast. Over that period, a succession of writers worked to construct a written past for Canada's westernmost province, one that would provide a source of identity, belonging, and legitimacy to the new society forming there. These efforts met with varying degrees of success, as historians struggled with the singular challenges presented by the province: the brevity of the European presence, its daunting geography, and a historical development that did not comfortably fit the contours of interpretations drafted and accepted elsewhere.

Despite the fact that British Columbia's historians consistently failed to provide an original, compelling vision of the province's past, a set of dominant themes did emerge, tying their work into a distinct, if rather loose, historiographical tradition. The most enduring of these themes were linked to British Columbia's historical and geographic position. Writers identified a sense of uniqueness, which they pointed to as the basis for the province's distinct identity. Locally, the meeting of mountains and ocean produced stirring images; globally, British Columbia was the place where East met West, representing the last chapter in the westward march of civilization. British Columbia's geographic isolation meant that, for far longer than other regions, it was kept out of history. Provincial historians were aware of their province's close proximity to prehistory, and they were much concerned with charting its move into history itself.

Geographic isolation also complicated the question of situating British Columbia in the world. Historians recognized that the province was caught between three competing pulls: American, British, and Canadian. The

United States was always close, its influence strong. Thus, provincial writers were anxious to distinguish the province from the American states to the south. Most usually, they contrasted the violence of the far west frontier in the United States with the putative peace and order north of the 49th parallel, pointing to the treatment of Native peoples north and south of the border as a litmus test for this. Meanwhile, the British imperial emphasis lingered on, while provincial historians more belatedly incorporated British Columbia's history into the story of Canada. The Canadian Pacific Railway, for instance, was seen more as an imperial road than as the central element of a new transcontinental Dominion. Throughout, these British Columbians looked over oceans or mountains for larger loyalties, while their relative isolation created a strong sense of being a place apart. The resulting perspective was what Allen Smith has identified as a "cosmopolitan regionalism," a paradoxical worldview that directly linked the local and particular to the global and universal.[1]

British Columbia's isolation from the rest of the world was matched by internal fragmentation as the province's geography split it into various regions that were only tenuously connected to each other. This challenging topography increased the importance of transportation in the eyes of BC writers as provincial unity and prosperity depended upon the physical links that bound British Columbia together. Yet local regionalism remained a potent force for historians, and they found it difficult, at times, to write of the province as a single entity.

Making a living has been another prominent theme in BC historical writing, and an abiding materialism runs through BC historiography. For historians, the exploitation of the province's natural resources brought the material prosperity that was an essential part of the promise that British Columbians saw in this new land. The power of material forces (e.g., geography, natural resources) remained strong in provincial writing. But this writing was not deterministic; individuals were not powerless in the face of these forces. Indeed, provincial historiography largely remained trapped in Romantic conventions that adhered to the image of a rugged, heroic individualism. By and large, the individual British Columbian faced the obstacles of geography and the frontier, overcoming nature in order to wrestle wealth from it.

Finally, provincial historians were concerned with defining British Columbia's social boundaries and identity. Most particularly, they sought to impose the hegemony of an Anglo group (those of British descent, from Britain, Canada, the Empire, even the United States) over the province's culturally plural, perennially fluid population. They disqualified Asians from membership in their new settler society and further worked to legitimate the dispossession of Native peoples. This could not be done through a single strategy of racial definition as Asians shared with Europeans the status of newcomers, while the province's Natives were indigenous to the region. Thus, while Asians were depicted as an alien people possessing a foreign history, Native peoples were denied a history altogether. Neither would be given an active role as historians worked to construct a written past for British Columbia.

This book examines how, from its beginnings until the middle of the twentieth century, BC historical writing was part of a larger imperial process. The historians studied here were engaged in much the same colonizing enterprise as were the European peoples they described – that of defining themselves as indigenous to their new home. It is not surprising, then, that they expended so much energy in attempts to apply the fundamental culture and motifs of the Old World to the New World. They had a ready-made global framework, and they sought to incorporate British Columbia into what they considered to be universal forces and identities: Empire, civilization, and history itself.

In the decades after 1958, this perspective was discarded as BC historical writing was remade by the same tectonic shifts that were revolutionizing the historical profession throughout the Western world. Taking up the conceptual tools of a new social history, BC historians now turned their gaze inward, to the internal workings and limited identities of the province's historical development. This shift from the universal to the particular produced an outpouring of work on Native peoples, ethnicity, and class, reflecting the province's particular, even unique, historical development. The skewed gender ratio that plagued British Columbia for much of its history led to a relative dearth of studies in this field. However, the more recent shift from "women's history" to "gender studies" allowed historians to conceptualize British Columbia's peculiar situation as concepts such as "gender" had to be constructed and negotiated in the relative absence of women.

Over the past decade, similar conceptual shifts have led to a new flourishing in BC historiography. Inspired by the burgeoning field of postcolonial studies, these historians have placed British Columbia's colonization at the centre of its history. They wish not to contribute to this colonizing process but, rather, to critique it. They recognize that British Columbia presents one of the richest fields in North America in which to study this process, particularly because of the relatively recent arrival of Europeans, which has meant that the modern and the premodern have collided here with unusual abruptness and clarity. Paradoxically, the postcolonial literature represents something of a move back towards a global, universal perspective. Now, though, historians wield a more critical edge as they seek to find those who had been left out of previous histories – written out by the very historians studied in this book. At the same time, though, there is a recognition that the colonial project unfolded differently in each time and place. Universal, global forces were at work, yes, but they worked in particular ways, unique to each historical moment.

One might imagine that, of the historians studied in this book, Frederic Howay and Margaret Ormsby would have been most capable of making the shift to this new perspective. They sensed that, at the core of British Columbia's history, was this meeting of two worlds – the European and the Native, civilization and wilderness. Of course, they did not conceptualize this as the meeting of the colonizer and the colonized for they did not think of themselves as colonizers. But they were acutely aware of British Columbia's novelty, and, like their colleagues, they laboured to construct a historical lineage for the new society that was also their home.

Notes

Abbreviations

AHSA	Art, Historical and Scientific Association (Vancouver)
BCA	British Columbia Archives (Victoria)
BL	Bancroft Library (University of California, Berkeley)
HP	Frederic Howay Papers (UBCA)
OOHP	Margaret Ormsby Oral History Papers (UBCA)
OP	Margaret Ormsby Papers (UBCA)
SP	Walter Sage Papers (UBCA)
UBCA	University of British Columbia Library, Special Collections and University Archives Division
VCA	Vancouver City Archives

Introduction

1 Rupert Brooke, *Rupert Brooke in Canada*, ed. Roger Hall and Sandra Martin (Toronto: Peter Martin Associates, 1978), 125.

2 Ibid., 125.

3 Alfred Crosby, *Ecological Imperialism: The Biological Expansion of Europe, 900-1900* (Cambridge: Cambridge University Press, 1986), 2.

4 Jack Hodgins, *The Invention of the World* (Toronto: Macmillan, 1977).

5 Cole Harris, *The Resettlement of British Columbia: Essays on Colonialism and Geographical Change* (Vancouver: UBC Press, 1997), 104.

6 Michael Kammen, *Mystic Chords of Memory: The Transformation of Tradition in American Culture* (New York: Knopf, 1991), 3.

7 Paul Carter, *The Road to Botany Bay: An Essay in Spatial History* (Boston: Faber, 1987), xvi.

8 Elizabeth Furniss, *The Burden of History: Colonialism and the Frontier Myth in a Rural Canadian Community* (Vancouver: UBC Press, 1999), 102.

9 Walter Mignolo, *The Darker Side of the Renaissance: Literacy, Territoriality, and Colonization* (Ann Arbor: University of Michigan Press, 1995), 169.

10 Cole Harris, "Social Power and Cultural Change in Pre-Colonial British Columbia," *BC Studies* 115/16 (1997-98): 47.

11 Edward Said, *Culture and Imperialism* (New York: Vintage Books, 1993), xii-xiii; *Orientalism* (New York: Vintage Books, 1978).

CHAPTER 1: THE EARLIEST PAGES OF HISTORY

1 Frederic Howay, "The Earliest Pages of the History of British Columbia," British Columbia Historical Association, *Report* (1923): 16-22; Margaret Ormsby, *British Columbia: A History* (Toronto: Macmillan, 1972 [1958]), 3-26.

2 E.O.S. Scholefield and F. Howay, *British Columbia from the Earliest Times to the Present* (Vancouver: S.J. Clarke, 1914), 1:73, 111; Walter Sage, "Unveiling of Memorial Tablet at Nootka Sound," BC Historical Association, *Report* (1924): 21.

3 See Bruce Trigger, *Natives and Newcomers: Canada's "Heroic Age" Reconsidered* (Montreal and Kingston: McGill-Queen's University Press, 1985); and Andrea LaForet and Annie York, *Spuzzum: Fraser Canyon Histories, 1808-1939* (Vancouver: UBC Press, 1998).

4 Supreme Court of British Columbia, *Reasons for the Judgement of the Honourable Chief Justice Allan McEachern* (1991); Don Monet, ed., *Colonialism on Trial: Indigenous Land Rights and the Gitksan Wet'suwet'en Sovereignty Case* (Gabriola Island: New Society Publishers, 1992).

5 Court of Appeal for British Columbia, *Reasons for Judgement: Between Delgamuukw, et al., and Her Majesty the Queen* (1993).

6 Supreme Court of Canada, "Judgements of the Supreme Court of Canada, *Delgamuukw v. BC*" (11 December 1997), http://csc.lexum.umontreal.ca/en/1997/1997rcs3-1010/1997rcs3-1010.html, 30 July 2008.

7 Walter Mignolo, *The Darker Side of the Renaissance: Literacy, Territoriality, and Colonization* (Ann Arbor: University of Michigan Press, 1995), 127.

8 Ibid., 323.

9 Trigger, *Natives and Newcomers*, 3.

10 John Norris, "The Strait of Anian and British North America: Cook's Third Voyage in Perspective," *BC Studies* 36 (1977-78): 6-18.

11 James Cook, *A Voyage to the Pacific Ocean*, 3 vols. and Atlas (London: W. & A. Strahan, 1784).

12 James Burney, *A Chronological History of North-Eastern Voyages of Discovery* (London: Payne & Foss, 1819); Patrick Tytler, *Historical Discovery on the More Northern Coasts of America, from the Earliest Period to the Present Time* (Edinburgh: Oliver & Boyd, 1832).

13 Robert Boyd, *The Coming of the Spirit of Pestilence: Introduced Infectious Diseases and Population Decline among Northwest Coast Indians, 1774-1874* (Vancouver: UBC Press, 1999), 204-7.

14 Ibid., 5, 263-65.

15 Peter Gay, *The Enlightenment: An Interpretation,* vol. 2, *The Science of Freedom* (London: Weidenfeld and Nicholson, 1969), 3, 58-125, 368-96; R.G. Collingwood, *The Idea of History* (New York: Oxford University Press, 1956), 52-85.

16 Paul Carter, *The Road to Botany Bay: An Essay in Spatial History* (Boston: Faber, 1987), 8.

17 Between 1845 and 1848, the United States seized over a million square miles, including one-third of Mexico after it forced war on its southern neighbour. David Pletcher, *The Diplomacy of Annexation: Texas, Oregon, and the Mexican War* (Columbia: University of Missouri Press, 1973), 577.

18 See Frederick Merk, *The Oregon Question: Essays in Anglo-American Diplomacy and Politics* (Cambridge: Harvard University Press, 1967); Donald Rakestraw, *For Honor or Destiny: The Anglo-American Crisis over the Oregon Territory* (New York: Peter Lang, 1995).

19 Robert Greenhow, *Memoir, Historical and Political, on the Northwest Coast of North America* (Washington: Blair & Rives, 1840); Robert Greenhow, *The History of Oregon and California, and the Other Territories on the North-West Coast of North America* (London: John Murray, 1844).

20 Thomas Farnham, *History of Oregon Territory, It Being a Demonstration of the Title to these United States of North America to the Same* (New York: New World Press, 1844); Ephraim Tucker, *History of Oregon* (Fairfield, WA: Galleon, 1970 [1844]); George Wilkes, *The History of Oregon, Geographical and Political* (New York: Colyer, 1845).

21 Reginald Stuart, *United States Expansionism and British North America, 1775-1871* (Chapel Hill: University of North Carolina Press, 1988), 36-37, 55, 58, 73, 79.

22 Wilkes, *The History of Oregon,* 3-6, 28.

23 Farnham, *History of Oregon Territory,* 5; Tucker, *History of Oregon,* 82-83.

24 Greenhow, *Memoir, Historical and Political,* 191-94; Tucker, *History of Oregon,* 53; Wilkes, *The History of Oregon,* 32-33.

25 Tucker, *History of Oregon,* 81.

26 Greenhow, *Memoir, Historical and Political,* 20; Greenhow, *The History of Oregon and California,* 31.

27 Greenhow, *Memoir, Historical and Political,* 90, 143-44; Greenhow, *The History of Oregon and California,* 266-68.

28 Wilkes, *The History of Oregon,* 44.

29 Tucker, *History of Oregon,* 82; Stuart, *United States Expansionism,* 36-37.

30 Albert Gallatin, *The Oregon Question* (New York: Bartlett & Welford, 1846); William Sturgis, *The Oregon Question* (Boston: Swift & Wiley, 1845).

31 Sturgis, *The Oregon Question*, 23-24, 32.

32 *Comparative Chronological Statement of the Events Connected with the Rights of Great Britain and the Claims of the United States to the Oregon Territory* (London, 1845); see also *Oregon Historical and Descriptive*, 3rd ed. (Bradford, 1846).

33 Thomas Falconer, *The Oregon Question* (London: Samuel Clarke, 1845); Travers Twiss, *The Oregon Territory, Its History and Discovery* (New York: Appleton, 1846). Falconer engaged in a spirited pamphlet debate with Greenhow, each faulting the other for various historical errors. See Greenhow, "Answer to the Strictures of Mr. Thomas Falconer," in Greenhow, *History* (3rd ed.); and "Mr. Falconer's Reply to Mr. Greenhow's Answer: With Mr. Greenhow's Rejoinder," published as a pamphlet in 1845 and reprinted as a postscript in Falconer, *Oregon Question* (2nd ed.).

34 John Dunn, *History of the Oregon Territory and British North American Fur Trade* (London: Edwards & Hughes, 1844); Charles Nicolay, *The Oregon Territory* (Fairfield, WA: Galleon, 1967 [1846]).

35 Falconer, *The Oregon Question*, 43.

36 *Comparative Chronological Statement*, 14; *Oregon Historical and Descriptive*, 8; Twiss, *The Oregon Territory*, 86-91; Falconer, *The Oregon Question*, 24.

37 *Comparative Chronological Statement*, 3; *Oregon Historical and Descriptive*, 2; Twiss, *The Oregon Territory*, 102-8; Falconer, *The Oregon Question*, 27-29.

38 *Oregon Historical and Descriptive*, 8; Twiss, *The Oregon Territory*, 61; Falconer, *The Oregon Question*, 19-24.

39 Dunn, *History of the Oregon Territory*, 12.

40 Nicolay, *The Oregon Territory*, 162-71.

41 Dunn, *History of the Oregon Territory*, 12.

42 Nicolay, *The Oregon Territory*, 220.

43 Elizabeth Furniss, *The Burden of History: Colonialism and the Frontier Myth in a Rural Canadian Community* (Vancouver: UBC Press, 1999), 187.

44 Bruce Trigger, "The Historians' Indian: Native Americans in Canadian Historical Writing from Charlevoix to the Present," *Canadian Historical Review* 67 (1986): 321.

45 Nicolay, *The Oregon Territory*, 224-25; Twiss, *The Oregon Territory*, 264.

46 Frederick Merk, *Manifest Destiny and Mission in American History: A Reconsideration* (New York: Alfred A. Knopf, 1963), 8-14.

47 Ibid., 4-10, chap. 2, passim.

48 Barbara Lowther, *A Bibliography of British Columbia: Laying the Foundations, 1849-1899* (Victoria: University of Victoria Press, 1968), 1-7.

49 Great Britain, House of Commons, *Report from the Select Committee on the Hudson's Bay Company*, [London, 1857].

50 See *British Columbia and Vancouver's Island: A Complete Handbook* (London: William Penny, 1858), 9-10; and R.C. Lundin Brown, *British Columbia: An Essay* (New Westminster: Royal Engineer Press, 1863), 35.

51 Merk, *The Oregon Question*, 139, 244n31; Pletcher, *The Diplomacy of Annexation*, 225, 243-44.

52 Edward Said, *Culture and Imperialism* (New York: Vintage Books, 1993), 164, 169-70; Suzanne Zeller, *Inventing Canada: Early Victorian Science and the Idea of a Transcontinental Nation* (Toronto: University of Toronto Press, 1987).

53 *Proceedings of the Royal Geographical Society*, vols. 1-6 (1857-62); *Journal of the Royal Geographical Society*, vols. 27 (1857) and 31 (1861).

54 W.C. Grant, "Description of Vancouver Island," *Journal of the Royal Geographical Society* 27 (1857): 268-320; and W.C. Grant, "Remarks on Vancouver Island," *Journal of the Royal Geographical Society* 31 (1861): 208-13.

55 William C. Hazlitt, *British Columbia and Vancouver Island: A Historical Sketch of the British Settlements in the North-West Coast of America* (London: Routledge, 1858), 199, 228.

56 Jean Barman, *The West beyond the West: A History of British Columbia*, rev. ed. (Toronto: University of Toronto Press, 1996), 363.

57 A.C. Anderson, *Hand-Book and Map to the Gold Region of Frazer's and Thompson's Rivers* (San Francisco: LeCount, 1858); Robert Ballantyne, ed., *Handbook to the New Gold Fields* (Edinburgh: Strahan, 1858); Kinahan Cornwallis, *The New El Dorado: or British Columbia* (London: Newby, 1858); John Domer, *New British Gold Fields: A Guide to British Columbia and Vancouver Island* (London: Angel, 1858); W.C. Hazlitt, *The Great Gold Fields of Cariboo* (Victoria: Klanak, 1974 [1862]); Alfred Waddington, *The Fraser Mines Vindicated, or the History of Four Months* (Vancouver: R.R. Reid, 1949 [1858]).

58 John Lutz and G. Young, *The Researcher's Guide to British Columbia: Nineteenth-century Directories, a Bibliography and Index* (Victoria: University of Victoria Public History Group, 1988), 2.

59 J. Despard Pemberton, *Facts and Figures Relating to Vancouver Island and British Columbia* (London: Longman, 1860).

60 *London International Exhibition, 1862: Catalogue of the Vancouver Contribution, with a Short Account of Vancouver Island and British Columbia* (London, 1862); London International Exhibition (1862), Executive Committee for Vancouver Island and BC, *Industrial Exhibition* [Victoria, 1861]; London International Exhibition, "An Open Letter" [Victoria, 1861].

61 Charles Forbes, *Prize Essay: Vancouver Island, Its Resources and Capabilities as a Colony* ([Victoria]: Colonial Government, 1862); Brown, *British Columbia*.

62 Richard Mayne, *Four Years in British Columbia and Vancouver Island* (London: John Murray, 1862); Alexander Rattray, *Vancouver Island and British Columbia: Where They Are, What They Are; and What They May Become* (London: Smith, Elder & Co., 1862). Mayne's reports appeared in *Journal of the Royal Geographical Society* 31 (1861): 213-23, 297-392, and 32 (1862): 529-35.

63 Rattray, *Vancouver Island and British Columbia*, 145-65.

64 Mayne, *Four Years in British Columbia*, 58, 157-59.

65 Duncan MacDonald, *British Columbia and Vancouver's Island: Comprising a Description of these Dependencies*, 3rd ed. (London: Longman, 1863), 28, 332; and Duncan MacDonald, *Lecture on British Columbia and Vancouver's Island* (London: Longman, 1863).

66 MacDonald, *British Columbia and Vancouver's Island*, 268.

67 Matthew Macfie, *Vancouver Island and British Columbia: Their History, Resources and Prospects* (London: Longman, 1865), 314; and Matthew Macfie, "The True Northwest Passage," *Fortnightly Review*, 1 December 1865, 227-39.

68 Macfie, *Vancouver Island and British Columbia*, 39.

69 Hazlitt, *British Columbia and Vancouver Island*, chaps. 8-11; Macfie, *Vancouver Island and British Columbia*, chap. 16; Mayne, *Four Years in British Columbia*, 211-304.

70 Hazlitt, *British Columbia and Vancouver Island*, 88-89; Mayne, *Four Years in British Columbia*, 211-19.

71 Macfie, *Vancouver Island and British Columbia*, 190, 461; Mayne, *Four Years in British Columbia*, 219.

72 MacDonald, *British Columbia and Vancouver's Island*, 70, chap. 7.

73 Brook Taylor, *Promoters, Patriots and Partisans: Historiography in Nineteenth-Century Canada* (Toronto: University of Toronto Press, 1989), 10-40.

CHAPTER 2: PIONEERS, RAILWAYS, AND CIVILIZATION

1 Adele Perry, *On the Edge of Empire: Gender, Race, and the Making of British Columbia* (Toronto: University of Toronto Press, 2001), 9.

2 Cole Harris, "Moving Amid the Mountains, 1870-1930," *BC Studies* 58 (Summer 1983): 4-13; Robert McDonald, "Victoria, Vancouver, and the Economic Development of British Columbia, 1886-1914," in *British Columbia: Historical Readings*, ed. P. Ward and R. McDonald, 370-75 (Vancouver: Douglas and McIntyre, 1981).

3 H.H. Bancroft, *History of British Columbia, 1792-1887* (San Francisco: History Co., 1887); H.H. Bancroft, *History of the Northwest Coast*, 2 vols. (San Francisco: A.L. Bancroft & Co., 1884).

4 John Caughey, *Hubert Howe Bancroft: Historian of the West* (Berkeley: University of California Press, 1946); Harry Clark, *A Venture in History: The Production, Publication and Sale of the Works of Hubert Howe Bancroft* (Berkeley: University of California Press, 1973). See also Bancroft's autobiographical *Literary Industries* (San Francisco: History Co., 1890).

5 W. Spalding (Postmaster General of British Columbia) to Bancroft, 19 March 1862, British Columbia Letters to H.H. Bancroft (1862-79), Bancroft Library (hereafter BL), P-C 43.

6 John Hittell, *Mining in the Pacific States of North America* (San Francisco: H.H. Bancroft & Co., 1861); William Knight, ed., *Hand-Book Almanac for the Pacific States: An Official Register and Business Directory*, 3 vols. (San Francisco: H.H. Bancroft & Co., 1862-64). The guidebooks were marketed as *Bancroft's Hand-Book of Mining for the Pacific States* and *Bancroft's Hand-Book Almanac for the Pacific States*, respectively. Also published during that time was W. Knight, comp., *Bancroft's Map of the Pacific States* (San Francisco: H.H. Bancroft & Co., 1863), which included the southwest corner of British Columbia and Vancouver Island.

7 Bancroft, *Literary Industries*, 229, 278.

8 Ibid., 180-81; Caughey, *Hubert Howe Bancroft*, 67-85.

9 Bancroft, *Literary Industries*, 230-44, 592-617; Clark, *A Venture in History,* 12-36; Caughey, *Hubert Howe Bancroft*, 99-117.

10 Caughey, *Hubert Howe Bancroft*, 227, 253-77; William Morris, "The Origin and Authorship of the Bancroft Pacific States Publications," *Oregon Historical Quarterly* 4 (1903): 313-14, 352-54; Bancroft, *Literary Industries*, 246-55, 267, 273.

11 Bancroft, *Literary Industries*, 530-39; *History of the Northwest Coast*, 1:vii-viii.

12 The HBC's London office refused to cooperate with Bancroft's researches: Secretary (HBC London) to Bancroft, 29 March 1879, BL, P-C 43. However, through the Victoria director of the Company, William Charles, Bancroft was given permission to copy HBC journals for Fort Langley and Fort Simpson. Hudson's Bay Company, "Journal ... Kept at Fort Langley during the Year 1827-29," BL, P-C 22; and "Journal at Fort Simpson (1834-37)," BL, P-C 23.

13 Bancroft's assistant transcribed a total of three bound volumes of the Douglas papers, catalogued as James Douglas, Private Papers (1827-61), BL, P-C 12-13; and James Douglas, Journals (1840-41), BL, P-C 11. Other records included: Simon Fraser, Journals and Letters (1806-8), BL, P-C 16-18; John Stuart, "Journal at the Rocky Mountains (1805-6)," BL, P-C 45; John Work, Journals (1824-34), BL, P-C 30; and W.F. Tolmie, "Journal during Residence on Puget Sound in 1833," BL, P-B 24.

14 Roderick Finlayson, "History of Vancouver Island and the Northwest Coast" (Victoria, 1878), BL, P-C 15; A.C. Anderson, "History of the Northwest Coast" (Victoria, 1878), BL, P-C 2; John Tod, "History of New Caledonia and the Northwest Coast" (Victoria, 1878), BL, P-C 27; Archibald McKinlay, "Narrative of a Chief Factor of the Hudson's Bay Company" (Victoria, 1878), BL, P-C 25; W.F. Tolmie, "History of the Puget Sound and the Northwest Coast" (Victoria, 1878), BL, P-B 25; and Joseph McKay, "Recollections of a Chief Trader in the Hudson's Bay Company" (Fort Simpson, 1878), BL, P-C 24.

15 James Cooper, "Maritime Matters on the Northwest Coast and Other Affairs of the Hudson's Bay Company in Early Times" (Victoria, 1878), BL, P-C 6; James Deans, "Settlement of Vancouver Island" (Victoria, 1878), BL, P-C 9; C.A. Bayley, "Early Life on Vancouver Island" (Victoria, 1878), BL, P-C 3.

16 Bancroft, *Literary Industries*, 285; G.M. Sproat, "History of British Columbia," G.M. Sproat Papers, British Columbia Archives (hereafter BCA), AM 257, file 7; E. Cridge, "Characteristics of James Douglas" (Victoria, 1878), BL, P-C 8; Amor De Cosmos, "The Governments of Vancouver Island and British Columbia" (San Francisco, 1878), BL, P-C 10; John Good, "British Columbia" (Victoria, 1878), BL, P-C 19; P.N. Compton, "Aboriginal British Columbia" (Victoria, 1878), BL, P-C 39; P.N. Compton, "Forts and Fort Life in New Caledonia under Hudson's Bay Company Regime" (Victoria, 1878), BL, P-C 5.

17 Bancroft, *Literary Industries*, 155.

18 Arthur Marwick, *The Nature of History* (New York: Alfred Knopf, 1971), 37-45; George Iggers, *New Directions in European Historiography* (Middleton: Wesleyan University Press, 1975), 17-26; Peter Novick, *That Noble Dream: The "Objectivity Question" and the American Historical Profession* (Cambridge: Cambridge University Press), 21-31.

19 Michael Kammen, *Mystic Chords of Memory: The Transformation of Tradition in American Culture* (New York: Knopf, 1991), 274.

20 Clark, *A Venture in History*, 118; H.H. Bancroft, *History of British Columbia, 1792-1887* (San Francisco: History Co., 1890).

21 Bancroft, *Literary Industries*, 2-11.

22 Ibid., 5-7.

23 Gerald Nash, *Creating the West: Historical Interpretations, 1890-1990* (Albuquerque: University of New Mexico Press, 1991), 200-8; Loren Baritz, "The Idea of the West," *American Historical Review* 66 (1961): 618-40.

24 Frederick Jackson Turner, "The Significance of the Frontier in American History," *Annual Report of the American Historical Association, 1893* (1894): 199-227.

25 Bancroft, *Literary Industries*, 133.

26 Walter Mignolo, *The Darker Side of the Renaissance: Literacy, Territoriality, and Colonization* (Ann Arbor: University of Michigan Press, 1995), 323.

27 Bancroft, *Literary Industries*, 151.

28 The History Company, *History of British Columbia. Bancroft's Works, Vol. xxxii* (San Francisco: History Co., 1887). This was a promotional pamphlet for the BC volume, located at Bancroft Library.

29 Bancroft, *History of the Northwest Coast*, 1:531-42, *History of British Columbia* (1887), 45-53.

30 Kay Anderson, *Vancouver's Chinatown: Racial Discourse in Canada, 1875-1980* (Montreal and Kingston: McGill-Queen's University Press, 1991), 41, 44.

31 Bancroft, *History of British Columbia* (1887), 719-27.

32 Bancroft, *History of the Northwest Coast*, 1:v, 2:317.

33 Ibid., 2:317, 697; Bancroft, *History of British Columbia* (1887), 391. For references to disease and liquor as "civilizing" agents, see Bancroft's *History of the Northwest Coast* 2:501-3, 534, 602, and *History of British Columbia*, 338.

34 Bancroft, *History of the Northwest Coast*, 2:569-70.

35 William Gray, *A History of Oregon, 1792-1849* (Portland: Harris & Holman, 1870), 4.

36 The History Company, *History of British Columbia. Bancroft's Works, Vol. xxxii.*

37 Bancroft, *History of British Columbia* (1887), 45-51, 423-26, 431-32.

38 Bancroft, *History of the Northwest Coast*, 2:534-35.

39 Caughey, *Hubert Howe Bancroft*, 209, 275-76.

40 The index of *History of BC* (1887) provides nearly twenty references to Chinese activities in the goldfields. These include dense footnotes in which Bancroft provided detailed information culled from primary sources.

41 Ibid., 682-83.

42 Ibid., 710.

43 Anderson, *Vancouver's Chinatown*, 44-61.

44 Bancroft, *History of British Columbia* (1887), 710-12.

45 Bancroft, *History of the Northwest Coast*, 1:404; *History of British Columbia* (1887), 54, 102-11, 134-56.

46 See Gray's *A History of Oregon*; Elwood Evans, *The Re-annexation of British Columbia to the United States, Right, Proper and Desirable: An Address* [Olympia, 1870].

47 Bancroft, *History of British Columbia* (1887), 202-13, 310-28.

48 Ibid., 64-66; Bancroft, *History of the Northwest Coast*, 2:536.

49 Bancroft, *History of British Columbia* (1887), 66, 203-12.

50 Bancroft, *History of the Northwest Coast*, 2:712.

51 Ibid., 2:316-416.

52 Ibid., 2:699.

53 Evans, *The Re-annexation of British Columbia to the United States;* David Wrobel, *The End of American Exceptionalism: Frontier Anxiety from the Old West to the New Deal* (Lawrence: University Press of Kansas, 1993), 20-22.

54 Bancroft, *History of British Columbia* (1887), 310-40, 582-604, 762.

55 Ibid., 757-58.

56 Ibid., ix, 640-95.

57 Ibid., 375.

58 Jean Barman, *The West beyond the West: A History of British Columbia*, rev. ed. (Toronto: University of Toronto Press, 1996), 364, 369.

59 John Kerr, *Biographical Dictionary of Well-Known British Columbians* (Vancouver: Kerr & Begg, 1890); Oliver Cogswell, *History of British Columbia* (Victoria: Colonist Press, 1893); Alexander Begg, *History of British Columbia: From Its Earliest Discovery to the Present Time* (Toronto: W. Briggs, 1894).

60 Cogswell, *History of British Columbia*, 3.

61 British Columbia, *Public Accounts for the Fiscal Year Ended 30th June 1894* (Victoria: Queen's Printer, 1894), 24, 145; "The Library," *Victoria Province*, 29 December 1894, 633.

62 Kerr, *Biographical Dictionary of Well-Known British Columbians,* preface.

63 Ibid., v-vi.

64 Ibid., v-xiii; Begg, *History of British Columbia*, 57, 98, 121, 190, 205-11.

65 Cogswell, *History of British Columbia*, 46-47; Begg, *History of British Columbia*, 115-21.

66 Kerr, *Biographical Dictionary of Well-Known British Columbians*, 58.

67 Begg, *History of British Columbia*, iii.

68 Kerr, *Biographical Dictionary of Well-Known British Columbians*, 1-2.

69 Ibid., 70-71; Begg, *History of British Columbia*, 7, 115-21.

70 Cole Harris, *Making Native Space: Colonialism, Resistance, and Reserves in British Columbia* (Vancouver: UBC Press, 2002), chaps. 3-7; Robin Fisher, *Contact and Conflict: Indian European Relations in British Columbia, 1774-1890*, 2nd ed. (Vancouver: UBC Press, 1992), 160-68.

71 Begg, *History of British Columbia*, 568; Cogswell, *History of British Columbia*, 10-11, 97-98; Kerr, *Biographical Dictionary of Well-Known British Columbians*, 67, 75.

72 David Chuenyan Lai, *Chinatowns: Towns within Cities in Canada* (Vancouver: UBC Press, 1988), 60-61; Barman, *The West beyond the West*, 379.

73 Kerr, *Biographical Dictionary of Well-Known British Columbians*, 72-73.

74 Ibid., 412.

Chapter 3: A Greater Britain on the Pacific

1 Jean Barman, *The West Beyond the West: A History of British Columbia*, rev. ed. (Toronto: University of Toronto Press, 1996), 380.

2 Robert McDonald, *Making Vancouver: Class, Status, and Social Boundaries, 1863-1913* (Vancouver: UBC Press, 1996), 146.

3 Ernst Breisach, *Historiography: Ancient, Medieval and Modern* (Chicago: University of Chicago Press, 1983), chaps. 15-19.

4 On the period's historiography, see also R.G. Collingwood, *The Idea of History* (New York: Oxford University Press, 1956), 143-47; Rosemary Jann, *The Art and Science of Victorian History* (Columbus: Ohio State University Press, 1985).

5 Natural History Society of BC, *Revised Constitution and List of Members* (Victoria: Colonist Press, 1901); R.E. Gosnell to J. Hosie, 8 April 1927, Provincial Library Correspondence, BCA, GR 726, box 1, file 3.

6 Natural History Society of BC, *Bulletin* 1-3 (1893, 1897, 1910); Peter Corley-Smith, *White Bears and Other Curiosities: The First 100 Years of the Royal British Columbia Museum* (Victoria: Royal BC Museum, 1989), 26-33, 45-46.

7 Gertrude Mellon, quoted in Alfred Hunt, "Mutual Enlightenment in Early Vancouver, 1886-1914" (PhD diss., University of British Columbia, 1987), 60; "Inventory," Art, Historical and Scientific Association of Vancouver Records (hereafter AHSA), Vancouver City Archives (hereafter VCA), AM 336.

8 AHSA, *Journal* (1917, 1921).

9 AHSA, *Historical Papers: Session 1907-1908* (Vancouver: AHSA, 1908).

10 AHSA, *Journal* (1921); AHSA, *Museum and Art Notes* (1926-31).

11 "List of Members (1908-28)," Natural History Society of BC Papers, BCA, AM 284, vols. 10-14.

12 AHSA, *Journal* (1917): 14-17.

13 F. Howay to E.O.S. Scholefield, 2 October 1911, Correspondence, BCA, GR 1738, box 74, file 5.

14 "Legislative Library and Bureau of Statistics Act, 1894," BC, *Statutes* (Victoria: Queen's Printer, 1894), 137-39.

15 Terry Eastwood, "R.E. Gosnell, E.O.S. Scholefield and the Founding of the Provincial Archives of British Columbia," *BC Studies* 54 (1982): 42; "Report on the Legislative Library," BC, *Sessional Papers* (1894), 1135-36; BC Provincial Library, *Report, 1899* and *1901* (Victoria: Queen's Printer, 1900, 1902).

16 R.E. Gosnell, "Memo for the Executive" [n.d.], BCA, GR 975, box 2, file 8; "Report for the Executive," 28 November 1896, BC Bureau of Statistics Papers, BCA, GR 153, box 1, file 1; Eastwood, "R.E. Gosnell, E.O.S. Scholefield," 45-8.

17 R.E. Gosnell, "A Plea for the Old Timer," *Victoria Daily Times* (1 August 1908), 11; "Fraser Centenary Display Tells Interesting Story of Growth in the West," *New Westminster Daily Columbian* (1 October 1908); BC Provincial Archives Department, *Simon Fraser Centenary, 1808-1908: Checklist of Books and Pamphlets* (Victoria: King's Printer, 1908).

18 "Vouchers Relating to Simon Fraser Centenary Celebration (1908, 1909)," BCA, C/D/30.1/Ar2; Eastwood, "R.E. Gosnell, E.O.S. Scholefield," 49.

19 Eastwood, "R.E. Gosnell, E.O.S. Scholefield," 55; W. Kaye Lamb, "Report on the State of the Library and Archives," 1934, BCA, C/D/30.8/L16, 18.

20 See, for instance, McBride to H.E. Young, 15 May 1914, BCA, GR 975, box 2, file 6; Scholefield to McBride, 6 June 1903, Correspondence, BCA, GR 146, box 1, file 1.

21 Eastwood, "R.E. Gosnell, E.O.S. Scholefield," 53-54; "Cariboo Reminiscences ... 1910 and 1912," box 1, file 3, and "Diary of a Trip through the Cariboo to Stuart Lake, 1913," box 1, file 4, both in E.O.S. Scholefield Papers, BCA, AM 491; BC Provincial Archives, *Report, 1910* (1911), 9.

22 BC Provincial Archives, *Report, 1913* (1914), 8-135.

23 C.F. Newcombe, *The First Circumnavigation of Vancouver Island*, Memoir 1 (Victoria: King's Printer, 1914); *Minutes of the Council of Vancouver Island [August 30, 1851 to February 6, 1861]*, Memoir 2 (Victoria: King's Printer, 1918); *Minutes of the House of Assembly of Vancouver Island, August 12, 1856 to September 25, 1858*, Memoir 3 (Victoria: King's Printer, 1918); and *House of Assembly Correspondence, August 12, 1856 to July 6, 1859*, Memoir 4 (Victoria: King's Printer, 1918).

24 E.O.S. Scholefield and F. Howay, *British Columbia from the Earliest Times to the Present* (Vancouver: S.J. Clarke, 1914), 1:xv-xlvi. The two bulletin bibliographies published were *A Bibliography of Publications on the War, contained in the Provincial Library*, Bulletin 1 (Victoria: King's Printer, 1916) and *A Bibliography of Publications on Ships,*

Shipbuilding and Ship Subsidies, contained in the *Provincial Library*, Bulletin 2 (Victoria: King's Printer, 1917).

25 E.O.S. Scholefield to F. Howay, 2 August 1911, Frederic Howay Papers (hereafter HP), box 6, file 7.

26 T.C. Elliott to F. Howay, 4 June 1911, HP, box 2, file 17.

27 "Reports of the Pacific Northwest History Department (1922, 1927-33)," BCA, C/D/30.1/Ar2.1.

28 The staunchly imperialist *British Columbia Magazine* lasted from 1907 to 1915. In its early years, it had also appeared first under the title *Westward Ho Magazine* and then *Man to Man Magazine*.

29 R.E. Gosnell, *A History of British Columbia* (n.p.: Lewis Publishing Co., 1906).

30 E.O.S. Scholefield and R.E. Gosnell, *Sixty Years of Progress: A History of British Columbia*, 2 vols. (Vancouver and Victoria: British Columbia Historical Association, 1913).

31 Scholefield and Howay, *British Columbia from the Earliest Times to the Present* (1914). To solicit subscriptions, Clarke put out a promotional tract for the Scholefield-Howay set in 1913 entitled *British Columbia, from the Earliest Times to the Present ... Profusely Illustrated* (Vancouver, Portland, San Francisco, Chicago: S.J. Clarke, [1913]).

32 A.O. MacRae, *History of the Province of Alberta*, 2 vols. (n.p.: Western Canadian History Co., 1913); N.F. Black, *History of Saskatchewan and the North West Territories*, 2 vols. (Regina: Saskatchewan Historical Co., 1913); F.H. Schofield, *The Story of Manitoba*, 3 vols. (Winnipeg: S.J. Clarke, 1913).

33 Such was the case with the British Columbia Historical Association, the publisher of *Sixty Years of Progress*. Thus, the company had no connection to the provincial historical society of the same name founded a decade later. The company charged each subscriber $100 to be included in the volume. J. Forsyth to W.K. Lamb, 22 June 1945, W. Kaye Lamb, documents, copies of originals obtained by author from W. Kaye Lamb.

34 E.O.S. Scholefield to F. Howay, 22 November 1911, HP, box 6, file 8; "Correspondence between E.O.S. Scholefield and BCH.A. re. publication of *Sixty Years of Progress* (1910-14), BCA, GR 726, box 1, file 1; Scholefield to BCH.A., 22 March 1910, BCA, GR 146, box 1, file 2; "Correspondence re. Howay and Scholefield's *British Columbia* (1914)," BCA, GR 1710, box 1, file 8.

35 W.K. Lamb to J. Forsyth, 25 June 1945, W. Kaye Lamb, documents.

36 *Report of the Provincial Archivist, 1910* (Victoria: King's Printer, 1911), 4-5.

37 R.E. Gosnell, "A Greater Britain on the Pacific," *British Columbia Magazine* 2, 1 (1908): 8.

38 Gosnell, *History of British Columbia*, 17; Frederic Howay, "British Columbia: A Historical Sketch," *The Fruit Magazine* 5 (1912): 291; Scholefield and Howay, *British Columbia from the Earliest Times to the Present* (1914), 1:73, 111.

39 Gosnell, *History of British Columbia*, 1-50; Scholefield and Howay, *British Columbia from the Earliest Times to the Present* (1914), 1:73-282.

40 Scholefield and Howay, *British Columbia from the Earliest Times to the Present* (1914), 1:19.

41 Ibid., 1:46-47; Howay, "British Columbia: A Historical Sketch," 291.

42 Scholefield and Howay, *British Columbia from the Earliest Times to the Present* (1914), 1:19.

43 Ibid., 1:388; E.O.S. Scholefield to F. Howay, 6 February 1914, BCA, GR 1710, box 1, file 8.

44 "Report on the Legislative Library, 1896," BC, *Sessional Papers* (Victoria: Queen's Printer, 1896), 615-18.

45 Scholefield and Gosnell, *Sixty Years of Progress*, 2:i.

46 Scholefield and Howay, *British Columbia from the Earliest Times to the Present* (1914), 1:1-17. Notably, Henry Wagner's classic, *The Cartography of the Northwest Coast of America to the Year 1800*, 2 vols. (Berkeley: University of California Press, 1937), used Scholefield's volume as the source for over a dozen maps and sketches.

47 Cole Harris, "Social Power and Cultural Change in Pre-Colonial British Columbia," *BC Studies* 115/116 (Autumn/Winter 1997-98): 48.

48 [E.O.S. Scholefield], British Columbia Provincial Library, *Report, 1909* (Victoria: King's Printer, 1910), 5.

49 Scholefield and Howay, *British Columbia from the Earliest Times to the Present* (1914), vol. 1, chaps. 3-4.

50 Ibid., 1:95-109.

51 Ibid., 1:64.

52 Ibid., 1:46-47; Scholefield and Gosnell, *Sixty Years of Progress*, 1:19-24.

53 R.E. Gosnell, "Colonial History, 1849-71," in *Canada and Its Provinces*, vol. 21, *The Pacific Province*, ed. A. Shortt and A. Doughty (Toronto: Glasgow, Brook & Company, 1914), 85; Scholefield and Howay, *British Columbia from the Earliest Times to the Present* (1914), 1:327-425; Gosnell, *History of British Columbia*, 71-98.

54 Scholefield and Howay, *British Columbia from the Earliest Times to the Present* (1914), 1:366; Gosnell, *History of British Columbia*, 83-85.

55 Scholefield and Howay, *British Columbia from the Earliest Times to the Present* (1914), 1:510-45; R. Gosnell and R. Coats, *Sir James Douglas* (Toronto: Morang, 1908), 90ff., 179-90; and Gosnell, "Colonial History, 1849-71," 124-25.

56 Gosnell and Coats, *Sir James Douglas*, 300-1.

57 Eastwood, "R.E. Gosnell, E.O.S. Scholefield," 40-45; "Gosnell, R.E.," Vertical File, BCA, reel 54, pp. 2261-65.

58 Gosnell, *History of British Columbia*, 146-223; Gosnell and Coats, *Sir James Douglas*, 207-301; Gosnell, "Colonial History, 1849-71," 75-176.

59 Scholefield and Gosnell, *Sixty Years of Progress*, 2:131-65; F. Howay, "Political History, 1871-1913," in *Canada and Its Provinces*, vol. 21, *The Pacific Province*, ed. A. Shortt and A. Doughty, 179-237 (Toronto: Glasgow, Brook & Company, 1914).

60   R.E. Gosnell, "Representation at Ottawa," *British Columbia Magazine* 6, 12 (December 1910): 1124.

61   R.E. Gosnell, *The Story of Confederation, with Postscript on Quebec Situation* (n.p., 1918), 151.

62   Gosnell, *History of British Columbia*, 206, 251-52; Scholefield and Gosnell, *Sixty Years of Progress*, 2:5; Scholefield and Gosnell, *Sixty Years of Progress*, 1:178-210.

63   R.E. Gosnell, "A Greater Britain on the Pacific," *British Columbia Magazine* 2, 1 (1908): 10.

64   Brook Taylor, *Promoters, Patriots and Partisans: Historiography in Nineteenth-Century Canada* (Toronto: University of Toronto Press, 1989), 166.

65   Carl Berger, *The Writing of Canadian History: Aspects of English-Canadian Historical Writing since 1900*, 2nd ed. (Toronto: University of Toronto Press, 1986), 28; Donald Wright, "The Professionalization of History in English Canada to the 1950s" (PhD diss., University of Ottawa, 1999), 85-90.

66   Coats to Lamb, 17 November 1944, W. Kaye Lamb, documents.

67   Charles Humphries, "The Banning of a Book in British Columbia," *BC Studies* 1 (1968-69): 1-12; and Humphries, "War and Patriotism: The *Lusitania* Riot," *British Columbia Historical News* 5, 1 (1971): 15-23.

68   E.O.S. Scholefield to Walter [Gilbert], 6 September, 27 September 1902; E.O.S. Scholefield to Wilfred Scholefield, 9 September 1902; E.O.S. Scholefield to Sir G. Moleworth, 24 March 1904; all BCA, GR 146, box 1, file 1.

69   R.E. Gosnell, *Reciprocity and Canada's Future* (Victoria, [1911]); R.E. Gosnell, "British Columbia and British International Relations," *Annals of the American Academy of Political and Social Science* 45 (January 1913): 18-19; Gosnell, *Story of Confederation*, 137-38, 149-52.

70   Gosnell, *Story of Confederation*, 137-38. See Carl Berger, *The Sense of Power: Studies in Ideas of Canadian Imperialism* (Toronto: University of Toronto Press, 1970).

71   Gosnell, *History of British Columbia*, 102; Scholefield and Howay, *British Columbia from the Earliest Times to the Present* (1914), 1:569; and Scholefield and Gosnell, *Sixty Years of Progress*, 1:154-56.

72   R.E. Gosnell, *The Alaska Boundary Question* (Toronto: Ontario Publishing Co., 1896); Gosnell, *History of British Columbia*, 51-70; Gosnell and Coats, *Sir James Douglas*, 156-68; Scholefield and Howay, *British Columbia from the Earliest Times to the Present* (1914), 1:432-53.

73   Gosnell and Coats, *Sir James Douglas*, 72.

74   Scholefield and Gosnell, *Sixty Years of Progress*, 196-97.

75   Scholefield and Howay, *British Columbia from the Earliest Times to the Present* (1914), 1:235.

76   R.E. Gosnell, "British Columbia," in *Immigration as Affecting Canada and Her Constituent Provinces*, ed. A.C. Flumerfelt [Victoria, 1908], 9-10.

77 Gosnell, *History of British Columbia*, 295-98; Scholefield and Gosnell, *Sixty Years of Progress*, 2:196-97.

78 Kay Anderson, *Vancouver's Chinatown: Racial Discourse in Canada, 1875-1980* (Montreal and Kingston: McGill-Queen's University Press, 1991), 38-44; Peter Ward, *White Canada Forever: Popular Attitudes towards Orientals in British Columbia*, 2nd ed. (Montreal and Kingston: McGill-Queen's University Press), 3-14.

79 Scholefield and Howay, *British Columbia from the Earliest Times to the Present* (1914), 1:116, 200, 235; Scholefield and Gosnell, *Sixty Years of Progress*, 1:106; Gosnell, "British Columbia," 11-14.

80 Gosnell and Coats, *Sir James Douglas*, 11, 41-46; Scholefield and Howay, *British Columbia from the Earliest Times to the Present* (1914), 1:132-33, 178-79.

81 Gosnell and Coats, *Sir James Douglas*, 336-37; Gosnell, "British Columbia," 11-14; Howay, "Political History, 1871-1913," 211-12.

82 Gosnell, "British Columbia and British International Relations," 11.

83 Ibid., 13.

84 Gosnell, "British Columbia," 11-14.

85 Along with Anderson and Ward, see Patricia Roy, *A White Man's Province: British Columbia Politicians and Chinese and Japanese Immigrants* (Vancouver: UBC Press, 1989) and *The Oriental Question: Consolidating a White Man's Province, 1914-1941* (Vancouver: UBC Press, 2003).

86 Quoted in Anderson, *Vancouver's Chinatown*, 71.

87 Ibid., 54.

88 Janet Cauthers, "The North American Indian as Portrayed by American and Canadian Historians, 1830-1930" (PhD diss., University of Washington, 1974), 251; Bruce Trigger, "The Historians' Indian: Native Americans in Canadian Historical Writing from Charlevoix to the Present," *Canadian Historical Review* 67 (1986): 316-22.

89 Barman, *The West beyond the West*, 379.

90 Cole Harris, *Making Native Space: Colonialism, Resistance, and Reserves in British Columbia* (Vancouver: UBC Press, 2002), 228-48.

91 R.E. Gosnell, "Indians and Indian Affairs in Canada," *Canadian Magazine* 56 (March 1921): 480-83.

92 Scholefield to Clarke Co., 14 January 1914, BCA, GR 1710, box 1, file 8; Scholefield and Howay, *British Columbia from the Earliest Times to the Present* (1914), 1:270.

93 Scholefield and Howay, *British Columbia from the Earliest Times to the Present* (1914), 1:69, 197; Scholefield and Gosnell, *Sixty Years of Progress*, 1:57; Gosnell and Coats, *Sir James Douglas*, 79-80.

94 Scholefield and Howay, *British Columbia from the Earliest Times to the Present* (1914), 1:293; Gosnell, *History of British Columbia*, 37-38.

95 Scholefield to E. Young, 12, 24 April 1911, BCA, GR 146, box 1, file 3.

96   Gosnell and Coats, *Sir James Douglas*, 81, 248; R.E. Gosnell, "Indians and Indian Affairs in Canada," *Canadian Magazine* 57 (May 1921): 39-43.

97   Gosnell, "Indians and Indian Affairs in Canada," 39-40.

98   Gosnell and Coats, *Sir James Douglas*, 266; Scholefield and Howay, *British Columbia from the Earliest Times to the Present* (1914), 1:387-88.

99   Elizabeth Furniss, *The Burden of History: Colonialism and the Frontier Myth in a Rural Canadian Community* (Vancouver: UBC Press, 1999), 63.

100 A.G. Morice, *Fifty Years in Western Canada: Being the Abridged Memoirs of Reverend A.G. Morice, O.M.I.* (Toronto: Ryerson Press, 1930), 187.

101 Adrien Morice, *The History of the Northern Interior of BC, formerly New Caledonia, 1660-1880* (Smithers: Interior Stationery, 1978 [1906]), 139-52.

102 A bibliography of Morice's ethnolinguistic works is provided in David Mulhall, *Will to Power: The Missionary Career of Father Morice* (Vancouver: UBC Press, 1986), 213-15. The most significant title in this contribution was *The Carrier Language (Dene Family): A Grammar and Dictionary*, 2 vols. (St. Gabriel-Molding, 1932).

103 Mulhall, *Will to Power,* 174.

104 Scholefield and Howay, *British Columbia from the Earliest Times to the Present* (1914), 1:249.

105 Scholefield and Gosnell, *Sixty Years of Progress,* 1:i; Michael Kammen, *Mystic Chords of Memory: The Transformation of Tradition in American Culture* (New York: Knopf, 1991), 274.

106 R.E. Gosnell, "A Plea for the Old-Timer," *Victoria Daily Times,* 1 August 1908, 11.

107 Gosnell, "A Plea for the Old-Timer," 11; Scholefield and Howay, *British Columbia from the Earliest Times to the Present* (1914), 1:261; Scholefield and Gosnell, *Sixty Years of Progress,* 1:177-78.

108 Scholefield and Gosnell, *Sixty Years of Progress,* 1:210.

109 R.E. Gosnell, *With the Compliments of R.E. Gosnell* (Ottawa, 1920); Gosnell, "A Plea for the Old-Timer," 11.

110 Nellie de Lugrin, *Pioneer Women of Vancouver Island, 1843-66* (Victoria: Women's Canadian Club of Victoria, 1928), 1.

111 Jean Barman, "'I walk my own track in life and no mere male can bump me off it': Constance Lindsay Skinner and the Work of History," in *Creating Historical Memory: English-Canadian Women and the Work of History,* ed. B. Boutilier and A. Prentice (Vancouver: UBC Press, 1997), 129.

112 Adele Perry, *On the Edge of Empire: Gender, Race, and the Making of British Columbia* (Toronto: University of Toronto Press, 2001), 165.

113 Scholefield and Howay, *British Columbia from the Earliest Times to the Present* (1914), 2:113-15.

114 Perry, *On the Edge of Empire,* 174.

115 Ibid., 183.

CHAPTER 4: THE DOMAIN OF HISTORY

1 W. Kaye Lamb, interviews by author, Vancouver, British Columbia, 6 December 1991, 24 January 1992.

2 Frederic Howay, "Memo made April 25, 1911 as to my family," HP, box 16, file 1. Other biographical details from HP, box 11, files 1-3. An invaluable source for this chapter was W. Kaye Lamb, "A Bibliography of the Printed Writings of Frederic William Howay," *British Columbia Historical Quarterly* 8 (1944): 27-51.

3 Frederic Howay to Torch Press Book Shop, 16 January 1914, HP, box 8, file 1.

4 Frederic Howay, "The Search for the Fraser by Sea and Land," Art, Historical and Scientific Association, *Historical Papers* (1907-8): 15-24; F. Howay, "Life and Adventures of Simon Fraser," *New Westminster Daily News*, Fraser Centennial Number, 30 September 1908, 9-11.

5 Frederic Howay, *Work of the Royal Engineers*, with a foreword by R. McBride (Victoria: King's Printer, 1910); R. McBride to F. Howay, 12 and 20 February 1909, 10 January 1910, HP, box 4, file 18. Howay and McBride appear to have kept up a semi-regular collaboration on matters of BC history, notably through the first years of the twentieth century. For instance, the pair discussed provincial historical work over dinner in 1908. See Gosnell to Howay, 26 June 1908, HP, box 3, file 15. Also, a "Memo for the Honorable Mr. McBride" [n.d.] (HP, box 32, file 3) appears to have been from Howay. The memo is a questionnaire asking McBride various questions about the political development of the province after 1900. Possibly, Howay used it for the sections on McBride in E.O.S. Scholefield and F. Howay, *British Columbia from the Earliest Times to the Present*, vol. 2 (Vancouver: S.J. Clarke, 1914).

6 Frederic Howay, "History of British Columbia," in *Elementary History of Canada*, ed. I. Gammel (Toronto: Educational Book Co., [1912]).

7 L. Pierce to F. Howay, 30 March, 28 November 1926, HP, box 5, file 28; Pierce to Howay, 3 June 1930, HP, box 6, file 2.

8 Frederic Howay et al., *Builders of the West: A Book of Heroes* (Toronto: Ryerson Press, 1929); F. Howay, *Captain George Vancouver* (Toronto: Ryerson Press, 1932).

9 Frederic Howay, "Building the Big Canoes," *The Beaver* 19, 3 (December 1939): 38. Howay's other *Beaver* articles appeared in 2, 2 (November 1921): 2-6; 8, 4 (March 1929): 155-56; 18, 1 (June 1938): 48-51.

10 Frederic Howay, review of *The Far West Coast*, by V.L. Denton, *Canadian Historical Review* 6 (1925): 84-85; F. Howay, review of *The Romance of British Columbia*, by A. Anstey, *Washington Historical Quarterly* 19 (1928): 66-67.

11 F. Howay to C. Stewart, 26 December 1922, HP, box 8, file 1.

12 Frederic Howay, "The Fur Trade as a Factor in the Development of the Northwest Coast," BC School Trustees Association, *Proceedings* (1915): 74.

13 Frederic Howay, "British Columbia: A Historical Sketch," *The Fruit Magazine* 5 (1912): 291; Howay, "Fur Trade as a Factor," 74.

14 Frederic Howay, "The Earliest Pages of the History of British Columbia," British Columbia Historical Association, *Report* (1923): 16-17.

15 Frederic Howay, *British Columbia: The Making of a Province* (Toronto: Ryerson Press, 1928), 1-2.

16 Robert McDonald, *Making Vancouver: Class, Status, and Social Boundaries, 1863-1913* (Vancouver: UBC Press, 1996), 162.

17 John Norris, "The Vancouver Island Coal Miners, 1912-1914: A Study of an Organizational Strike," *BC Studies* 45 (Spring 1980): 56-72; Paul Phillips, *No Power Greater: A Century of Labour in British Columbia* (Vancouver: BC Federation of Labour, 1967), 55-61.

18 Howay's records on the riot trial are in the file "Ladysmith Riot," HP, box 30, file 15. Note particularly, "Rex v. Allsopp ..." (23 October 1913); and Howay to Minister of Justice, "Re: Nanaimo Riot Cases," [n.d.].

19 Phillips, *No Power Greater*, 60.

20 Scholefield and Howay, *British Columbia from the Earliest Times to the Present* (1914), 2:388, 448.

21 Ibid., 2:chaps. 3-4.

22 Ibid., 2:244.

23 Ibid., 2:116, 262, 484.

24 Ibid., 2: chaps. 33-34.

25 Ibid., 2:222.

26 Ibid., 2:222-29, 277-78.

27 Ibid., 2:142-48, 496-97, 526-27.

28 Howay, *Work of the Royal Engineers*, 1.

29 Scholefield and Howay, *British Columbia from the Earliest Times to the Present* (1914), 2:155-6.

30 Ibid., 2:354-55, 376, 441.

31 Ibid., 2:451.

32 Ibid., 2:344-52, 394, 538-44.

33 Ibid., 2:426-28.

34 Frederic Howay, "Political History, 1871-1913," in *Canada and Its Provinces*, vol. 21, *The Pacific Province*, ed. A. Shortt and A. Doughty (Toronto: Glasgow, Brook & Company, 1914), 215.

35 Scholefield and Howay, *British Columbia from the Earliest Times to the Present* (1914), 2:451.

36 Ibid., 1:chap. 7; 2:chaps. 18, 27, 31.

37 Ibid., 2:619.

38 Ibid., 2:34ff., 177-89.

39 Frederic Howay, "The Royal Engineers in British Columbia," Corporation of BC Land Surveyors, *Report of the Proceedings of the Nineteenth Annual General Meeting* (1924): 18.

40 S.J. Clarke to E.O.S. Scholefield, 15 January 1914, BCA, GR 1710, box 1, file 8.

41 Harris, *Making Native Space*, xxi-xxiii.

42 Frederic Howay, "Chairman's Address," BC Historical Association, *Report* (1924): 24; F. Howay, "International Aspects of the Maritime Fur-Trade," Royal Society of Canada, *Transactions*, ser. 3, 36 (1942): 59-78.

43 "Subject File: Songhees Reserve," HP, box 36, file 6.

44 Scholefield and Howay, *British Columbia from the Earliest Times to the Present* (1914), 2:chap. 24.

45 Ibid., 2:169, 233, 235, 567.

46 Ibid., chap. 32.

47 Ibid., 2:571-73.

48 Frederic Howay, "The Settlement and Progress of BC, 1871-1914," in *The Cambridge History of the British Empire,* vol. 6, *Canada and Newfoundland* (Cambridge: Cambridge University Press, 1930), 563-65.

49 Howay, *British Columbia: The Making of a Province*, 264-66.

50 Walter Sage, "Frederic William Howay: Historian of British Columbia," *British Columbia Historical Quarterly* 8 (1944): 5.

51 Scholefield and Howay, *British Columbia from the Earliest Times to the Present* (1914), 1:116, 235.

52 Ibid., 2:244.

53 Scholefield to S.J. Clarke, 9 June 1914, BCA, GR 1710, box 1, file 8.

54 Frederic Howay, "A List of Trading Vessels in the Maritime Fur Trade, 1785-1825," Royal Society of Canada, *Transactions*, ser. 3, 24 (1930), sec. 2: 111-34; ser. 3, 25 (1931), sec. 2: 117-49; ser. 3, 26 (1932), sec. 2: 43-86; ser. 3, 27 (1933), sec. 2: 119-47; ser. 3, 28 (1934), sec. 2: 11-49. These were republished in a single volume, edited by R.A. Pierce, *A List of Trading Vessels in the Maritime Fur Trade, 1785-1825* (Kingston: Limestone Press, 1973).

55 See Howay's introductions and editorial notes to *The Dixon-Meares Controversy* (Toronto: Ryerson Press, 1929); *Zimmerman's Captain Cook* (Toronto: Ryerson Press, 1930); *The Journal of Captain James Colnett Aboard the Argonaut* (Toronto: Champlain Society, 1940); and *Voyages of the Columbia to the Northwest Coast, 1787-90 and 1790-93* (Boston: Massachusetts Historical Society, 1941).

56 Howay, *Voyages of the Columbia to the Northwest Coast*, v.

57 Howay, *List of Trading Vessels*, 1-3, 26-27, 95-96, 104-6, 134; F. Howay, "Early Days of the Maritime Fur-Trade on the Northwest Coast," *Canadian Historical Review* 4 (1923): 26-44; F. Howay, "An Outline Sketch of the Maritime Fur Trade," *Report of the Canadian Historical Association* (1932): 5-14.

58 Howay, "An Outline Sketch," 14.

59 Howay, "International Aspects of the Maritime Fur-Trade," 59-78.

60 Robin Fisher, *Contact and Conflict: Indian-European Relations in British Columbia, 1774-1890*, 2nd ed. (Vancouver: UBC Press, 1992), 1; C. Archer, review of *Voyages of the "Columbia" to the Northwest Coast, 1787-90 and 1790-93*, ed. Frederic Howay, *BC Studies* 93 (Spring 1992): 81; James Gibson, *Otter Skins, Boston Ships, and China Goods: the Maritime Fur Trade of the Northwest Coast, 1785-1841* (Montreal and Kingston: McGill-Queen's University Press, 1992), xii. Howay's research is the main source for "Plate 66: New Caledonia and Columbia," in *Historical Atlas of Canada*, vol. 1, *From the Beginning to 1800*, ed. R. Cole Harris (Toronto: University of Toronto Press, 1987).

61 Frederic Howay, W. Sage, and H.F. Angus, *British Columbia and the United States: The North Pacific Slope from Fur Trade to Aviation* (Toronto: Ryerson Press, 1942), 13; Fisher, *Contact and Conflict*, 1.

62 On violence: "The Attempt to Capture the Brig Otter," *Western Historical Quarterly* 21 (1930): 179-88; "Indian Attacks upon Maritime Traders of the North-West Coast, 1785-1805," *Canadian Historical Review* 6 (1925): 287-309; and the last of the "List of Trading Vessels" entries, Royal Society of Canada, *Transactions*, ser. 3, 28 (1934), sec. 2: 11-49. On liquor: "The Introduction of Intoxicating Liquors amongst the Indians of the Northwest Coast," *British Columbia Historical Quarterly* 6 (1942): 157-69.

63 Frederic Howay, "The First Use of the Sail by the Indians of the Northwest Coast," *American Neptune* 1 (1941): 374-80; F. Howay, "The Origin of the Chinook Jargon," *British Columbia Historical Quarterly* 6 (1942): 225-50.

64 Howay, "Origin of the Chinook Jargon," 243.

65 Howay, *British Columbia: The Making of a Province*, 9ff.

66 Scholefield and Howay, *British Columbia from the Earliest Times to the Present* (1914), 2:619.

67 Frederic Howay, "Crowfoot: The Great Chief of the Blackfeet," *Report of the Canadian Historical Association* (1930): 107-12; F. Howay, "Sekani," in *Encyclopedia of Canada*, vol. 5 (Toronto: University Associates of Canada, 1937), 371.

68 Howay, "A List of Trading Vessels" (1934), 34; Howay, "Indian Attacks upon Maritime Traders," 287-309; Frederic Howay, "An Early Account of the Loss of the Boston in 1803," *Western Historical Quarterly* 17 (1926): 280-88.

69 Howay, "Settlement and Progress of BC," 253-54.

70 Howay, *British Columbia: The Making of a Province*, 8.

71 Howay, "The Attempt to Capture the Brig Otter," 180-81; Howay, "Indian Attacks upon Maritime Traders," 287-309.

72 The Seven Oaks incident was part of the increasingly violent conflict between the North West Company and the Hudson Bay Company for control of the region around the Red River Settlement. On 19 June 1816, a party of Métis employees of the North West Company was confronted by the local HBC governor and a score of his own men and settlers. One of the parties fired – we still do not know which – and the

ensuing firefight was as quick as it was one-sided: all of the HBC men were killed; one Métis was injured. The incident remained a controversial one in the following century and more. Most historians (themselves products of an Anglo settler society) were sympathetic to the HBC party, with a minority coming down on the side of the Métis and the North West Company.

73 Lyle Dick, "The Seven Oaks Incident and the Construction of a Historical Tradition, 1816-1970," *Journal of the Canadian Historical Association* 2 (1991): 91-113.

74 John Willis, *A History of Dalhousie Law School* (Toronto: University of Toronto Press, 1979), 3-66; John McLaren, "The History of Legal Education in Common Law Canada," in *Legal Education in Canada*, ed. R. Matas and D. McCawley, 111-45 (Montreal: Federation of Law Societies of Canada, 1987).

75 S. Waddams and J. Brierly, "Law," in *Canadian Encyclopedia*, 2nd ed. (Edmonton: Hurtig, 1988), 1185-87.

76 Walter Sage, "Judge Frederic William Howay (1867-1943): Pioneer Historical Critic," *British Columbia Library Quarterly* 22 (1944): 51.

77 Frederic Howay, review of *Union List of Manuscripts in Libraries of the Pacific Northwest*, by C.W. Smith, *Canadian Historical Review* 13 (1932): 82-83; F. Howay, "Captains Gray and Kendrik: The Barrell Letters," *Washington Historical Quarterly* 12 (1921): 243.

78 Frederic Howay, "Historical Research in BC," 4 October 1926, HP, box 29, file 4; F. Howay to R. Bishop, 29 October 1928, HP, box 8, file 14.

79 Peter Novick, *That Noble Dream: The "Objectivity Question" and the American Historical Profession* (Cambridge: Cambridge University Press, 1988), 1-2.

80 Frederic Howay, review of *The Oregon Missions*, by J.W. Bashford, *Review of Historical Publications Relating to Canada* 22 (1919): 126-28.

81 Frederic Howay, review of *History of Alaska*, by H.W. Clark, *Canadian Historical Review* 11 (1930): 354-56.

82 *Report of the Canadian Historical Association* (1922): 18.

83 Frederic Howay to Wallace, 25 January, 18 April 1927, HP, box 8, file 11.

84 W. Sage to H. Gerrans, 24 March 1921, SP, box 31, file 32; F. Howay to W. Sage, 8 April 1927, SP, box 6, file 5.

85 F. Howay to Pierce, 2 November 1926, I IP, box 8, file 9, University of British Columbia, *Calendar* (1929-55).

86 James Pilton, comp., "A Handbook and Guide to the Howay-Reid and Northwest Collections of Canadiana," University of British Columbia Library (1951); Laurenda Daniells, "The Special Collections of the Library of UBC," *British Columbia Library Quarterly* 36, 4 (1973): 45-47.

87 Frederic Howay, "William Sturgis: The Northwest Fur Trade," *British Columbia Historical Quarterly* 8 (1944): 11-25.

88 Frederic Howay, "An Early Colonization Scheme in British Columbia," *British Columbia Historical Quarterly* 3 (1939): 51-63; F. Howay, "The Voyage of the Captain

Cook and the Experiment," *British Columbia Historical Quarterly* 5 (1941): 285-96; F. Howay, "Four Letters from Richard Cadman Etches to Sir Joseph Banks," *British Columbia Historical Quarterly* 6 (1942): 125-39.

89 Frederic Howay, "Early Shipping in Burrard Inlet," *British Columbia Historical Quarterly* 1 (1937): 3-20; F. Howay, "Early Settlement on Burrard Inlet," *British Columbia Historical Quarterly* 1 (1937): 101-14; F. Howay, "Coal-Mining on Burrard Inlet," *British Columbia Historical Quarterly* 4 (1940): 1-20.

90 Frederic Howay, "The Negro Immigration into Vancouver Island in 1858," *British Columbia Historical Quarterly* 3 (1939): 101-13.

91 Howay, "The Introduction of Intoxicating Liquors"; Howay, "Origin of the Chinook Jargon."

92 Lamb, interviews.

93 F. Howay to Elliott, 31 March 1930, HP, box 8, file 20; 29 March 1936, HP, box 9, file 10; 4 February 1937, HP, box 9, file 13; 17 March 1941, HP, box 10, file 1.

94 Howay to Elliott, 13 January 1938, HP, box 9, file 16.

95 Carl Berger, *The Writing of Canadian History: Aspects of English-Canadian Historical Writing since 1900*, 2nd ed. (Toronto: University of Toronto Press, 1986), 1-31; Brook Taylor, *Promoters, Patriots and Partisans: Historiography in Nineteenth-Century Canada* (Toronto: University of Toronto Press, 1989), 265-66; A.B. McKillop, "Historiography," *Canadian Encyclopedia*, 2nd ed. (Edmonton: Hurtig, 1988), 993.

96 Berger, *The Writing of Canadian History*, 140-59; Marlene Shore, *The Science of Social Redemption: McGill, the Chicago School, and the Origins of Social Research in Canada* (Toronto: University of Toronto Press, 1987), 202-3, 301n84.

97 Quoted in Donald Wright, "The Professionalization of History in English Canada to the 1950s" (PhD diss., University of Ottawa, 1999), 276-77.

98 F. Howay to Elliott, 24 July 1935, HP, box 9, file 9; Angus to Howay, 18 January 1934, HP, box 1, file 5; Sage to Howay, 16 March, 9 April 1934, HP, box 6, file 5. Henry Angus, "My First Seventy-Five Years (1891-1966)," Angus Family Papers, University of British Columbia Library, Special Collections and University Archives Division, box 1, files 1-2, p. 247.

99 Howay, Sage, and Angus, *British Columbia and the United States*, 1-13.

100 Ibid., chaps. 5-6.

101 Ibid., 38, 43, 64, 173-74, 177.

102 Ibid., 67.

103 Ibid., 116, 125.

104 Ibid., 123.

105 Frederic Howay, review of *Oregon Geographic Names*, by L.A. McArthur, *Canadian Historical Review* 10 (1929): 169-70; F. Howay, "Memo in Notes and Manuscripts," 9 February 1942, HP, box 19, file 1.

106 Howay, Sage, and Angus, *British Columbia and the United States*, 376, 408.

107 "New Westminster Stands Solid for Conservatives," *New Westminster Daily Columbian*, 1 February 1907, 1; Howay, "Early Days of the Maritime Fur-Trade," 26; F. Howay, "The Early Literature of the Northwest Coast," Royal Society of Canada, *Transactions*, ser. 3, 18 (1924), sec. 2: 1.

108 Howay to Elliott, 29 March 1935, HP, box 9, file 10.

109 Wright, "The Professionalization of History in English Canada," 277-78.

Chapter 5: A Professional Past

1 Frederick Soward, "Early History of the University of British Columbia" (1930), University of British Columbia Library, Special Collections and University Archives Division (hereafter UBCA); Harry T. Logan, *Tuum Est: A History of the University of British Columbia* (Vancouver: UBC Press, 1958); and Lee Stewart, *"It's Up to You": Women at UBC in the Early Years* (Vancouver: UBC Press, 1990).

2 Lawrence Veysey, *Emergence of the American University* (Chicago: University of Chicago Press, 1965); A.B. McKillop, *Matters of Mind: The University in Ontario, 1791-1951* (Toronto: University of Toronto Press, 1994); Konrad Jarausch, ed., *The Transformation of Higher Learning, 1860-1930: Expansion, Diversification, Social Opening and Professionalization in England, Germany, Russia and the US* (Chicago: University of Chicago Press, 1983).

3 See Burton Bledstein, *The Culture of Professionalism: The Middle Class and the Development of Higher Education in America* (New York: W.W. Norton and Co., 1978); Peter Novick, *That Noble Dream: The "Objectivity Question" and the American Historical Profession* (Cambridge: Cambridge University Press, 1988), chap. 2.

4 Novick, *That Noble Dream*, 1-2.

5 "Biography – General," SP, box 6, file 1; Walter Sage, "Statement Regarding Credentials of W.N. Sage," 1928, President's Office Correspondence, UBCA, roll 180.

6 Margaret Hayward [Sage's daughter], interview by author, Vancouver, BC, 10 December 1992; W. Sage to H. Gerrans, 13 February 1910, SP, box 31, file 28.

7 Carl Berger, *The Writing of Canadian History: Aspects of English-Canadian Historical Writing since 1900*, 2nd ed. (Toronto: University of Toronto Press, 1986), 8-53; Donald Wright, "The Professionalization of History in English Canada to the 1950s" (PhD diss., University of Ottawa, 1999), 74-76; Robert Bothwell, *Laying the Foundation: A Century of History at the University of Toronto* (Toronto: University of Toronto Press, 1991), 47-48.

8 Sage to Gerrans, 6 June 1904, SP, box 31, file 28.

9 George Iggers, *New Directions in European Historiography* (Middleton: Wesleyan University Press, 1975), 153-57; Rosemary Jann, *The Art and Science of Victorian History* (Columbus: Ohio State University Press, 1985), 224.

10 Henry Angus, "My First Seventy-Five Years (1891-1966)," Angus Family Papers, UBCA, box 1, files 1-2, pp. 81-83.

11 H.F. Angus and W. Sage, "The Homecoming: A Comedy in Four Acts," Oxford, 1914, SP, box 33, file 6.

12 W. Sage to H. Gerrans, 18 September, 22 October 1918, SP, box 31, file 31.

13 W. Sage to H. Gerrans, 10 November 1917, SP, box 31, file 31.

14 Ibid. Sage's early research was the basis for his "Sir George Arthur and His Administration of Upper Canada," *Queen's Quarterly* 26 (1918): 22-53.

15 W. Sage to H. Gerrans, 2 June 1920, SP, box 31, file 32.

16 W. Sage to H. Gerrans, 3 June 1920, and W. Sage to H. Gerrans, 23 April 1921, SP, box 31, file 31; W. Sage to G. Wrong, 11 October 1921, President's Office Correspondence, UBCA, roll 180.

17 W. Sage to H. Gerrans, 24 March 1921, SP, box 31, file 31; F. Howay to Sage, 8 April 1927, SP, box 6, file 5.

18 W. Sage to H. Gerrans, 24 March 1921, SP, box 31, file 31; Bothwell, *Laying the Foundation*, 67.

19 Walter Sage, *Sir James Douglas and British Columbia* (Toronto: University of Toronto Press, 1930), 347-51. A valuable source on Sage's writings is Helen Boutilier, "A Bibliography of the Printed Writings of Walter Noble Sage," *British Columbia Historical Quarterly* 17 (1953): 127-37.

20 Sage, *Sir James Douglas*, 289, 347-51.

21 "Theses, Papers, etc. towards Qualifications for Degrees (Sage, 1925)," University of Toronto, Department of History Records, University of Toronto Archives, A70-0025, box 10, file 116.

22 "Correspondence – Incoming and Outgoing Re: *Sir James Douglas and British Columbia* (1928-30)," SP, box 31, file 5.

23 Walter Sage, "The Gold Colony of British Columbia," *Canadian Historical Review* 2 (1921): 340-59; W. Sage, "The Early Days of Representative Government in British Columbia," *Canadian Historical Review* 3 (1922): 143-80; W. Sage, "Spanish Explorers of the British Columbian Coast," *Canadian Historical Review* 12 (1931): 390-406.

24 Sage, "The Early Days of Representative Government," 143-80; Sage, *Sir James Douglas*, chaps. 6-9; W. Sage, "From Colony to Province: The Introduction of Responsible Government in British Columbia," *British Columbia Historical Quarterly* 3 (1939): 1-14.

25 Walter Sage, C. Martin, and G. Wrong, *The Story of Canada* (Toronto: Ryerson Press, 1929).

26 Sage, *Sir James Douglas*, 258.

27 Walter Sage, "Federal Parties and Provincial Political Groups in British Columbia, 1871-1903," *British Columbia Historical Quarterly* 12 (1948): 153-56; Frederic Howay, W. Sage, and H.F. Angus, *British Columbia and the United States: The North Pacific Slope from Fur Trade to Aviation* (Toronto: Ryerson Press, 1942), 192.

28 Sage, *Sir James Douglas*, 171, 289; Sage, "Federal Parties and Provincial Political Groups in British Columbia," 151-69.

29 Walter Sage, "The Critical Period of British Columbia History, 1866-71," *Pacific Historical Review* 1 (1932): 424-43; W. Sage, "The Annexationist Movement in British Columbia," Royal Society of Canada, *Transactions*, ser. 3, 21 (1927), sec. 2: 97-110; Howay, Sage, and Angus, *British Columbia and the United States*, chap. 8.

30 Walter Sage, "British Columbia and Confederation," *British Columbia Historical Quarterly* 15 (1951): 81-84.

31 Howay, Sage, and Angus, *British Columbia and the United States*, 237-38, 242.

32 Walter Sage, "British Columbia Becomes Canadian (1871-1901)," *Queen's Quarterly* 52 (1945): 174-83.

33 Ibid., 169; Walter Sage, "Canada on the Pacific: 1866-1925," *Washington Historical Quarterly* 17 (1926): 91-104; W. Sage, *Canada from Sea to Sea* (Toronto: University of Toronto Press, 1940), 15-16.

34 Sage, "Canada on the Pacific," 98-101, 104; W. Sage, "British Problems on the Pacific," [1927], in SP, box 32, file 14.

35 Sage, "The Early Days of Representative Government," 143.

36 W. Sage to Angus, 17 February 1942, SP, box 8, file 10.

37 Notable articles included "The Kyoto Conference on Pacific Relations," *BC Teacher* (1930); "Underprivileged Canadians," *Queen's Quarterly* (1931); "A Contribution to International Ill-Will," *Dalhousie Review* (1931); "The Legal Status in BC of Residents of Oriental Race and Their Descendants," *Canadian Bar Review* (1937); "Effect of the War on Oriental Minorities," *Canadian Journal of Economics and Political Science* (1941); and East Indians in Canada," *International Journal* (1946). Copies of these are found in Angus Papers, UBCA, box 3. Angus's prominent role in the campaign to overturn anti-Asian legislation is described in Kay Anderson, *Vancouver's Chinatown: Racial Discourse in Canada, 1875-1980* (Montreal and Kingston: McGill-Queen's University Press, 1991), 152-53; and Patricia Roy, *The Oriental Question: Consolidating a White Man's Province, 1914-1941* (Vancouver: UBC Press, 2003), 154-55, 216.

38 Angus, "My First Seventy-Five Years," 302-3, 319-22.

39 Angus, "Kyoto Conference," 21-25.

40 Anderson, *Vancouver's Chinatown*, 152.

41 Walter Sage, "Canadian History," 1927, SP, box 34, file 1; Sage's review of *Building of the Canadian Nation* (1942), by G. Brown, SP, box 33, file 5; W. Sage to H. Gerrans, 12 December 1918, SP, box 31, file 31.

42 W. Sage to Bolton, 24 March 1933, SP, box 33, file 1.

43 Sage, *Canada from Sea to Sea*, 17; W. Sage, "Towards Broader Horizons in Canadian History," 1938, SP, box 32, file 29.

44 Walter Sage, "Where Stands Canadian History?" *Report of the Canadian Historical Association* (1945): 5-6; W. Sage, "Towards New Horizons in Canadian History," *Pacific Historical Review* 8 (1939): 51-53.

45 W. Sage to L.S. Klinck, 14 July, 28 July 1927, President's Office Correspondence, UBCA, roll 272.

46 Donald Worcester, "Herbert Eugene Bolton: The Making of a Western Historian," in *Writing of Western History: Essays on Major Western Historians*, ed. R. Etulain, 193-214 (Albuquerque: University of New Mexico Press, 1991); Berger, *The Writing of Canadian History*, 148.

47 Walter Sage, "Some Aspects of the Frontier in Canadian History," *Report of the Canadian Historical Association* (1928): 62-72.

48 Berger, *The Writing of Canadian History*, 119.

49 Sage, *Canada from Sea to Sea*, 31; Sage, "Towards New Horizons in Canadian History," 47-57.

50 Sage, *Canada from Sea to Sea*, 32; W. Sage, "History 3: Canada West of the Great Lakes," [1937], SP, box 9, file 6; Howay, Sage, and Angus, *British Columbia and the United States*, 288-98.

51 Walter Sage, "Vancouver: The Rise of a City," *Dalhousie Review* 17 (1937): 49-50.

52 Walter Sage, "Trip to Nootka Sound," August 1924, SP, box 31, file 6.

53 Walter Sage, "Unveiling of Memorial Tablet at Nootka Sound," BC Historical Association, *Report* (1924): 17-22.

54 Gerald Nash, *Creating the West: Historical Interpretations, 1890-1990* (Albuquerque: University of New Mexico Press, 1991), chap. 2.

55 James Walker, "The Indian in Canadian Historical Writing," *Historical Papers of the Canadian Historical Association* (1971): 38-40; Bruce Trigger, "The Historians' Indian: Native Americans in Canadian Historical Writing from Charlevoix to the Present," *Canadian Historical Review* 67 (1986): 322-25; Berger, *The Writing of Canadian History*, 286, 298-301.

56 Adele Perry, *On the Edge of Empire: Gender, Race, and the Making of British Columbia* (Toronto: University of Toronto Press, 2001), 196.

57 Walter Mignolo, *The Darker Side of the Renaissance: Literacy, Territoriality, and Colonization* (Ann Arbor: University of Michigan Press, 1995), 127.

58 J.L. McDougall, "The Frontier School and Canadian History," *Report of the Canadian Historical Association* (1929): 121-25.

59 Morris Zaslow, "The Frontier Thesis in Recent Historiography," *Canadian Historical Review* 29 (1948): 153-67; Berger, *The Writing of Canadian History*, 118-21, 174-75.

60 Donald Creighton, *The Commercial Empire of the St. Lawrence, 1760-1850* (Toronto: Ryerson Press, 1937).

61 Harold Innis, *The Fur Trade in Canada: An Introduction to Canadian Economic History*, rev. ed. (Toronto: University of Toronto Press, 1970), 393.

62 Harold Innis, "Field Notes: Toronto to BC, 1932," Harold Innis Papers, University of Toronto Archives, B72-0003, box 6, file 15.

63 Harold Innis, *A History of the Canadian Pacific Railway* (Toronto: University of Toronto Press, 1970 [1923]), 3-21; H. Innis, *Settlement and the Mining Frontier*, Canadian Frontiers of Settlement Series, vol. 9, pt. 2 (Toronto: Macmillan, 1936).

64 H. Innis to W. Sage, 2 February 1935, SP, box 6, file 6; W. Sage, "Harold A. Innis, 1894-1952," *British Columbia Historical Quarterly* 17 (1953): 149-51.

65 W.A. Carrothers, *The British Columbia Fisheries* (Toronto: University of Toronto Press, 1941); W.A. Carrothers, "Forest Industries of British Columbia," in *The North American Assault on the Canadian Forest*, ed. A.R.M. Lower, 227-344 (New Haven: Yale University Press, 1938).

66 H. Angus, "A Summary of Economic Problems Awaiting Investigation in British Columbia," *Contributions to Canadian Economics* 2 (1929) 45-51.

67 Howay, Sage, and Angus, *British Columbia and the United States*, 376.

68 Ibid., 228, 268.

69 Ibid., 298.

70 W.L. Morton, "Clio in Canada: The Interpretation of Canadian History," in *Approaches to Canadian History*, ed. C. Berger, 42-49 (Toronto: University of Toronto Press, 1967).

71 Walter Sage, review of *The Commercial Empire of the St. Lawrence*, by Donald Creighton, *British Columbia Historical Quarterly* 3 (1939): 135-45.

72 Walter Sage, "Geographical and Cultural Aspects of the Five Canadas," *Report of the Canadian Historical Association* (1937): 28-34.

73 André Siegfried, *Canada*, trans. H. Hemming and D. Hemming (London: Jonathan Cape, 1937).

74 Sage, *Canada from Sea to Sea*, 15.

75 Walter Sage, "Is British Columbia American?" 1955, SP, box 10, file 8.

76 Hayward, interview.

77 Walter Sage, "The Oregon Treaty of 1846," *Canadian Historical Review* 27 (1946): 349-67; W. Sage, "Canada: The Neighbour to the North," *Pacific Historical Review* 20 (1951): 111-21.

78 Walter Sage, "Britain's Contribution to the World," 1948, SP, box 32, file 43; W. Sage, "Canada from Sea to Sea," [n.d.], SP, box 32, file 21.

79 Walter Sage, "The Historical Peculiarities of Canada with Regard to Hemisphere Defence," *Pacific Historical Review* 10 (1941): 16.

80 Walter Sage, "The British Commonwealth and the Collective System," *Pacific Historical Review* 3 (1934): 156-63; W. Sage, "British Problems on the Pacific," 1927, SP, box 32, file 14.

81 Howay, Sage, and Angus, *British Columbia and the United States*, 192; W. Sage, "History 203: Canada West of the Great Lakes," 1957, SP, box 9, file 7.

82 "Biographical Material," S. Mack Eastman Papers, UBCA, box 1, file 1. Eastman's dissertation was published as *Church and State in Early Canada* (Edinburgh: University Press, 1915).

83 Mack Eastman, "Report of the History Department, for 1921-22," 7 October 1922, President's Office Correspondence, UBCA, roll 323; W. Sage, "Department of History," 1952, SP, box 32, file 7; UBC, *Calendar* (1915-26).

84 Sylvia Thrupp, *The Merchant Class of Medieval London, 1300-1500* (Chicago: University of Chicago Press, 1948); S. Thrupp, *Society and History: Essays* (Ann Arbor: University of Michigan Press, 1977). Thrupp also founded and edited the journal *Comparative Studies in Society and History*, one of the most important journals in her field.

85 Sylvia Thrupp, "A Guide for Graduate Students Working for Their MA Degree in History," [1942]; and S. Thrupp, "History Honours, Third Year, Seminar Outline: An Introduction to History Method," [1942]; both in SP, box 10, file 3.

86 Ormsby to Eastman, [1965], Eastman Papers, UBCA, box 1, file 12.

87 "History – 32: Suggestions re. Men in History," President's Office Correspondence, UBCA, roll 33.

88 Sage, "Department of History," 1952; UBC, *Calendar* (1925-32).

89 Harvey to Howay, 3 April 1928, HP, box 3, file 17.

90 D.C. Harvey, "The Department of History, the UBC," 22 July 1931, SP, box 4, file 21.

91 McKillop, *Matters of Mind*, 106; Paul Phillips, *Britain's Past in Canada: The Teaching and Writing of British History* (Vancouver: UBC Press, 1989).

92 See Frances Woodward, *Theses on British Columbia History and Related Subjects* (Vancouver: University of British Columbia Library, 1969), 9-16, for a listing of early BA essays.

93 W. Sage, "[Honours] Seminar in the History of British Columbia," [1927], SP, box 10, file 6.

94 UBC, *Calendar* (1929), 132-33; W. Sage, "Seminar Outline in British Columbia History" (Vancouver: University of British Columbia, 1930); Sage, "Seminar in the History of BC," [1927].

95 Walter Sage, "School of Historians," *Vancouver World*, 7 November 1920, found in Faculty Addresses [1915-22], UBC Scrapbook no. 7, UBCA.

96 UBC, *Calendar* (1936), 122-23; W. Sage, "History 3: Canada West of the Great Lakes," [1937], SP, box 9, file 6.

97 Mack Eastman, quoted in Wright, "The Professionalization of History in English Canada," 129; W. Sage, "Report on the Department of History," 2 April 1928, SP, box 2, file 21; UBC, *Calendar* (1920-40).

98 UBC, *Calendar* (1919), 32; UBC, *Calendar* (1926), 79-80.

99 Sage, "Canadian History," 1927.

100 S.M. Eastman to G. Davidson, 4 June 1921, SP, box 32, file 9.

101 Walter Sage, "British Columbia as a Field for Historical Authorship," 1933, SP, box 32, file 19.

102 UBC, *Calendar* (1936), 81-82.

103 Walter Sage, "MA Seminar in the History of British Columbia," [n.d.], SP, box 10, file 6.

104 See, for instance, W. Sage to H. Johns, 6 November 1934, SP, box 4, file 25; and Sage to W.K. Lamb, 8 February 1935, SP, box 32, file 3.

105 Walter Sage, "Studies Completed and Fields Assigned in British Columbia History," May 1937, Margaret Ormsby Papers, UBCA (hereafter OP), box 7, file 12.

106 UBC Special Collections card file "Theses – MA – A8 (H-Phil)" lists all the MA theses completed in the history department; Woodward (*Theses*, 9-16) lists honours and graduate theses on BC topics.

107 University of Victoria, Department of History, "List of Graduate Essays and Theses Relating to British Columbia History," July 1969, OP, box 7, file 17.

Chapter 6: Lamb, Ormsby, and a First Generation of BC Historians

1 In 1929, fewer than one hundred of UBC's 1,885 students came from outside the province, with the largest number of these arriving from the rest of Canada. See "Memorandum Prepared for the Honourable Minister of Education and Transmitted to Him by the President of the University," 18 December 1929, President's Office Correspondence, UBCA, roll 26.

2 "The Historical Society, UBC, [Programs, 1921-39]," Historical Society of UBC Records, UBCA, box 1, file 4; "Historical Society of UBC, Minutes (1928-32)," SP, box 35, file 9.

3 Margaret Ormsby, interviews by author, Coldstream, British Columbia, 2-3 November 1992.

4 Graduate Historical Society Records (1934-44), UBCA; W. Sage, "Historical Renaissance in BC," *Canadian Historical Review* 17 (1936): 417.

5 Doug Owram, *The Government Generation: Canadian Intellectuals and the State, 1900-45* (Toronto: University of Toronto Press, 1986), 164, 188, 223, 309-10.

6 Biographical information on W. Kaye Lamb from interviews by author, Vancouver, British Columbia, 6 December 1991, 24 January 1992; Elizabeth Eso, "W. Kaye Lamb and the Provincial Archives of British Columbia, 1934-39" (MA thesis, University of British Columbia, 1984), 14-20; Wilfred Smith, "W. Kaye Lamb," *Archivaria* 15 (Winter 1982-83): 9-15. The same issue of *Archivaria* also published Gwynneth Evans, E. Hawkins, and J. Honeywell, "Bibliography of the Printed Works of William Kaye Lamb," 131-44.

7 William Ormsby, "The Public Archives of Canada, 1948-1968," *Archivaria* 15 (Winter 1982-83): 36-46; Don Downey, "National Archivist Was Custodian of Canada's History," *Globe and Mail*, 30 August 1999, A19; "In Memoriam: William Kaye Lamb, OC, FRSC, 1904-1999," *Archivaria* 45 (Spring 1999): 176-84.

8 W. Kaye Lamb, "Report on the State of the Library and Archives," 1934, 25-26, BCA, C/D/30.8/L16, 18.

9 Willard Ireland, "The Provincial Archives," [n.d.], BCA, box 2, file 3; Lamb, "Report on the State," 1934, 23-25; Eso, "W. Kaye Lamb and the Provincial Archives," 31-36.

10 "British Columbia Historical Quarterly," [1958], *British Columbia Historical Associa-tion Papers* (1923-70), BCA, AM 2779, box 5, file 1; Lamb, interviews; Eso, "W. Kaye Lamb and the Provincial Archives," 44-51.

11 Lamb, interviews.

12 For example, F.V. Longstaff and W. Kaye Lamb, "The Royal Navy on the Northwest Coast, 1813-50," *British Columbia Historical Quarterly* 9 (1945): 1-24, 113-28; F.W. Laing and W.K. Lamb, "The Fire Companies of Old Victoria," *British Columbia Historical Quarterly* 10 (1946): 43-75.

13 W. Kaye Lamb, "The Census of Vancouver Island, 1855," *British Columbia Historical Quarterly* 4 (1940): 51-58; "Memoirs and Documents Relating to Judge Begbie," *British Columbia Historical Quarterly* 5 (1941): 125-47; "Correspondence Relating to the Establishment of a Naval Base at Esquimalt, 1851-57," *British Columbia Historical Quarterly* 6 (1942): 277-96; "Diary of Robert Melrose [1852-57]," *British Columbia Historical Quarterly* 7 (1943): 119-34, 199-218, 283-95.

14 W. Kaye Lamb, ed., *Sixteen Years in the Indian Country: The Journal of Daniel Williams Harmon, 1800-1816* (Toronto: Macmillan, 1957); W.K. Lamb, *The Letters and Journals of Simon Fraser, 1806-1808* (Toronto: Macmillan, 1960); W.K. Lamb, *The Journals and Letters of Sir Alexander Mackenzie* (Toronto: Macmillan, 1970); W.K. Lamb, *A Voyage of Discovery to the North Pacific Ocean and Round the World, 1791-1795*, 4 vols. (London: Hakluyt Society, 1984).

15 W. Kaye Lamb, "The Advent of the Beaver," *British Columbia Historical Quarterly* 2 (1938): 163-84; "The Founding of Fort Victoria," *British Columbia Historical Quarterly* 7 (1943): 71-92; "Introduction," in *The Letters of John McLouglin from Fort Vancouver to the Governor and Committee*, vol. 1, ed. E.E. Rich, 1-59 (Toronto: Champlain Society, 1941).

16 W. Kaye Lamb, "The Governorship of Richard Blanshard," *British Columbia Historical Quarterly* 14 (1950): 1-40.

17 W. Kaye Lamb, "Early Lumbering on Vancouver Island [1844-66]," *British Columbia Historical Quarterly* 2 (1938): 31-53, 95-121.

18 W. Kaye Lamb, "The Pioneer Days of the Trans-Pacific Service: 1887-91," *British Columbia Historical Quarterly* 1 (1937): 143-64; W.K. Lamb, "Empress to the Orient," *British Columbia Historical Quarterly* 4 (1940): 29-50, 79-110; W.K. Lamb, "Empress Odyssey: A History of the Canadian Pacific Service to the Orient, 1913-45," *British Columbia Historical Quarterly* 12 (1948): 1-78.

19 W. Kaye Lamb, *History of the Canadian Pacific Railway* (New York: Macmillan, 1977).

20 Ormsby, interviews.

21 W. Kaye Lamb, "Presidential Address," *Report of the Canadian Historical Association* (1958): 1-12.

22 Biographical information on Ormsby is taken from Ormsby, interviews; John Norris, "Margaret Ormsby," *BC Studies* 32 (Winter 1976-77): 11-27; Margaret Ormsby, "My Irish Father," Okanagan Historical Society, *Report* 47 (1983): 82-87; and M. Ormsby,

"My Irish Father – George Lewis Ormsby, Part II," Okanagan Historical Society, *Report* 48 (1984): 130-33.

23 Ormsby, interviews.

24 Margaret Ormsby, "The History of the Okanagan Valley" (BA thesis, University of British Columbia, 1929); M. Ormsby, "A Study of the Okanagan Valley of British Columbia" (MA thesis, University of British Columbia, 1931).

25 Ormsby, interviews.

26 Ibid.

27 Some of her more notable publications in the journal included "Pre-exemption Claims in Okanagan Valley," 6 (1935): 177-84; "The Significance of the Hudson's Bay Brigade Trail," 13 (1949): 28-37; and "Captain Houghton's Exploratory Trip, 1864," 13 (1949): 38-44.

28 Ormsby to Margaret Ormsby [mother], [March 1940], OP, box 23, file 5.

29 John Conway, interview by Ruth Sandwell, 11 June 1999, in Margaret Ormsby Oral History Papers, UBCA (hereafter OOHP), box 1, file 26.

30 Ormsby, interviews.

31 Margaret Ormsby, "Relations Between British Columbia and the Dominion of Canada, 1871-1885" (PhD diss., Bryn Mawr, 1937); Ormsby to Sage, 13 December 1931, SP, box 4, file 36; Sage to Ormsby, 21 December 1931, SP, box 4, file 26.

32 Ormsby, interviews; Margaret Ormsby, "Prime Minister Mackenzie, the Liberal Party and the Bargain with British Columbia," *Canadian Historical Review* 26 (1945): 148-73.

33 Quoted in Marlene Shore, ed., *The Contested Past: Reading Canada's History* (Toronto: University of Toronto Press, 2002), 14.

34 Ormsby, interviews.

35 Ormsby to Sage, 23 June 1943, SP, box 9, file 3.

36 Paul Axelrod, *Making a Middle Class: Student Life in English Canada during the Thirties* (Montreal and Kingston: McGill-Queen's University Press, 1990), 21; "UBC Student Enrolment Figures: 1915-present," UBC Library, http://www.library.ubc.ca/archives/enrolmnt.html, 14 May 2003.

37 Lee Stewart, *"It's Up to You": Women at UBC in the Early Years* (Vancouver: UBC Press, 1990), chaps. 4-5.

38 Alison Prentice, "Laying Siege to the History Professoriate," in *Creating Historical Memory: English-Canadian Women and the Work of History*, B. Boutilier and A. Prentice (Vancouver: UBC Press, 1997), 225n18.

39 Frances Woodward, *Theses on British Columbia History and Related Subjects* (Vancouver: University of British Columbia Library, 1969); UBC Special Collections card file, "Theses – MA – A8 (H-Phil)."

40 Prentice lists the eight, with school and date of their PhD: from UBC class of 1924, Lillian Gates (Radcliffe, 1956) and Winnifred Ramsell (Wisconsin, 1931); from 1925, Sylvia Thrupp (London, 1931); from 1926, Marion Spector (Columbia, 1940) and Marion Mitchell (Columbia, 1938); from 1929, Margaret Ormsby (Bryn Mawr, 1938);

from 1931, Idele Wilson (Toronto, 1944); and from 1932, Norah Hughes (Chicago, 1945). Prentice, "Laying Siege," 211-16, 225n17.

41   Prentice, "Laying Siege," 202, 225n18.

42   Robert Bothwell, *Laying the Foundation: A Century of History at the University of Toronto* (Toronto: University of Toronto Press, 1991), 51-56, 133, 140.

43   Stewart, *"It's Up to You,"* 115.

44   John Norris, interview by Ruth Sandwell, 26 May 1999, OOHP, box 1, file 17.

45   "Appointment Sheets: Sylvia Thrupp," President's Office Papers, UBCA, box 206; Sage to G. Ridgeway, 27 March 1941, SP, box 8, file 7.

46   Sage to Dean Buchanan, 3 May 1937, President's Office Correspondence, UBCA, roll 180; Sage to Ridgeway, 27 March 1941, SP, box 8, file 7. H.K. Ralston, interview by author, Vancouver, British Columbia, 29 October 1992; Ormsby, interviews; Norris, interview.

47   Michael Horn, *Academic Freedom in Canada: A History* (Toronto: University of Toronto Press, 1999), 213; Prentice, "Laying Siege," 220-21, 231n101. Jean Murray in Saskatchewan likewise escorted that university's president (who was her father) to official functions. Donald Wright, "Gender and the Professionalization of History in English Canada before 1960," *Canadian Historical Review* 81 (2000): 53-59.

48   Mary Kinnear, *In Subordination: Professional Women, 1870-1970* (Montreal and Kingston: McGill-Queen's University Press, 1995), 17, 48-50.

49   Prentice, "Laying Siege," 231n104.

50   Quoted in ibid., 212.

51   Wright, "Gender and the Professionalization of History," 40.

52   Ormsby, interviews.

53   Ibid.

54   Neil Sutherland, interview by author, Vancouver, British Columbia, 16 July 1992.

55   UBC, *Calendar* (1968); Ralston, interview.

56   UBC, *Calendar* (1948-62); Ormsby, interviews.

57   Patricia Roy, interview by Ruth Sandwell, 31 July 1999, OOHP, box 1, file 39.

58   University of Victoria, Department of History, "List of Graduate Essays and Theses Relating to BC History," July 1969, OP, box 7, file 17.

59   Ormsby, "Curriculum Vitae," June 1975, OOHP, box 1, file 3.

60   Ormsby, interviews.

61   Roy, interview; Jean Friesen, interview by Ruth Sandwell, 19 January 1999, OOHP, box 1, file 36.

62   Margaret Prang, interview by Ruth Sandwell, 18 May 1999, OOHP, box 1, file 14; Jean Elder, interview by Ruth Sandwell, 24 July 1999, OOHP, box 1, file 37.

63   Roy, interview.

64   Norris, interview.

65   Prang, interview; Conway, interview; Norris, interview; Keith Ralston, interviews by Ruth Sandwell, 4 May, 11 June 1999, OOHP, box 1, file 11; John Bosher, interview

by Ruth Sandwell, 15 June 1999, OOHP, box 1, file 28; Ivan Avacumovic, interview by Ruth Sandwell, 18 August 1999, OOHP, box 1, file 42; Robin Fisher, interview by Ruth Sandwell, 29 June 1999, OOHP, box 1, file 31.

66 Fisher, interview.

67 "British Columbia Centennial Committee: Minutes," 26 January 1956, British Columbia Centennial Committee Records, BCA, GR 1448, box 16 P/H 4.

68 Ormsby, interviews.

69 Ormsby's research team included future academics Neil Sutherland, Gordon Elliott, and Dorothy Blakey Smith; archivist John Bovey; and politician Brian Smith.

70 M. Ormsby to L. Wallace, 28 August 1956, BCA, GR 1448, box 16 P/H 4.

71 Ormsby, "Historians' View Points," *Canadian Literature* 3 (Winter 1960): 65-67.

72 Hayden White, *The Content of the Form: Narrative Discourse and Historical Representation* (Baltimore: Johns Hopkins University Press, 1987); Dominick LaCapra, *History and Criticism* (Ithaca: Cornell University Press, 1985); Louis Mink, "Narrative Form as a Cognitive Instrument," in *The Writing of History: Literary Form and Historical Understanding*, ed. R. Canary and H. Kozick, 129-49 (Madison: University of Wisconsin Press, 1978).

73 Carl Berger, *The Writing of Canadian History: Aspects of English-Canadian Historical Writing since 1900*, 2nd ed. (Toronto: University of Toronto Press, 1986), chap. 7; Peter Novick, *That Noble Dream: The "Objectivity Question" and the American Historical Profession* (Cambridge: Cambridge University Press), chap. 10.

74 Berger, *The Writing of Canadian History*, 220.

75 Margaret Ormsby, "Humanized History," *Canadian Literature* 9 (Summer 1961): 53-56.

76 Margaret Ormsby, *British Columbia: A History* (Toronto: Macmillan, 1972 [1958]), 494.

77 Ibid., 336.

78 Ibid., 484.

79 Ibid., 300.

80 Norris, "Margaret Ormsby," 17.

81 See Ormsby, *British Columbia*, chaps. 11 and 15, particularly 304-7, 331-32, 408-11.

82 Novick, *That Noble Dream*, 92-97, 239-41.

83 Ormsby, *British Columbia*, 251.

84 Ibid., 485-86, 438-39.

85 Margaret Ormsby, "A Horizontal View: Presidential Address," Canadian Historical Association, *Historical Papers* (1966): 4.

86 Ormsby, *British Columbia*, 117, 159-62, 185-89, 353-61, 452-79. See also M. Ormsby, "T. Dufferin Pattullo and the Little New Deal," *Canadian Historical Review* 43 (1962): 277-97.

87 Ormsby, *British Columbia*, 491.

88 Ibid., 412.

89 Margaret Ormsby, "Neglected Aspects of British Columbia's History," *British Columbia Library Quarterly* 23, 4 (1960): 11.
90 Ormsby, *British Columbia*, 344, 441, 465.
91 Ibid., chaps. 1-2.
92 For the tension between the HBC and settlers, see Ormsby, *British Columbia*, chaps. 4-5; between British and Canadian factions, ibid., chaps. 6-8. See also Margaret Ormsby, "Canada and the New British Columbia," *Report of the Canadian Historical Association* (1948): 74-77.
93 Ormsby, *British Columbia*, 199, 217-30, 259-92.
94 Ibid., 361.
95 Ibid., 438-39.
96 M. Ormsby to M. Ormsby [mother], [March 1940], OP, box 23, file 5; Margaret Ormsby, "Agricultural Development in British Columbia," *Agricultural History* 19 (January 1945): 11-29; M. Ormsby, "Fruit Marketing in the Okanagan Valley of British Columbia," *Agricultural History* 9 (1935): 80-97; M. Ormsby, "The History of Agriculture in British Columbia," *Scientific Agriculture* 20, 1 (September 1939): 61-72; M. Ormsby, "The United Farmers of BC: An Abortive Third-Party Movement," *British Columbia Historical Quarterly* 17 (1958): 53-73.
97 Ormsby, *British Columbia*, 70, 125-27, 203-4, 343-44, 493-94.
98 Ibid., 94-95, 113-14, 255.
99 Ormsby, interviews; Stephen Hume, "Ormsby: Still the Scholar Supreme," *Vancouver Sun*, 10 June 1992, A17.
100 Ormsby, "My Irish Father," 133.
101 Ormsby, interviews.
102 Joan Scott, "History and Difference," *Daedalus* 116, 4 (1987): 98.
103 Novick, *That Noble Dream*, 510.
104 Kay Anderson, *Vancouver's Chinatown: Racial Discourse in Canada, 1875-1980* (Montreal and Kingston: McGill-Queen's University Press), 170-71.
105 See, for instance, Frederick Soward, "Canada and the Far Eastern Crisis," 1933, Soward Papers, UBCA, box 3, file 1. On Henry Angus, see Chapter 5.
106 "The Historical Society, UBC, [Programs, 1921-39]."
107 Ormsby, *British Columbia*, 167, 273, 299-300, 493.
108 Ibid., 491-93.
109 Ibid., 349-53.
110 Ibid., 336.
111 Roderick Haig-Brown, "Review of *British Columbia: A History*," CBC Information Services, Vancouver, 2 December 1958, OP, box 3, file 3.
112 Ormsby, "History of the Okanagan Valley," 19-49; Ormsby, "Study of the Okanagan Valley," 8-12.
113 Ormsby, interviews.

114 Ormsby, *British Columbia*, 33, 127.

115 Margaret Ormsby, "The Ten Encampments," Okanagan Historical Society, *Report* 3 (1929): 19; Ormsby, *British Columbia*, 127.

116 Ormsby, *British Columbia*, 284, 52.

117 Ormsby, "Canada and the New British Columbia," 85.

118 Ormsby, *British Columbia*, 144, 246.

119 Ibid., 124, 131, 194-95.

120 Ibid., 478, 491.

121 Ormsby, "Horizontal View," 9.

122 Ormsby, *British Columbia*, 371, 375, 458; Ormsby, "Horizontal View," 3, 8.

123 W.L. Morton, *Manitoba: A History*, 2nd ed. (Toronto: University of Toronto Press, 1967), 250.

124 Ibid., ix.

125 See Berger, *The Writing of Canadian History*, chap. 10.

126 Quoted in Lyle Dick, "'A Growing Necessity for Canada': W.L. Morton's Centenary Series and the Forms of National History, 1955-80," *Canadian Historical Review* 82 (2001): 235.

127 Quoted in ibid., 235.

128 Ormsby, *British Columbia*, 129, 136, 185-86, 235-36.

129 Ibid., chaps. 4-9; Ormsby, "Neglected Aspects of British Columbia's History," 10.

130 For example, see Ormsby's *Coldstream – Nulli Secundus* (Vernon: Friesen, 1990), 32ff.; and her "Introduction," in M. Ormsby, ed., *A Pioneer Gentlewoman in British Columbia: The Recollections of Susan Allison* (Vancouver: UBC Press, 1976).

131 Ormsby, "Horizontal View," 7.

132 Ibid., 2.

133 Ibid., 12.

CONCLUSION

1 Allen Smith, "The Writing of British Columbia History," *BC Studies* 45 (Spring 1980): 102.

Bibliography of Primary Sources

ARCHIVAL SOURCES

Bancroft Library

Anderson, A.C. "History of the Northwest Coast." Victoria, 1878. P-C 2.

Bayley, C.A. "Early Life on Vancouver Island." Victoria, 1878. P-C 3.

British Columbia Letters to H.H. Bancroft (1862-79). P-C 43.

Compton, P.N. "Aboriginal British Columbia." Victoria, 1878. P-C 39.

–. "Forts and Fort Life in New Caledonia under Hudson's Bay Company Regime." Victoria, 1878. P-C 5.

Cooper, James. "Maritime Matters on the Northwest Coast and Other Affairs of the Hudson's Bay Company in Early Times." Victoria, 1878. P-C 6.

Cridge, Edward. "Characteristics of James Douglas." Victoria, 1878. P-C 8.

De Cosmos, Amor. "The Governments of Vancouver Island and British Columbia." San Francisco, 1878. P-C 10.

Deans, James. "Settlement of Vancouver Island." Victoria, 1878. P-C 9.

Douglas, James. Private Papers (1827-61). P-C 12-13.

–. Journals (1840-41). P-C 11.

Finlayson, Roderick. "History of Vancouver Island and the Northwest Coast." Victoria, 1878. P-C 15.

Fraser, Simon. Journals and Letters (1806-8). P-C 16-18.

Good, John B. "British Columbia." Victoria, 1878. P-C 19.

Hudson's Bay Company. "Journal ... Kept at Fort Langley during the Year 1827-29." P-C 22.

–. "Journal at Fort Simpson (1834-37)." P-C 23.

McKay, Joseph. "Recollections of a Chief Trader in the Hudson's Bay Company." Fort Simpson, 1878. P-C 24.

McKinlay, Archibald. "Narrative of a Chief Factor of the Hudson's Bay Company." Victoria, 1878. P-C 25.

Stuart, John. "Journal at the Rocky Mountains (1805-6)." P-C 45.

Tod, John. "History of New Caledonia and the Northwest Coast." Victoria, 1878. P-C 27.

Tolmie, W.F. "History of the Puget Sound and the Northwest Coast." Victoria, 1878. P-B 25.

–. "Journal during Residence on Puget Sound in 1833." P-B 24.

Work, John. Journals (1824-34). P-C 30.

British Columbia Archives

British Columbia Bureau of Statistics Papers. GR 153.

British Columbia Centennial Committee Records. GR 1448.

British Columbia Historical Association Papers (1900-76). AM 2736.

–. (1923-70). AM 2779.

British Columbia Provincial Archives Correspondence. GR 1738.

British Columbia Provincial Archives Papers. GR 975.

British Columbia Provincial Library Correspondence. GR 146.

–. GR 726.

British Columbia Provincial Library Papers. GR 1710.

Lamb, W. Kaye. "Report on the State of the Library and Archives." 1934. C/D/30.8/L16.

Natural History Society of British Columbia Papers. AM 284.

"Reports of the Pacific Northwest History Department (1922, 1927-33)." C/D/30.1/Ar2.1.

Scholefield, E.O.S. Papers. AM 491.

Sproat, G.M. Papers. AM 257.

"Vouchers Relating to Simon Fraser Centenary Celebration (1908, 1909)." C/D/30.1/Ar2.

University of British Columbia Archives

Angus Family Papers.

Eastman, S. Mack. Papers.

Graduate Historical Society Records (1934-44).

Historical Society of the University of British Columbia Records.

Howay, Frederic. Papers.

Ormsby, Margaret. Oral History Project Papers.

–. Papers.

President's Office Correspondence.

President's Office Papers.

Sage, Walter. Papers.

Soward, Frederick. "Early History of the University of British Columbia." 1930.

–. Papers.

University of British Columbia Scrapbook No. 7.

University of Toronto Archives

Innis, Harold. Papers. B72-0003.
University of Toronto, Department of History Records. A70-0025.

Vancouver City Archives

Art, Historical and Scientific Association of Vancouver Records. AM 336.

INTERVIEWS

Hayward, Margaret. Interview by author. Vancouver, British Columbia, 10 December 1992.
Lamb, W. Kaye. Interviews by author. Vancouver, British Columbia, 6 December 1991, 24 January 1992.
Ormsby, Margaret. Interviews by author. Coldstream, British Columbia, 2-3 November 1992.
Ralston, H.K. Interview by author. Vancouver, British Columbia, 29 October 1992.
Sutherland, Neil. Interview by author. Vancouver, British Columbia, 16 July 1992.

OTHER PRIMARY SOURCES

Anderson, A.C. *Hand-Book and Map to the Gold Region of Frazer's and Thompson's Rivers*. San Francisco: LeCount, 1858.
Angus, Henry Forbes. *Citizenship in British Columbia*. Victoria: King's Printer, 1926.
–. "A Summary of Economic Problems Awaiting Investigation in British Columbia." *Contributions to Canadian Economics* 2 (1929): 45-51.
Art, Historical and Scientific Association of Vancouver. *Historical Papers: Session 1907-1908*. Vancouver, 1908.
–. *Journal* (1917-21).
–. *Museum and Art Notes* (1926-32).
Ballantyne, Robert, ed. *Handbook to the New Gold Fields*. Edinburgh: Strahan, 1858.
Bancroft, Hubert Howe. *History of British Columbia, 1792-1887*. San Francisco: History Co., 1887.
–. *History of British Columbia, 1792-1887*. San Francisco: History Co., 1890.
–. *History of the Northwest Coast*. 2 vols. San Francisco: A.L. Bancroft & Co., 1884.
–. *History of the Northwest Coast*. 2 vols. San Francisco: History Co., 1890.
–. *Literary Industries*. San Francisco: History Co., 1890.
Begg, Alexander. *History of British Columbia: From Its Earliest Discovery to the Present Time*. Toronto: W. Briggs, 1894.
Black, N.F. *History of Saskatchewan and the North West Territories*. 2 vols. Regina: Saskatchewan Historical Co., 1913.

British Columbia. *Public Accounts for the Fiscal Year Ended 30th June 1894.* Victoria: Queen's Printer, 1894.

British Columbia. *Sessional Papers.* Victoria: Queen's Printer, 1894-97.

British Columbia. *Statutes.* Victoria: Queen's Printer, 1894.

British Columbia and Vancouver's Island: A Complete Handbook. London: William Penny, [1858].

British Columbia Historical Association. *Report.* 1923-29.

British Columbia Magazine. 1907-15.

British Columbia Provincial Archives. *Report, 1910-13.* Victoria: King's Printer, 1911-14.

British Columbia Provincial Archives Department. *Simon Fraser Centenary, 1808-1908: Checklist of Books and Pamphlets.* Victoria: King's Printer, 1908.

British Columbia Provincial Library. *A Bibliography of Publications on Ships, Shipbuilding and Ship Subsidies, contained in the Provincial Library.* Bulletin 2. Victoria: King's Printer, 1917.

–. *A Bibliography of Publications on the War, Contained in the Provincial Library.* Bulletin 1. Victoria: King's Printer, 1916.

–. *Report, 1898-1909.* Victoria: Queen's/King's Printer, 1899-1910.

Brooke, Rupert. *Rupert Brooke in Canada.* Toronto: Peter Martin Associates, 1978.

Brown, R.C. Lundin. *British Columbia: An Essay.* New Westminster: Royal Engineer Press, 1863.

Burney, James. *A Chronological History of North-Eastern Voyages of Discovery.* London: Payne & Foss, 1819.

Carrothers, W.A. *The British Columbia Fisheries.* Toronto: University of Toronto Press, 1941.

–. "Forest Industries of British Columbia." In *The North American Assault on the Canadian Forest,* ed. A.R.M. Lower, 227-344. New Haven: Yale University Press, 1938.

Cogswell, Oliver. *History of British Columbia.* Victoria: Colonist Press, 1893.

Comparative Chronological Statement of the Events Connected with the Rights of Great Britain and the Claims of the United States to the Oregon Territory. London [1845].

Cook, James. *A Voyage to the Pacific Ocean.* 3 vols. and Atlas. London: W. & A. Strahan, 1784.

Cornwallis, Kinahan. *The New El Dorado: or British Columbia.* London: Newby, 1858.

Court of Appeal for British Columbia. *Reasons for Judgement: Between Delgamuukw, et al., and Her Majesty the Queen.* 1993.

Creighton, Donald. *The Commercial Empire of the St. Lawrence, 1760-1850.* Toronto: Ryerson Press, 1937.

Domer, John. *New British Gold Fields: A Guide to British Columbia and Vancouver Island.* London: Angel, [1858].

Dunn, John. *History of the Oregon Territory and British North American Fur Trade.* London: Edwards & Hughes, 1844.

Eastman, S. Mack. *Church and State in Early Canada.* Edinburgh: University Press, 1915.

Evans, Elwood. *The Re-annexation of British Columbia to the United States, Right, Proper and Desirable: An Address.* [Olympia, 1870].

Falconer, Thomas. *On the Discovery of the Mississippi, and On the South-Western, Oregon, and North-Western Boundary.* London: Samuel Clarke, 1844.

–. *The Oregon Question.* London: Samuel Clarke, 1845.

Farnham, Thomas. *History of Oregon Territory, It Being a Demonstration of the Title to These United States of North America to the Same.* New York: New World Press, 1844.

Forbes, Charles. *Prize Essay: Vancouver Island, Its Resources and Capabilities as a Colony.* [Victoria]: Colonial Government, 1862.

Gallatin, Albert. *The Oregon Question.* New York: Bartlett & Welford, 1846.

Gosnell, R. Edward. *The Alaska Boundary Question.* Toronto: Ontario Publishing Co., 1896.

–. "British Columbia." In *Immigration as Affecting Canada and Her Constituent Provinces,* ed. A.C. Flumerfelt. [Victoria, 1908].

–. "British Columbia and British International Relations." *Annals of the American Academy of Political and Social Science* 45 (January 1913): 1-19.

–. "Colonial History, 1849-71." In *Canada and Its Provinces.* Vol. 21, *The Pacific Provinces,* ed. A. Shortt and A. Doughty, 75-176. Toronto: Glasgow, Brook & Company, 1914.

–. "A Greater Britain on the Pacific." *British Columbia Magazine* 2, 1 (1908): 7-12.

–. *A History of British Columbia.* N.p.: Lewis Publishing Co., 1906.

–. "Indians and Indian Affairs in Canada," *Canadian Magazine,* 56, no. 6 (1921): 480-83; 57, no. 1 (1921): 39-43.

–. "A Plea for the Old-Timer." *Victoria Daily Times,* 1 August 1908, 11.

–. *Reciprocity and Canada's Future.* Victoria, [1911].

–. "Representation at Ottawa." *British Columbia Magazine* 6, 12 (December 1910): 1120-24.

–. *The Story of Confederation, with Postscript on Quebec Situation.* N.p., 1918.

–. *With the Compliments of R.E. Gosnell.* Ottawa, 1920.

–, and R. Coats. *Sir James Douglas.* Toronto: Morang, 1908.

Grant, W.C. "Description of Vancouver Island." *Journal of the Royal Geographical Society* 27 (1857): 268-320.

–. "Remarks on Vancouver Island." *Journal of the Royal Geographical Society* 31 (1861): 208-13.

Gray, William H. *A History of Oregon, 1792-1849.* Portland/San Francisco: Harris & Holman/H.H. Bancroft & Co., 1870.

Great Britain. House of Commons. *Report from the Select Committee on the Hudson's Bay Company.* [London, 1857].

Greenhow, Robert. *The History of Oregon and California, and the Other Territories on the North-West Coast of North America.* London: John Murray, 1844.

—. *Memoir, Historical and Political, on the Northwest Coast of North America*. Washington: Blair & Rives, 1840.

Hazlitt, William C. *British Columbia and Vancouver Island: A Historical Sketch of the British Settlements in the North-West Coast of America*. London: Routledge, 1858.

—. *The Great Gold Fields of Cariboo*. 1862. Reprint, Victoria: Klanak, 1974.

History Company, The. *History of British Columbia. Bancroft's Works, Vol. xxxII*. San Francisco: History Co., 1887.

Hittell, John. *Mining in the Pacific States of North America*. San Francisco: H.H. Bancroft & Co., 1861.

House of Assembly Correspondence, August 12, 1856 to July 6, 1859. British Columbia Provincial Archives, Memoir 4. Victoria: King's Printer, 1918.

Howay, Frederic. "The Attempt to Capture the Brig Otter." *Western Historical Quarterly* 21 (1930): 179-88.

—. "British Columbia: A Historical Sketch." *The Fruit Magazine* 5 (1912): 291-93.

—. *British Columbia: The Making of a Province*. Toronto: Ryerson Press, 1928.

—. "Building the Big Canoes." *The Beaver* 19, 3 (December 1939): 38-42.

—. *Captain George Vancouver*. Toronto: Ryerson Press, 1932.

—. "Captains Gray and Kendrik: The Barrell Letters." *Washington Historical Quarterly* 12 (1921): 243-71.

—. "Chairman's Address." British Columbia Historical Association. *Report* (1924): 22-25.

—. "Coal-Mining on Burrard Inlet." *British Columbia Historical Quarterly* 4 (1940): 1-20.

—. "Crowfoot: The Great Chief of the Blackfeet." *Report of the Canadian Historical Association* (1930): 107-12.

—. "The Earliest Pages of the History of British Columbia." British Columbia Historical Association. *Report* (1923): 16-22.

—. "An Early Account of the Loss of the Boston in 1803." *Western Historical Quarterly* 17 (1926): 280-88.

—. "An Early Colonization Scheme in British Columbia." *British Columbia Historical Quarterly* 3 (1939): 51-63.

—. "Early Days of the Maritime Fur-Trade on the Northwest Coast." *Canadian Historical Review* 4 (1923): 26-44.

—. "The Early Literature of the Northwest Coast." Royal Society of Canada, *Transactions*, ser. 3, 18 (1924), sec. 2: 1-31.

—. "Early Settlement on Burrard Inlet." *British Columbia Historical Quarterly* 1 (1937): 101-14.

—. "Early Shipping in Burrard Inlet." *British Columbia Historical Quarterly* 1 (1937): 3-20.

—. "The First Use of the Sail by the Indians of the Northwest Coast." *American Neptune* 1 (1941): 374-80.

–. "Four Letters from Richard Cadman Etches to Sir Joseph Banks." *British Columbia Historical Quarterly* 6 (1942): 125-39.

–. "The Fur Trade as a Factor in the Development of the Northwest Coast." British Columbia School Trustees Association. *Proceedings* (1915): 74-81.

–. "History of British Columbia." In *Elementary History of Canada*, ed. I. Gammel. Toronto: Educational Book Co., [1912].

–. "Indian Attacks upon Maritime Traders of the North-West Coast, 1785-1805." *Canadian Historical Review* 6 (1925): 287-309.

–. "International Aspects of the Maritime Fur-Trade." Royal Society of Canada. *Transactions*, ser. 3, 36 (1942): 59-78.

–. "The Introduction of Intoxicating Liquors amongst the Indians of the Northwest Coast." *British Columbia Historical Quarterly* 6 (1942): 157-69.

–. "Life and Adventures of Simon Fraser." *New Westminster Daily News*, Fraser Centennial Number, 30 September 1908, 9-11.

–. "A List of Trading Vessels in the Maritime Fur Trade, 1785-1825." Royal Society of Canada. *Transactions*, ser. 3, 24 (1930) sec. 2: 111-34; ser. 3, 25 (1931) sec. 2: 117-49; ser. 3, 26 (1932) sec. 2: 43-86; ser. 3, 27 (1933) sec. 2: 119-47; ser. 3, 28 (1934) sec. 2: 11-49.

–. *A List of Trading Vessels in the Maritime Fur Trade, 1785-1825.* Ed. R.A. Pierce. Kingston: Limestone Press, 1973.

–. "The Negro Immigration into Vancouver Island in 1858." *British Columbia Historical Quarterly* 3 (1939): 101-13.

–. "The Origin of the Chinook Jargon." *British Columbia Historical Quarterly* 6 (1942): 225-50.

–. "An Outline Sketch of the Maritime Fur Trade." *Report of the Canadian Historical Association* (1932): 5-14.

–. "Political History, 1871-1913." In *Canada and Its Provinces.* Vol. 21, *The Pacific Province*, ed. A. Shortt and A. Doughty, 179-237. Toronto: Glasgow, Brook & Company, 1914.

–. Review of *History of Alaska*, by H.W. Clark. *Canadian Historical Review* 11 (1930): 354-56.

–. Review of *Oregon Geographic Names*, by L.A. McArthur. *Canadian Historical Review* 10 (1929): 169-70.

–. Review of *The Far West Coast*, by V.L. Denton. *Canadian Historical Review* 6 (1925): 84-85.

–. Review of *The Oregon Missions*, by J.W. Bashford. *Review of Historical Publications Relating to Canada* 22 (1919): 126-28.

–. Review of *The Romance of British Columbia*, by A. Anstey. *Washington Historical Quarterly* 19 (1928): 66-67.

–. Review of *Union List of Manuscripts in Libraries of the Pacific Northwest*, by C.W. Smith. *Canadian Historical Review* 13 (1932): 82-83.

–. "The Royal Engineers in British Columbia." Corporation of BC Land Surveyors. *Report of the Proceedings of the Nineteenth Annual General Meeting* (1924): 18-24.

–. "The Search for the Fraser by Sea and Land." Art, Historical and Scientific Association. *Historical Papers* (1907-8): 15-24.

–. "Sekani." In *Encyclopedia of Canada*. Vol. 5. Toronto: University Associates of Canada, 1937.

–. "The Settlement and Progress of British Columbia, 1871-1914." In *The Cambridge History of the British Empire*. Vol. 6, *Canada and Newfoundland*. Cambridge: Cambridge University Press, 1930.

–. "The Voyage of the Captain Cook and the Experiment." *British Columbia Historical Quarterly* 5 (1941): 285-96.

–. "William Sturgis: The Northwest Fur Trade." *British Columbia Historical Quarterly* 8 (1944): 11-25.

–. *Work of the Royal Engineers*. Victoria: King's Printer, 1910.

–, ed. *The Dixon-Meares Controversy*. Toronto: Ryerson Press, 1929.

–, ed. *The Journal of Captain James Colnett Aboard the Argonaut*. Toronto: Champlain Society, 1940.

–, ed. *Voyages of the Columbia to the Northwest Coast, 1787-90 and 1790-93*. Boston: Massachusetts Historical Society, 1941.

–, ed. *Zimmerman's Captain Cook*. Toronto: Ryerson Press, 1930.

–, W.M. Stevens, W. Sage, N. Robinson, and R. Reid. *Builders of the West: A Book of Heroes*. Toronto: Ryerson Press, 1929.

–, W. Sage, and H.F. Angus. *British Columbia and the United States: The North Pacific Slope from Fur Trade to Aviation*. Toronto: Ryerson Press, 1942.

Innis, Harold. *The Fur Trade in Canada: An Introduction to Canadian Economic History*. Rev. ed. Toronto: University of Toronto Press, 1970.

–. *A History of the Canadian Pacific Railway*. 1923. Reprint, Toronto: University of Toronto Press, 1970.

–. *Settlement and the Mining Frontier*. Canadian Frontiers of Settlement Series, vol. 9, pt. 2. Toronto: Macmillan, 1936.

Journal of the Royal Geographical Society (1857-61).

Keenleyside, Hugh. *Memoirs of Hugh L. Keenleyside*. 2 vols. Toronto: McClelland and Stewart, 1981-82.

Kerr, John. *Biographical Dictionary of Well-Known British Columbians*. Vancouver: Kerr & Begg, 1890.

Knight, William, comp. *Bancroft's Map of the Pacific States*. San Francisco: H.H. Bancroft & Co., 1863.

–, ed. *Hand-Book Almanac for the Pacific States: An Official Register and Business Directory*. 3 vols. San Francisco: H.H. Bancroft & Co., 1862-64.

Laing, F.W., and W.K. Lamb. "The Fire Companies of Old Victoria." *British Columbia Historical Quarterly* 10 (1946): 43-75.

Lamb, W. Kaye. "The Advent of the Beaver." *British Columbia Historical Quarterly* 2 (1938): 163-84.

–. "The Census of Vancouver Island, 1855." *British Columbia Historical Quarterly* 4 (1940): 51-58.

–. "Correspondence Relating to the Establishment of a Naval Base at Esquimalt, 1851-57." *British Columbia Historical Quarterly* 6 (1942): 277-96.

–. "Diary of Robert Melrose [1852-57]." *British Columbia Historical Quarterly* 7 (1943): 119-34, 199-218, 283-95.

–. Documents. Copies of originals obtained by author from W. Kaye Lamb.

–. "Early Lumbering on Vancouver Island [1844-66]." *British Columbia Historical Quarterly* 2 (1938): 31-53, 95-121.

–. "Empress Odyssey: A History of the Canadian Pacific Service to the Orient, 1913-45." *British Columbia Historical Quarterly* 12 (1948): 1-78.

–. "Empress to the Orient." *British Columbia Historical Quarterly* 4 (1940): 29-50, 79-110.

–. "The Founding of Fort Victoria." *British Columbia Historical Quarterly* 7 (1943): 71-92.

–. "The Governorship of Richard Blanshard." *British Columbia Historical Quarterly* 14 (1950): 1-40.

–. *History of the Canadian Pacific Railway.* New York: Macmillan, 1977.

–. "Introduction." In *The Letters of John McLoughlin from Fort Vancouver to the Governor and Committee.* Ed. E.E. Rich. Vol. 1. Toronto: Champlain Society, 1941.

–. "Memoirs and Documents Relating to Judge Begbie." *British Columbia Historical Quarterly* 5 (1941): 125-47.

–. "The Pioneer Days of the Trans-Pacific Service: 1887-91." *British Columbia Historical Quarterly* 1 (1937): 143-64.

–. "Presidential Address." *Report of the Canadian Historical Association* (1958): 1-12.

–, ed. *A Voyage of Discovery to the North Pacific Ocean and Round the World, 1791-1795.* 4 vols. London: Hakluyt Society, 1984.

–, ed. *Sixteen Years in the Indian Country: The Journal of Daniel Williams Harmon, 1800-1816.* Toronto: Macmillan, 1957.

–, ed. *The Journals and Letters of Sir Alexander Mackenzie.* Toronto: Macmillan, 1970.

–, ed. *The Letters and Journals of Simon Fraser, 1806-1808.* Toronto: Macmillan, 1960.

London International Exhibition (1862), Executive Committee for Vancouver Island and British Columbia. "An Open Letter." [Victoria, 1861].

–. *Industrial Exhibition.* [Victoria, 1861].

London International Exhibition, 1862: Catalogue of the Vancouver Contribution, with a Short Account of Vancouver Island and British Columbia. London, 1862.

Longstaff, F.V., and W.K. Lamb. "The Royal Navy on the Northwest Coast, 1813-50." *British Columbia Historical Quarterly* 9 (1945): 1-24, 113-28.

Lugrin, Nellie de. *Pioneer Women of Vancouver Island, 1843-66.* Victoria: Women's Canadian Club of Victoria, 1928.

MacDonald, Duncan. *British Columbia and Vancouver's Island: Comprising a Description of these Dependencies.* 3rd ed. London: Longman, 1863.

–. *Lecture on British Columbia and Vancouver's Island.* London: Longman, 1863.

Macfie, Matthew. "The True Northwest Passage." *Fortnightly Review,* 1 December 1865, 227-39.

–. *Vancouver Island and British Columbia: Their History, Resources and Prospects.* London: Longman, 1865.

MacRae, A.O. *History of the Province of Alberta.* 2 vols. N.p.: Western Canadian History Co., 1913.

Mayne, Richard. *Four Years in British Columbia and Vancouver Island.* London: John Murray, 1862.

McDougall, J.L. "The Frontier School and Canadian History." *Report of the Canadian Historical Association* (1929): 121-25.

Minutes of the Council of Vancouver Island [August 30, 1851 to February 6, 1861]. British Columbia Provincial Archives, Memoir 2. Victoria: King's Printer, 1918.

Minutes of the House of Assembly of Vancouver Island, August 12, 1856 to September 25, 1858. British Columbia Provincial Archives, Memoir 3. Victoria: King's Printer, 1918.

Monet, Don, ed. *Colonialism on Trial: Indigenous Land Rights and the Gitksan Wet'suwet'en Sovereignty Case.* Gabriola Island: New Society Publishers, 1992.

Morice, Adrien. *The Carrier Language (Dene Family): A Grammar and Dictionary.* 2 vols. St. Gabriel-Molding, 1932.

–. *Fifty Years in Western Canada: Being the Abridged Memoirs of Reverend A.G. Morice, O.M.I.* Toronto: Ryerson Press, 1930.

–. *The History of the Northern Interior of British Columbia, formerly New Caledonia, 1660-1880.* 1906. Reprint, Smithers, BC: Interior Stationery, 1978.

Morton, W.L. *Manitoba: A History.* 2nd ed. Toronto: University of Toronto Press, 1967.

Natural History Society of British Columbia. *Bulletin* (1893-1910).

–. *Papers and Communications* (1891).

Newcombe, C.F. *The First Circumnavigation of Vancouver Island.* British Columbia Provincial Archives, Memoir 1. Victoria: King's Printer, 1914.

Nicolay, Charles. *The Oregon Territory.* 1846. Reprint, Fairfield, WA: Galleon, 1967.

Oregon Historical and Descriptive. 3rd ed. Bradford, 1846.

Ormsby, Margaret. "Agricultural Development in British Columbia." *Agricultural History* 19 (January 1945): 11-29.

–. *British Columbia: A History.* 1958. Reprint, Toronto: MacMillan, 1972.

–. "Canada and the New British Columbia." *Report of the Canadian Historical Association* (1948): 74-85.

–. "Captain Houghton's Exploratory Trip, 1864." Okanagan Historical Society. *Report* 13 (1949): 38-44.

–. *Coldstream – Nulli Secundus.* Vernon: Friesen, 1990.

–. "Fruit Marketing in the Okanagan Valley of British Columbia." *Agricultural History* 9 (1935): 80-97.

–. "Historians' View Points." *Canadian Literature* 3 (Winter 1960): 65-67.

–. "The History of Agriculture in British Columbia." *Scientific Agriculture* 20, 1 (September 1939): 61-72.

–. "The History of the Okanagan Valley." BA thesis, University of British Columbia, 1929.

–. "A Horizontal View: Presidential Address." Canadian Historical Association. *Historical Papers* (1966): 1-13.

–. "Humanized History." *Canadian Literature* 9 (Summer 1961): 53-56.

–. "My Irish Father." Okanagan Historical Society. *Report* 47 (1983): 82-87.

–. "My Irish Father – George Lewis Ormsby, Part II." Okanagan Historical Society. *Report* 48 (1984): 130-33.

–. "Neglected Aspects of British Columbia's History." *British Columbia Library Quarterly* 23, 4 (1960): 9-12.

–. "Pre-exemption Claims in Okanagan Valley." Okanagan Historical Society. *Report* 6 (1935): 177-84.

–. "Prime Minister Mackenzie, the Liberal Party and the Bargain with British Columbia." *Canadian Historical Review* 26 (1945): 148-73.

–. "Relations Between British Columbia and the Dominion of Canada, 1871-1885." PhD diss., Bryn Mawr, 1937.

–. "The Significance of the Hudson's Bay Brigade Trail." Okanagan Historical Society. *Report* 13 (1949): 28-37.

–. "A Study of the Okanagan Valley of British Columbia." MA thesis, University of British Columbia, 1931.

–. "T. Dufferin Pattullo and the Little New Deal." *Canadian Historical Review* 43 (1962): 277-97.

–. "The Ten Encampments," Okanagan Historical Society. *Report* 3 (1929): 18-19.

–. "The United Farmers of BC: An Abortive Third-Party Movement." *British Columbia Historical Quarterly* 17 (1958): 53-73.

–, ed. *A Pioneer Gentlewoman in British Columbia: The Recollections of Susan Allison.* Vancouver: UBC Press, 1976.

Pemberton, J. Despard. *Facts and Figures Relating to Vancouver Island and British Columbia.* London: Longman, 1860.

Proceedings of the Royal Geographical Society (1857-62).

Rattray, Alexander. *Vancouver Island and British Columbia: Where They Are, What They Are; and What They May Become.* London: Smith, Elder & Co., 1862.

Report of the Canadian Historical Association (1922-58).

Report of the Provincial Archivist, 1910. Victoria: King's Printer, 1911.

Sage, Walter. "The Annexationist Movement in British Columbia." Royal Society of Canada. *Transactions*, ser. 3, 21 (1927), sec. 2: 97-110.

–. "British Columbia and Confederation." *British Columbia Historical Quarterly* 15 (1951): 71-84.

–. "British Columbia Becomes Canadian (1871-1901)." *Queen's Quarterly* 52 (1945): 168-83.

–. "The British Commonwealth and the Collective System." *Pacific Historical Review* 3 (1934): 156-63.

–. *Canada From Sea to Sea*. Toronto: University of Toronto Press, 1940.

–. "Canada on the Pacific: 1866-1925." *Washington Historical Quarterly* 17 (1926): 91-104.

–. "Canada: The Neighbour to the North." *Pacific Historical Review* 20 (1951): 111-21.

–. "The Critical Period of British Columbia History, 1866-71." *Pacific Historical Review* 1 (1932): 424-43.

–. "The Early Days of Representative Government in British Columbia." *Canadian Historical Review* 3 (1922): 143-80.

–. "Federal Parties and Provincial Political Groups in British Columbia, 1871-1903." *British Columbia Historical Quarterly* 12 (1948): 151-69.

–. "From Colony to Province: The Introduction of Responsible Government in British Columbia." *British Columbia Historical Quarterly* 3 (1939): 1-14.

–. "Geographical and Cultural Aspects of the Five Canadas." *Report of the Canadian Historical Association* (1937): 28-34.

–. "The Gold Colony of British Columbia." *Canadian Historical Review* 2 (1921): 340-59.

–. "The Historical Peculiarities of Canada with Regard to Hemisphere Defence." *Pacific Historical Review* 10 (1941): 15-27.

–. "Historical Renaissance in British Columbia." *Canadian Historical Review* 17 (1936): 415-18.

–. "The Oregon Treaty of 1846." *Canadian Historical Review* 27 (1946): 349-67.

–. Review of *The Commercial Empire of the St. Lawrence*, by Donald Creighton. *British Columbia Historical Quarterly* 3 (1939): 135-45.

–. "Seminar Outline in British Columbia History." Vancouver: University of British Columbia, 1930.

–. "Sir George Arthur and His Administration of Upper Canada." *Queen's Quarterly* 26 (1918): 22-53.

–. *Sir James Douglas and British Columbia*. Toronto: University of Toronto Press, 1930.

–. "Some Aspects of the Frontier in Canadian History." *Report of the Canadian Historical Association* (1928): 62-72.

–. "Spanish Explorers of the British Columbian Coast." *Canadian Historical Review* 12 (1931): 390-406.

–. "Towards New Horizons in Canadian History." *Pacific Historical Review* 8 (1939): 47-57.

–. "Vancouver: The Rise of a City." *Dalhousie Review* 17 (1937): 49-54.

–. "Where Stands Canadian History?" *Report of the Canadian Historical Association* (1945): 5-14.

–, G. Wrong, and C. Martin. *The Story of Canada*. Toronto: Ryerson Press, 1929.

Schofield, F.H. *The Story of Manitoba*. 3 vols. Winnipeg: S.J. Clarke, 1913.

Scholefield, E.O.S., and R.E. Gosnell. *Sixty Years of Progress: A History of British Columbia*. 2 vols. Vancouver/Victoria: British Columbia Historical Association, 1913.

–, and F. Howay. *British Columbia from the Earliest Times to the Present*. 2 vols. Vancouver: S.J. Clarke, 1914.

–, and F. Howay. *British Columbia, from the Earliest Times to the Present ... Profusely Illustrated*. Vancouver, Portland, San Francisco, Chicago: S.J. Clarke, [1913].

Shortt, A., and A. Doughty, eds. *Canada and Its Provinces*. Vols. 21-22, *The Pacific Province*. Toronto: Glasgow, Brook & Company, 1914.

Siegfried, André. *Canada*. Trans. H. Hemming and D. Hemming. London: Jonathan Cape, 1937.

Sturgis, William. *The Oregon Question*. Boston: Swift & Wiley, 1845.

Supreme Court of British Columbia. *Reasons for the Judgement of the Honourable Chief Justice Allan McEachern*. 1991.

Supreme Court of Canada. "Judgements of the Supreme Court of Canada, *Delgamuukw v. BC*." 11 December 1997. http://csc.lexum.umontreal.ca/en/1997/1997rcs3-1010/1997rcs3-1010.html, viewed 30 July 2008.

Thrupp, Sylvia. *The Merchant Class of Medieval London, 1300-1500*. Chicago: University of Chicago Press, 1948.

–. *Society and History: Essays*. Ann Arbor: University of Michigan Press, 1977.

Tucker, Ephraim. *History of Oregon*. 1844. Reprint, Fairfield, WA: Galleon, 1970.

Turner, Frederick Jackson. "The Significance of the Frontier in American History." *Annual Report of the American Historical Association, 1893* (1894): 199-227.

Twiss, Travers. *The Oregon Territory, Its History and Discovery*. New York: Appleton, 1846.

Tytler, Patrick. *Historical Discovery on the More Northern Coasts of America, from the Earliest Period to the Present Time*. Edinburgh: Oliver & Boyd, 1832.

University of British Columbia. *Calendar* (1915-60).

–. "University of British Columbia Student Enrolment Figures: 1915-present," University of British Columbia Library. http://www.library.ubc.ca/archives/enrolmnt.html, 14 May 2003.

Waddington, Alfred. *The Fraser Mines Vindicated, or the History of Four Months*. 1858. Reprint, Vancouver: R.R. Reid, 1949.

Wagner, Henry. *The Cartography of the Northwest Coast of America to the Year 1800*. 2 vols. Berkeley: University of California Press, 1937.

Wilkes, George. *The History of Oregon, Geographical and Political*. New York: Colyer, 1845.

Index

Skelton, O.D., 99
Smith, Allen, 150
Songhees Reserve case (1914), 80-81, 88
Sorbonne University, 115, 122
Soward, Frederick, 97, 121, 128
Spain, 13, 16, 19, 56, 61, 84,
Sproat, G.M., 33
staples thesis, 110-12
Stewart, Lee, 129
Stuart, John, 33
Sturgis, William, 18
Supreme Court of Canada, 12
Swift, Jonathan, 13, 54

Taylor, Brook, 28
technologies of power, 7, 55
Teit, James, 85
Thrupp, Sylvia, 116, 118, 119, 121, 129-30
Tod, John, 33
Tolmie, W.F., 123
Trigger, Bruce, 13, 20
Tucker, Ephraim, 17-18
Turner, Frederick Jackson, 105
Twiss, Travers, 18-19

United States: anti-colonial myth, 20-21; as City on the Hill, 35-36;

criticism of US Native policy, 18, 19-20, 28, 37-38; Edwardian historians on, 59-60; Howay on, 92-93; Manifest Destiny, 20-21, 29, 40; Mayne on, 26; Oregon boundary dispute, 15-16; Ormsby on, 146; Sage on, 113-14
universities, Europe and North America, 95-96
University of British Columbia (UBC), 9, 89, 95
University of Toronto, 97-98, 128-30
University of Toronto Press, 100, 101

Vancouver, George, 14, 19, 56, 67, 123
Vancouver Riot (1907), 62

Wagner, Henry, 123, 165n46
Wilkes, George, 17-18
women: as agents of British Empire, 69-70; dearth in population, 69; historical writers in British Columbia, 68-69; as history faculty, 129-30, 131-32; as history students, 128-29, 131-32; in modern historical writing, 133, 141; Ormsby on, 140-41; at UBC, 128
Work, John, 123
Wrong, George, 97, 101, 128